THE BEST
TRUE CRIME
STORIES
OF THE YEAR
2025

THE BEST
TRUE CRIME
STORIES
OF THE YEAR
2025

INTRODUCTION BY
DOUGLAS PRESTON

FOREWORD BY
PETER CROOKS, SERIES EDITOR

CRIME INK
NEW YORK

First edition

Interior design by Maria Fernandez

Library of Congress Control Number: 2025935477

Hardcover ISBN: 978-1-61316-709-0
Paperback ISBN:978-1-61316-710-6
eBook ISBN: 978-1-61316-711-3

10 9 8 7 6 5 4 3 2 1

Printed in the United States of America

CONTENTS

Foreword

by Peter Crooks

As a writer and editor for a regional magazine during the past twenty-five years, I've had the opportunity to publish a range of stories that serve readers in different ways. Some of my most successful efforts have been true crime reports in the San Francisco Bay Area. A series of articles I presented in 2011 received international acclaim, national media coverage, and a magazine award.

Among many important issues, the articles exposed serious police corruption and led to the conviction of the highest-ranking law enforcement officer in California history to be arrested for selling drugs. Another favorite assignment let me profile a Bay Area investigator named Paul Holes, who spent decades reviewing cold case files and chasing an insidious criminal known as the Golden State Killer. The investigator's tenaciousness—and the evolution and use of DNA technology—led to the arrest and conviction of this serial killer and rapist just two months after the profile was published, a serendipitous event that occurred thanks to the tireless work by Holes and other law enforcement professionals.

When I started as the true crime editor for the Crime Ink imprint of Penzler Publishers in the fall of 2024, my first assignment was to find the material for this anthology, *The Best True Crime Stories of the Year.* One steadfast rule was that all the stories needed to be published during the calendar year. I spent many days in the Berkeley Public Library deep-diving into the pages of various magazines and newspapers, and evenings scouring websites to find a dynamic collection of stories published in 2024.

While the stories needed to be published within the year, the stories did not need to take place in the present day. Some of these events occurred many years ago. For example, Patricia Wen's story from the *Boston Globe Magazine*, "The Heiress at Harvard," let readers turn back time to the late 1800s—and halfway through the following century—to meet the remarkable Frances Glessner Lee, a divorced, wealthy mother who made an enormous impact on police work. Wen writes about Lee's determination to "pursue her mission of professionalizing murder investigations with single-minded focus, despite significant odds stacked against her at Harvard and in local police departments across the country. She contributed much of her personal fortune, political acumen, and even her artistic talents to making sure all victims—man or woman, rich or poor—got investigations that were full and fair."

Another story from yesteryear is Joe Pompeo's *Vanity Fair* page-turner, "Death and the Masque." This piece takes readers back to the punk rock music scene in Los Angeles in the late 1970s, when bands like the Go-Gos and the Germs were packing nightclubs with Travis Bickle types thrashing about in mosh pits. This colorful setting becomes diabolical as Pompeo recounts additional mayhem caused by a slippery serial killer stalking the punk community.

Some of the pieces investigate ripped-from-the-headlines issues. Jordan Michael Smith's story for *Harper's*, "The Forever Cure," explores controversial civil commitment treatments for convicted sex offenders and asks if these treatments actually rehabilitate criminals, or continue to punish them.

Maclean's writer Lana Hall's illuminating "The Incel Terrorist" investigates a horrific crime committed by a seventeen-year-old man in Toronto who took a sword into one of the city's erotic massage parlors and butchered a sex worker. The story reveals many issues—the anger and violence that involuntarily celibate young men, the sometimes dangerous reality of sex workplaces, and whether a tragedy such as this should be prosecuted as terrorism, due to the hate crime against women. That Hall draws from her own experiences working in the massage parlor world adds empathy and understanding to an otherwise unthinkable set of circumstances.

I was determined to include a story from *Texas Monthly*, a regional magazine from the Lone Star State that offers exceptional content on every page with particular excellence in its true crime reporting. I am delighted to share "The Problem with Erik: Privilege, Blackmail, and Murder For Hire in Austin" by Katy Vine and Ana Worrel. Vine and Worrel's deeply reported and brilliantly written epic is cinematic, so much so that I hope it finds its way to the brothers Coen or Safdie for a silver screen treatment. Vine and Worrel also told the story in a gripping podcast format, which added new dimensions to the print version.

Readers will want to head north to rural Minnesota to dive into John Rosengren's stunning mystery, "Anatomy of a Murder," originally printed in *The Atavist*. Rosengren had two stories that I considered for the anthology—the other was a heartbreaking report about an innocent man on death row. Another guideline for this annual collection was that I could use only one piece per writer, and when Rosengren mentioned that the murder weapon in the Minnesota tale was a moose antler, I knew which story to reprint.

While traditional print media sources provided much of the anthology's content, new media also played a role. Slate.com journalist Luke Winkie went to the Gaylord Opryland Resort in Nashville to cover CrimeCon, a popular attraction for true crime aficionados who spend more than $200 to listen to talks by Investigation Discovery personalities and investigators, and to meet the relatives of victims and criminals. Winkie's story, "The BTK Killer's Daughter. Gabby Petito's Parents. JonBenét's Dad," informs readers about the big business that true crime has become. Who knew that five decades after Paddy Chayefsky's *Network* hit movie theaters its brilliant satire would transform into prescient drama?

A longtime colleague, *San Francisco Standard* editor Jon Steinberg, sent me a link to his digital newspaper's must-read headline, "Nudists Fight Off Pirate Terrorist." The story, an absolute classic of San Francisco Castro District culture, features a pair of heroic, totally nude neighborhood fellas who had to think fast and act quickly when a mentally ill man began threatening a tourist with a blowtorch. Reporter Tomoki Chien let me know that when he met one of the story's protagonists in a Castro coffee shop, "he was nude for the duration of the interview, with the exception of a courtesy sock he donned when our (slightly flabbergasted) photo intern began taking his portrait."

While I'm excited to present the content in *The Best True Crime Stories of the Year*, I'm hesitant to offer these brief spoiler alert teasers. Each of these stories stands on its own and each writer's voice deserves to be heard as it was originally published—the collection showcases diversity in subject matter and storytelling style. These true crime pieces are immediately thrilling, deeply provocative, and ultimately enlightening, with the common thread that they are reported by journalists at the top of their game. I'm thankful for each contributor's participation in this project, and I am certain that readers will be surprised, shocked, and entertained by their efforts.

—Peter Crooks

Introduction:
The Pleasures of Revenge

by Douglas Preston

As a writer of crime stories—both true and fictional—I've often been asked why I think people enjoy reading about crime and punishment, murder and mayhem, violence and wrongdoing. Why do human beings in cultures across the globe love dark stories? Isn't enjoying stories of violence, crime, murder, and cruelty a sign of mental sickness or psychological imbalance? Why do our most treasured works of literature involve death, violence, tragedy, war, and criminality? This is true of the great works of literature across the ages, from Homer and Shakespeare to Tolstoy, Dostoyevsky, Dickens, Melville, Conan Doyle, all the way up to Stephen King.

Indeed, it's almost impossible to think of a "nice" book in the literary canon. One of the sweetest books in the canon would have to be *Pollyanna*, the treacly novel by Eleanor H. Porter, in which the heroine's very name became a slur against overly optimistic people. Even in that sappy novel, the heroine is cruelly abused by her aunt and later hit by a car and paralyzed.

In his *Divine Comedy*, Dante leads the reader through both Heaven in the *Paradiso* and Hell in the *Inferno*. But which of these works do we read today? Certainly not the *Paradiso*, with its mind-numbing and tiresome descriptions of joyous souls dancing in Heaven around God. No—we delight in the *Inferno*, with its horrifying, gruesome, and garish depictions of the tortures of Hell.

Dark stories of crime and punishment have always been popular, going back to the very birth of literature. *Beowulf* is not a nice story, nor is the *Iliad*, *Gilgamesh*, or the stories in the Bible. Long before there was writing, there were stories told around the fire, and they were not pretty stories about kindhearted people having a lovely time.

Of all the dark stories, the darkest are true crime. True crime stories limn the extremes of human behavior. It's been said that we've recently been experiencing an explosion of interest in true crime stories and that this interest may be a reflection of a growing malignancy in our society, perhaps induced by cultural fragmentation, political polarization, or the pernicious effects of the internet. But this is wildly wrong. These stories have been with humanity from the beginning.

So we're back to the question: why do readers love dark stories? Why do we prefer stories of evil to stories of good folk doing fine things? When I've been asked this question at book-signings, my answers have usually been on the glib side.

We love reading scary stories because they give us the frisson of danger without the actual threat. Stories of crime and violence provide a thrilling escape from the dullness of everyday life. Such stories teach us about human nature and the sources of evil. Dark stories are a psychologically safe way for us to explore the shadowy side in our own psyches. Reading about crime and violence teaches us how to avoid becoming a victim. We like solving the puzzles presented in a murder mystery. And so forth.

These answers are not wrong, but they don't go deep enough. The real answer lies in our evolution as a species. We are, fundamentally, a *storytelling* species. Evolutionary biologists believe that a love of storytelling (and story-listening) is hardwired into our genes.

The theory goes like this: as language developed among our early hominin ancestors, those tribal groups that began to tell stories about themselves had an evolutionary advantage over those groups who didn't. Stories transmit cultural values, information, and beliefs from one generation to the next. They are vital for group cohesion and identity.

But even more profoundly, stories are the basis of religious belief. Religion is built on stories that tell of gods and demons, that explain why bad things happen, and that provide comfort and support by making sense of the random cruelty of existence. You don't have to be an evolutionary biologist to see the enormous benefit of storytelling in our evolutionary past. And anyone who's been a parent knows that even the littlest of children, scarcely able to talk, already have an insatiable hunger for stories.

So why are humans invariably attracted to stories of violence and crime? Why, as a storytelling species, do we enjoy reading about the dark side of human nature? The deep answer lies in the evolution of altruism, cooperation, and a phenomenon known as "third-party punishment." This is a complex and unfamiliar evolutionary argument, so bear with me.

Katrin Riedl from the Max Planck Institute for Evolutionary Anthropology in Leipzig, Germany, performed a curious experiment with chimpanzees. She set up a situation where a chimpanzee, using a set of pulleys and traps, could steal food from another chimp. A third chimpanzee, observing the theft, could then "punish" the thief by pulling on a rope, depriving the thief of its ill-gotten food. The idea was to see if chimps engaged in "third-party punishment"—that is, if a chimp would punish another chimp for wronging a third chimp. But the third chimp never punished the thief—not even when the victim was a close relative.

This experiment and others showed that chimpanzees do not engage in third-party punishment. If a chimp steals food or commits a wrong against another, the victim will retaliate. But bystanders, even close relatives, will not intervene.

This is starkly different from human behavior. All human societies have set up elaborate systems of third-party punishment.

In our society, third-party punishment is the task of an elaborate criminal justice system, with its codified laws, police forces that investigate wrongdoing and arrest transgressors, a system of courts, judges, lawyers, and juries to establish responsibility, and an extensive prison system to punish.

The desire to punish wrongdoers is deeply embedded in our psyche: experiments have shown that by three years of age, children already demonstrate a strong, innate propensity to react to and punish third-party transgressions. We authors all know how powerful the emotion of revenge is in driving along a good story. Revenge is a combination of two things: the desire to punish and the satisfaction of seeing it carried out.

Some anthropologists call third-party punishment "altruistic punishment." Why "altruistic"? For most of our evolution, we lived in small groups of perhaps a hundred individuals. A person who commits a crime in such a small human society is usually punished not by direct retaliation by the victim, but by third-party individuals who take it upon themselves to discipline the transgressor.

The punisher derives no direct benefit from doing it himself. His actions, rather, benefit the group as a whole by enhancing fairness, order and stability. An individual who punishes a third party who has not harmed him directly but has transgressed the norms of the group, does so *altruistically*—that is, he acts for the good of the group with no personal gain. Furthermore, he also does so at personal risk, as the targeted individual may resist or retaliate. Since this behavior is unknown among the great apes, it suggests that altruistic punishment is a unique product of human evolution.

Punishment and cooperation go hand in hand. Human cooperation provides a huge evolutionary benefit through group evolution. A group that cooperates will prevail over a group of selfish people living a "Lord of the Flies" existence, each out for themselves.

But when evolutionary biologists mathematically modeled the evolutionary benefit of straight-up cooperation, they found it to be weak if not nonexistent. Groups of *merely* cooperative individuals don't evolve in a strongly cooperative direction. Why? Because of the problem of criminals and slackers.

In a group of cooperators with no punishers, it becomes advantageous to be a freeloader or criminal. The slacker is the guy who sleeps under a bush while the rest go out hunting the mammoth but then partakes in the feast afterward, or who hangs back and lets others fight the battle. The criminal is the one who rapes someone's daughter, or steals food, or otherwise harms others for his own benefit.

To counteract freeloaders, slackers, and criminals, a cooperative group *must* have punishers. The group needs someone to say, *Hey, pal, you didn't hunt, so you don't eat.* Or, *You raped that woman so you're going to be put to death.*

Now, in a game theory analysis, if you mathematically add in the benefit of *punishment* in a society of cooperators, suddenly you see that cooperation and altruism evolve rapidly and strongly within the group. It becomes advantageous for members of the group to obey the rules, cooperate, and pull their weight—otherwise they will be punished. Punishment is the secret sauce that drives the development of cooperation and altruism. Without punishment, cooperation and altruism in human society would not have evolved.

In other words, one of our most treasured human qualities—cooperation—evolved only because of the existence of punishment.

This brings us to the second stage of the evolutionary argument. Many humans *like* punishing wrongdoers or seeing them get punished. A number of classic experiments have shown that the desire to punish is hardwired into our brains.

In these experiments, subjects were given the opportunity to punish wrongdoing in a series of games involving money, sharing, and cooperation. These experiments have shown that when people punish—especially at a cost to themselves—the dorsal striatum, a reward part of the brain, lights up. Those subjects who sacrificed the most to punish got the biggest charge from it. Unlike chimps, humans get a biological reward in their brains from punishing wrongdoers. We *like* to see wrongdoers getting what they deserve. This is why revenge is such a powerful motivator in so many of our stories. Such plots light up the dorsal striatum.

So now we can start to see why humans have a peculiar interest in dark stories—especially ones involving true crime. These stories involve crime *and punishment*. The pleasures derived from reading such stories are manifold and embedded within our genes. These kinds of stories transmit crucial societal values of stability, order, rules of behavior, cooperation, unselfishness, and helping others. These are the core values with which we evolved to become human beings. We are keenly and profoundly interested in stories that show those values being affirmed. But we are also acutely interested in—and rewarded by—witnessing punishment of those who violate those values. Our dorsal striatum lights up with pleasure when, for example, we see the bad guys getting their just deserts in a novel like *The Count of Monte Cristo*, for example, or the *Odyssey*, or *Macbeth*, or *Carrie*.

In any story, in order for there to be bad guys who must be punished, you've also got to have a dramatic transgression—in other words, a crime. In this way, dark stories affirm the fundamental human values of cooperation, altruism, and punishment in ways that nice stories do not. That is why we prefer to read about sinners being savagely tortured in the Circles of Hell than the blissful souls flying around God in Heaven. Our interest in true crime, far from being a sign of social malignancy, is actually an indication of societal health and psychological well-being.

Which is to say: You may read and enjoy these true crime stories with a guilt-free conscience, knowing you are affirming some of humanity's deepest cultural values.

What Really Happened to Baby Christina?

by Matthew Bremner

Twenty-five years ago, Barton McNeil called 911 to report that his three-year-old daughter had died in the night. It was the worst thing that could ever happen to any parent. Then a new nightmare began.

At around 7:00 A.M. on June 16, 1998, Barton McNeil a 39-year-old divorced father, woke up on the couch after a muggy, stormy night.

It was the beginning of one of those long summers in Bloomington, Illinois, the air so heavy you could chew it.

The evening before, he and his girlfriend, Misook Nowlin, had broken up. They'd gone out to Avanti's, a local Italian restaurant, and gotten into it yet again. The previous year, Nowlin had been convicted of domestic battery against McNeil, and he was due in court the next day to testify at her sentencing hearing.

Nowlin wanted McNeil to speak on her behalf, and at first he'd planned to. Even though he'd testified against her at trial, he felt sorry for her and didn't want her going to prison. But at the restaurant his feelings had changed. She'd confessed that jealousy had driven her to snoop around his garbage and his phone records, convinced he was having an affair. He ended the meal early and left, furious. Besides, it was his night with his three-year-old daughter, Christina, and he had to pick her up at his ex-wife's house.

Mulling the fight over in the morning, McNeil couldn't shake the image of Nowlin trembling with anger as they paid the check, or of her pleading with him to talk it through as he rushed from the restaurant. She'd even followed him out of the parking lot. When he stopped the car and demanded to know what she was doing, she said she wanted to warn him his tailpipe was smoking.

McNeil, medium height, lanky, and balding, stretched out on the sofa and felt his lack of sleep—after the fight, he'd been up late online chatting with a woman in the Philippines. Now he heaved himself upright and stumbled to his desk to check his email. Nothing of interest.

McNeil traipsed to the bathroom and called out to wake Christina in the bedroom next door. It was time to get up and get dressed. She didn't stir. McNeil, a prep cook at the nearby Red Lobster restaurant, had less than an hour to drop Christina off at day care and get to work.

He smoked a cigarette on the toilet and called to Christina one more time. Still nothing. So he took a shower, then checked his email again, and finally crept into the bedroom. There she lay, wrapped in the swirl of her flower-patterned sheets, a copy of *Go, Dog. Go!* beside her. Her eyes were open, her skin clammy and the color of slate.

McNeil froze. His stomach churned. Panic took the wind out of his lungs.

He scrambled for the phone and dialed 911.

"911, what's your emergency?" answered the dispatcher.

"I need an ambulance! I need it fast. 1106 North Evans. My daughter is dying . . ." McNeil wheezed.

The dispatcher's voice was monotone. "Okay . . . you got to help me out here now."

McNeil whimpered in agreement.

"Try to stay calm. How old is your daughter?"

"Three . . . I think she's dead!"

McNeil attempted CPR, but blowing into Christina's mouth made a hideous, whining sound; blood ran from her nose, and her body sagged in his arms. "It's Christina, it's Christina, it's Christina!" he howled. "*Ohhhhhh*, Christina!"

The paramedics arrived minutes later, and McNeil sank to the kitchen floor, stupefied. They shouted instructions to each other over the thud and clatter of their work. Patrol officers trampled through the living room. McNeil could still see Christina lying in his Red Lobster T-shirt and her white underpants with the word MONDAY written across them.

Paramedics remember him wailing, "frantic," but that they saw "no tears." When officers asked him for the number of Christina's mother, his ex-wife Tita McNeil, he had trouble remembering it, even though he called her home almost daily.

According to police, when she eventually arrived, she screamed at McNeil, "What did you do to my child?" (McNeil does not recall this.) She then crouched next to Christina's limp body and began stroking her daughter's arm. McNeil sat beside her, staring, disconnected, disbelieving.

Just after 9:19 A.M., the coroner's office removed the girl's body from the apartment. Less than fifteen minutes later, believing they'd seen nothing suspicious, the police released the scene.

⊶

The place was empty. Friends had taken Tita away, and the authorities were gone. McNeil sat on his porch smoking cigarette after cigarette. How could he go back inside and face the things Christina had left behind? Her nebulizer. The book she had been looking at the night before. The tiny white dress hanging on his bedroom door that she would have worn that morning to day care.

From the front porch, McNeil thought he saw—*could it be her?*—Nowlin. She'd shown up earlier that morning while the police were there and he'd asked her to leave. Now she was back. Nowlin pulled over a few doors down from McNeil's home and approached him. She was cold and matter-of-fact, which wasn't at all like her. But the strangest thing of all came next: McNeil claims she said, "Well, could Christina have been murdered?" (Nowlin denies having said this.)

After a brief conversation, which Nowlin says took place inside but McNeil insists happened outside, she left for work, as if nothing unusual had happened.

McNeil was confused. *Had Christina been murdered? What was Misook saying?* But he was also anesthetized by shock, unable to think straight. And, anyway, he couldn't stand to be at the apartment any longer, so he headed for the home of his ex-wife, Christina's mother, the only person in the world who he trusted was in as much pain as he was. But he found little respite there. His mind kept returning to the breakup and the hours after. *Why had Misook called him last night, asking if he was home with Christina and where she was sleeping?* (Phone records confirmed that Nowlin called McNeil that night, but she later said she could not remember the call.) *Why had she arrived unannounced that morning and stayed until after the police left?*

Could Misook have killed Christina?

McNeil's mind raced. It wasn't likely that anyone entered the apartment through the front door; he was sleeping on the sofa next to it. Besides, anticipating that Nowlin might return wanting to keep arguing, McNeil had secured the screen door the night before, which he didn't usually do.

He could only imagine that she might have entered through Christina's bedroom window. Come to think of it, there had been something off in Christina's room that morning. He just couldn't figure out what . . . The fan. When he entered Christina's room that morning, it had been on the floor, not mounted to the window, where it had been most of the spring. But, McNeil thought, to get to the fan, the killer would have to first get past the latched window screen. Opening the screen from outside would be impossible without damaging the window.

McNeil excused himself from Tita's and returned to his home on North Evans Street. He walked up a narrow cement path lined with bushes and messy shrubbery, toward the window of Christina's bedroom. He saw holes in the storm screen's lower corners, and the screen appeared completely off its track.

At 5:16 P.M., ten hours after he'd found Christina dead, he called 911 again. "My name is Bart McNeil," he told the dispatcher. "My daughter was found dead by me this morning at this address. The detectives were here, the coroner, everything. I need a detective—the homicide detective. I have reason to believe she was murdered. . . ."

In the late nineties, the twin cities of Bloomington and Normal were a good place to grow up and raise a family, in a white-picket-fence sort of way. The cities are in the middle of the state, about halfway between Chicago and St. Louis, with brightly colored Victorians lined up quietly and politely. Some of the streets are cobbled. In the 1990s, the cities had such a low murder rate that the Bloomington police had no specialized homicide department.

In fact, when McNeil made his second 911 call, the officers were in such disbelief at his story that the shift lieutenant sounded annoyed. McNeil kept calling and calling, insisting that they investigate a murder. "What the hell's his problem?" the lieutenant snapped at the dispatcher.

A detective arrived at McNeil's home nearly forty-five minutes after the first call. McNeil waved him down from the sidewalk outside his home and showed him the window screen. McNeil told the detective that he thought Nowlin had done it and that she had killed his daughter. He was almost hyperventilating as he spoke.

The detective sent McNeil to the police station to be interviewed. The detective would stay behind to meet the crime scene technician who had been there in the morning. When the technician arrived, he said he'd seen a hole in the screen that morning, but just one. He later reported that he'd also noticed spiderwebs connecting the window frame to the screen.

At the police station, McNeil recounted the previous night: After leaving Nowlin, he reached his ex-wife's place at about 7:00 P.M. to collect Christina. She hadn't had dinner, so McNeil drove her to McDonald's for a Happy Meal and then home. By 10:30, McNeil had begun the bedtime routine, and fifteen minutes later, Christina was tucked in.

McNeil then logged on to his computer and started chatting with the woman from the Philippines until around midnight, when he said he heard a voice coming from Christina's room. He found his daughter sitting up in bed, grinning. He tucked her in once more.

A little before 2:00 A.M., McNeil crashed on the couch after a last peek at Christina. The rumble of a brewing thunderstorm kept him awake until about 2:45 A.M.

McNeil was more interested in getting the detectives to understand his theory than in explaining his routine. He insisted they look at Nowlin. She was obsessive, he claimed, capable of violence, and even "maniacal." The night before, she'd been apoplectic during their breakup. Killing Christina must have been some sort of revenge, McNeil asserted. Still, as he drove home that night, he felt that his theory had fallen on deaf ears.

McNeil returned to the police station the next day. In his only recorded interview with the police—despite his insistence that everything be recorded—he was combative from the start. He criticized the police work: "My only daughter is lying on a cold-ass slab of concrete, and you guys are sitting on your ass. I want that fucking forensics team down there now!" he shouted at one point.

Detectives also interviewed Nowlin, who said she'd gone home after the fight at Avanti's and was later joined by three friends. Around 8:00 P.M., they ventured out to a local pool hall and stayed until about 9:30, when Nowlin returned home with her friend Susie Kaiser. The pair stayed up gossiping and eating Korean food for at least another ninety minutes. The topic was McNeil: The breakup had left Nowlin shattered, sad, and angry. "I really love him," she told detectives. Kaiser said Nowlin had told her she wanted to visit McNeil that night; she advised against it.

After Kaiser left, phone records confirm that Nowlin received a call at 12:21 A.M. She'd hoped it was McNeil. She was desperate to talk to him. Instead, it was her brother in Korea on the line, and they only spoke for sixty-two seconds. Nowlin claimed she fell asleep, exhausted and disappointed. She didn't wake until her ex-husband Andy Nowlin came around to drop off clothes for their daughter about 6:00 A.M. (Andy Nowlin corroborated this visit but said he went to pick the clothes up, not to drop them off.)

In a separate room, things were not going well for McNeil. He kept referring to himself as a "suspect" and insisted that police should "arrest him [rather] than arrest nobody at all." He said, "Even though I don't know the autopsy [results], I already know what they are: died by asphyxiation."

The timing of that comment couldn't have been worse for him. Later that morning, Dr. Violette Hnilica, the forensic pathologist, released the autopsy results: Christina had died from smothering. Dr. Hnilica identified swelling of the vagina and anus. She suspected sexual molestation.

Later that day, investigators interviewed McNeil again, this time for some eight hours. No recordings or transcripts of this interview are available, just police narratives summarizing the event, and the Bloomington Police

Department did not reply to questions about its investigation. But according to those summaries, the police found McNeil's claims impossible. There were spiderwebs on the window frame, for one, and it had stormed the night before, for another. An intruder surely would have left muddy footprints, but the carpets in the apartment had all been dry.

In the investigators' view, Christina and McNeil were together inside a locked residence and there was no evidence that anyone else had been there that night. McNeil must have killed Christina. The motive: sexual abuse. Maybe he'd been molesting his daughter and things had gone too far. Maybe he didn't want people to find out, so he'd killed her to cover his tracks. "You're not a bad guy," the detectives told him during the interrogation. "We all make mistakes." No, McNeil insisted, he would never confess "in a million years"; it was Nowlin.

After hours in the interview room, the detectives asked if McNeil was hungry. He was. Detectives returned a while later with a scrunched-up McDonald's brown paper bag. Inside was a kid-sized burger, fries, and a lobster Beanie Baby—identical to Christina's last meal. Even the toy was the same. Then the police told McNeil that they were interviewing Nowlin, too, simultaneously. He begged detectives to put them together in a room. They agreed.

"Why are you accusing me?" Nowlin challenged him, according to police narratives. "I loved you."

McNeil shot back, his eyes red, "You killed Christina! You're a psycho-bitch!"

"No, you murdered Christina!" Nowlin yelled.

The police intervened. Nowlin was released but informed she'd have to take a polygraph test eventually. Some minutes later, she fainted in the police parking lot.

McNeil would spend that night in the county jail on suicide watch after being arrested and charged with the murder of his daughter.

○——◆——○

On Christmas Eve 2022, my three-year-old tried to pick up his baby brother and accidentally dropped him.

On the way to the hospital, our baby was peaceful. His tiny hand locked around my pinky as he peered out the window at the orange blur of the streetlights in the nighttime drizzle. I felt guilty for a thousand things: for not intervening sooner, for not turning around a second earlier. It wasn't my older son's fault; it was mine. Normalcy was so fragile—one minute, things were fine, then they weren't. Harmony and horror seemed divided by nothing more than an instant. I felt I'd failed to protect my baby in that instant.

Over the hacking coughs and squeak of rubber soles in the ER, the doctor told us he probably had a fractured skull. Results of a CAT scan would tell us if he had internal bleeding. I prepared for a tomorrow in which I loathed myself forever.

But somehow, he was fine. I'd narrowly missed what I supposed was the worst thing that can happen to a person. He would need to be monitored for a while, but my relief was immediate. I burst into tears. I'd never cried like that before.

A day later, crammed into a chair beside my son's hospital bed, amid the click and drip of hospital machinery, the submarine pulses, I remembered a story I'd heard about a father in Illinois who'd spent the last quarter century in prison for the murder of his three-year-old daughter. He claimed he was innocent.

I'd heard it maybe a month before, but the man's story came back to me now, as my son slept beside me, still wrapped in a tangle of tubes as I contemplated what nearly happened to him, to me. If what I'd read was true and Barton McNeil was innocent of killing his daughter, then it occurred to me that I'd been wrong the night before. Losing a child was not the worst thing that could happen to a person: Being unjustly locked up for it was.

But could it be true? For months, the question wouldn't leave my mind. I read court documents, scrutinized police reports, and exchanged countless emails with lawyers and criminal experts. Spoke to McNeil on the phone at least once a week. As luck would have it, there would be a hearing in November 2023 to decide if his lawyers could convince a judge to order a retrial of McNeil's case—a chance, decades later, to prove his innocence.

If McNeil hadn't killed Christina, then who did? And if he hadn't, what had those years been like since the moment his old life ended in one horrible instant?

In June 2023, I visited him at the Pinckneyville prison in southern Illinois. I entered a large, austere room, with round tables and fixed steel stools. McNeil's remaining hair was now gray; he seemed skinnier than in photos, a blue shirt stretched across his bony shoulders. His voice was nasal but steady: "Good to finally meet you in person."

McNeil told me that after his arrest, of all the people he was desperate to convince he hadn't done it, none mattered more than Christina's mother. He frequently wrote to her from county jail, pleading for her forgiveness. "This is the most important and saddest letter of my life," he wrote. "My eyes are rivers of tears as I write this to you. I am begging you, Tita, on the ashes of our beloved Christina and on the grave of my late mother. I never harmed our baby, Tita. I never ever harmed my one and only precious baby. I am on my knees begging you Tita, to believe me."

On the night of her death, McNeil had custody of Christina as part of his shared parenting arrangement with Tita. After their breakup, she had become more trusting in his ability to care for their daughter, and McNeil, in turn, had taken great pride in raising Christina. She had given McNeil a purpose beyond satisfying his whims—in the main, getting drunk, or chasing women in bars after work. She made him happy to be at home and determined to be better than he was—or, at the very least, better than his parents had been.

His childhood wasn't horrendous, but it lacked warmth. His parents divorced when he was just six years old, and he and his brother moved from Bloomington to live near family in Wisconsin. Soon after, his mother was discovered dead on the kitchen floor, a bottle of pills nearby.

McNeil and his brother moved back to Bloomington to live with their father, an icy, indifferent man, and his father's new partner. As a teen, McNeil drank beer and smoked weed. He dropped out of school, believing he could never graduate. He tried college but dropped out of there, too. He worked a few low-paid jobs at old folks' homes and local restaurants. In 1979, he was arrested for dealing prescription pills.

There were movements of promise, though. In his late twenties, McNeil aced the GED test. He got a Pell Grant to attend Illinois State, and he almost graduated. There was emotional stability, too.

McNeil had a thing for "Asian gals," as he once told me. And in the late eighties, after a colleague at Red Lobster introduced them, he started writing to Tita, a Filipina woman who worked as a midwife in Saudi Arabia. She was bright and kind and spoke many languages. It wasn't long before he proposed to her during a visit to the Philippines. And while some of McNeil's friends saw the situation as a little mail-order-bride-ish, he was insulted by the insinuation. Tita eventually came to live in Bloomington in May 1993.

They had good times together, but there were fights, too. Tita told the police he could be cruel and indifferent, and one time, she told them, McNeil even "grabbed her by the hair and shook her around." That fight ended in Tita taking out a restraining order against him. McNeil told me he was deeply ashamed of these actions. (Despite attempts to contact Tita McNeil for this article, I could not reach her.)

McNeil had been a scumbag to Tita; he knew it. In fact, he was having an affair with Nowlin during Tita's pregnancy with Christina. Although he ended up leaving her for Nowlin, in the spring of 1998, he'd been trying to set things right. But by June 16 of that year, all hope for the future was gone. He'd lost his daughter, and he was losing himself. "And then for Tita to now condemn me, I mean, I just, my whole life was destroyed," McNeil told me, his voice breaking.

For several weeks after his arrest, McNeil convinced himself the police would eventually realize their mistake. That changed after his indictment, when he began to feel that the system, and even the community, was against him. A journalist for the local paper, *The Pantagraph*, asked him, "Is it not more likely you did it? Maybe you're mentally ill. . . . Maybe demons haunt and control you." His family scattered, telling him to stop pointing the finger at Nowlin. But he refused. McNeil wrote letters to friends and journalists, pleading for their intervention. He wrote to the lead detective in the case, Larry Shepherd, whom he begged to investigate Nowlin. "I have always been certain that some of you believe what I have told you," he wrote in mid-July 1998, with a combination of hope and frustration. "I have learned that the investigation is ongoing and that Misook is still a suspect. For that, I'm very thankful."

McNeil was right. Detectives were aware of Nowlin's conviction for domestic violence against him. Police searched her home and seized two vibrators, items McNeil alleged she might have used to assault Christina sexually. But none of Christina's DNA was found on them. They subjected Nowlin to a polygraph test (an investigatory tool that's now widely considered to be unreliable). During the test, she denied entering McNeil's apartment on the night of Christina's death and denied suffocating her. The examiner noted Nowlin's difficulty with English and her "erratic and inconsistent responses," which made it impossible for him to offer an opinion on her answers.

Then, in mid-September 1998, the lead detective on McNeil's case began an unrelated investigation of Nowlin. Her nine-year-old daughter, Michelle Nowlin, had told her school principal, Aissa Frasier, that Nowlin was abusing her. Frasier sounded the alarm to social services. In pretrial testimony in that case, Frasier said: "[Michelle] had a bruise on her thigh that was several inches long, maybe three inches long or so. . . . It was apparent that it had been there for a while."

Frasier told the court that Michelle claimed that her mother had vowed to end her life while pinching her nose and clamping a hand over her mouth. "She needed to behave or the same thing that happened to her sister [Christina] would happen to her," Frasier said in court.

Years later she remembered, "I said, 'What do you mean "happened to Christina"?' And she goes, 'That's my sister. She died this summer.' And that's the first time I realized. Oh my God."

Michelle also told Department of Children and Family Services caseworkers that after Christina's death, Nowlin said she found the bed Christina had died in at a local Salvation Army, where Nowlin was doing community service. Michelle informed DCFS workers and police that her mother had told her she might take it home, saying she wanted to "remember" Christina. While Michelle said she didn't feel threatened, a DCFS investigator wrote in a report that in her view, the bed was a way of "taunting Michelle with the murder of Christina." Both Michelle and Nowlin told me that their memories of these events were hazy. Nowlin said that Michelle was a young girl at the time and guessed the story was an attempt at revenge after Nowlin had hit her.

McNeil had access to this DCFS report and the police report about the incident through his lawyer. In the county jail, he was becoming more and more impatient. He knew that forensics revealed an absence of semen on the bedsheets, on Christina's clothing, and within her body. That surely discredited the state's theory of sexual molestation, he assumed. The detective found hairs in Christina's hand, which hinted at a struggle.

It was McNeil's intention to bring all of this up at trial in his own defense. But in December 1998, the state's attorney filed a motion seeking to exclude any evidence and arguments that implicated Nowlin in Christina's death. "In this case, the defendant's assertions against Misook are founded entirely on speculation and unsupported by the evidence," the state wrote in its motion.

McNeil's lawyer countered by presenting numerous witnesses at a March pretrial hearing, known as an "offer of proof" hearing. Their goal was the opposite of the state's: to persuade the judge to admit all evidence pointing to Nowlin.

Among the witnesses the defense called was the DCFS investigator, who testified that nine-year-old Michelle told her that her mother had beaten her and covered her mouth, threatening, "I will kill you tonight." (Nowlin denies that she said this.)

The defense also called Misook Nowlin's former husband Andy Nowlin, who told the court that the night before Christina's death, he'd received a call from Nowlin. She wanted to "set up" McNeil by planting marijuana in his car. Andy figured she wanted revenge against McNeil for not testifying at her domestic-battery hearing and for breaking up with her. In her testimony, Nowlin claimed not to remember if she'd called Andy, but phone records showed that she rang him three times that night, the last time at 10:52 P.M.

Nowlin denied going to McNeil's apartment that night and denied that she'd asked Andy for marijuana. But in the same line of questioning, she seemed to contradict herself. "I asked him maybe—I just joke around with him. I don't ask him seriously, you know," she qualified. She claimed that she'd shown up at McNeil's home the morning after

Christina's death for some computer help, and "also I just kind of miss him."

In a huge blow to McNeil's defense, the court ruled that evidence of Nowlin's potential involvement would be excluded from his trial. The trial date was confirmed for June 1999. McNeil opted for a bench trial, afraid a jury might be too "emotional."

McNeil wrote Tita again after the judge's ruling, pleading for help. She hadn't replied to any of his previous letters. "Defending myself is making me weary," he wrote. "My own conscience is clean, but I wish others knew the truth, too."

At trial, the defense called three witnesses, including McNeil. The state called fifteen. The prosecution pointed out that he was home with her that night and dismissed the notion of an intruder; the hole in the bedroom window screen could have been there long before. (Two detectives did confirm the presence of more than one hole, and one detective mentioned that the screen seemed slightly off its track and "just fell out" when the police attempted to move it.)

Dr. Hnilica, the forensic pathologist, testified that swelling in Christina's vaginal area was "in the realm of molestation." She established a time of death based on digested stomach contents (a technique that even in the late 1990s was known to be imprecise), which indicated to her that the death must have occurred at 10:30 P.M. This seemed to invalidate McNeil's story about seeing his daughter awake at midnight. It also gave Nowlin an alibi.

When a frustrated McNeil took the stand in his defense, he told the court that the police had "paid absolutely no attention whatsoever to what [I] had to say . . . since day one of my daughter's death until this, and pardon me for saying this, it has been a bunch of crap."

He wanted to point the finger at Nowlin, but a judge had already ruled that he couldn't. Indeed, the judge found there was "no evidence that someone else entered the home" and, referring to the pathologist's estimated time of death of between 10:30 and 12:30, "certainly not during the time Christina died." The judge couldn't dismiss McNeil's proximity to his daughter that night, nor the possible motive: that McNeil was trying to cover up sexual molestation. He also pointed to McNeil's suspicious behavior during police interviews: "The video provides important evidence. . . . It shows a man conscious that a murder had been committed, knew that he was a suspect, and who had formulated a defense."

McNeil was found guilty of the murder of a three-year-old girl in a Red Lobster T-shirt and day-of-the-week underwear. He was sentenced to life in prison.

○━━━○

After McNeil's conviction, the state's word was the word of God to many. Tita didn't respond to any of his letters, convinced that he had sexually abused and murdered her daughter. His father and brother showed little interest in continuing their relationships. After the trial, McNeil never heard from his father again. He died in 2017.

Between 2002 and 2011, McNeil's case languished. His appeals were rejected, and no innocence networks would help him. Only his cousin Grace Schlafer was a beacon of hope during this time. She filed FOIA requests, sent letters to forensic pathologists, and made efforts to locate witnesses. But soon, life interfered when she began caring for her father full-time, and her support waned. Isolated, McNeil started to send letters to random people in the hope of company: "They were addresses from this pen-pal website, but none of them turned out to be real addresses. Every letter was returned to me unopened." The world seemed to have forgotten about him.

There were many times during those years when McNeil wanted to kill himself. Everything had been taken from him—his daughter's life and, in many ways, his own. He hadn't even been able to grieve for Christina; how could anyone do so while fighting for their own innocence? He was locked up the day after her death. He hadn't even been allowed at her funeral. Guilt gnawed at him. He may not have killed Christina, but he'd let the person who he believed did into his life and into hers. That person, whom he'd fallen in love with because she looked like a "Hollywood star" from a bygone age, had ruined his life.

Reaching Nowlin for this article wasn't easy. It was months before she replied to my emails. When she eventually did, she was hesitant to talk. She didn't want her words twisted. As something of a precondition, she wanted to know, "Do you think I killed Christina?" I wrote back that I hoped talking with her would help me answer that.

The weeks dragged on with no answer, until, finally, Nowlin agreed to talk to me over the phone. Although she was worried that I wouldn't understand her English, she talked quickly.

She told me she was born on the outskirts of Seoul to a middle-class family. Her mother died when she was young, and Nowlin had suffered physical abuse as a child. At nineteen, she'd gotten pregnant by a much older man and unwittingly gave up the child for adoption in a postpartum haze.

A new chapter began when she met Andy Nowlin, an American serviceman. Their relationship swiftly progressed to marriage, prompting her relocation to Illinois. The couple soon had a daughter, Michelle. But life in the States wasn't an immediate fit. Nowlin sometimes spent money without thinking. "It was all about money," Andy told me. "If there was money there, life is good. There's no money there. And then it's all hell." She even shoplifted for the thrill of it, for which she was convicted twice, first in 1991 and again in 1996.

While Nowlin admitted she had a temper, others claimed she could be just plain violent. She said she saw this as a part of the culture in which she'd been brought up; it was how her father raised her. Michelle told me, "She was physical for sure. There was a paper-towel holder that was wooden; she would mainly hit me in my thighs and my midsection."

After her domestic-abuse charge, Nowlin said, she "never touched [Michelle] again."

On the night of Christina's death, she told me, she was with her friends. She said that yes, she could be jealous, and yes, she had a temper, but that didn't make her Christina's killer. She did not crawl through the window that night: "I couldn't get past that myself, no way.... Someone would have to have pulled me up."

She said she did not suffocate Christina, whom she called her "daughter," despite having no biological or legal relation to her: "I never do that to her.... She's too precious to me." When I asked what she thought of McNeil's belief that she killed Christina, she replied: "One time, I loved him very much. So I understand what he's doing.... If that's me in his situation, I'd do the same thing, probably."

When I contacted Nowlin, it was through the Illinois Department of Corrections' email system. She's in prison now—but not for anything having to do with Christina McNeil.

In September 2011, seventy-year-old Linda Tyda, a respected Chinese interpreter, went missing after leaving her home for a job in Bloomington. A week later, a Chinese-speaking restaurant hostess approached the police, claiming that Nowlin—then married to Tyda's son—paid her twenty dollars to act as a client and arrange a meeting with Linda Tyda. Tyda agreed to meet this "client" in a grocery store parking lot.

Surveillance footage revealed that instead of the hostess, Nowlin met Tyda in the parking lot. They argued, and Nowlin grabbed Tyda's arm and purse. After the altercation, both women left in their cars. Tyda followed Nowlin to her sewing shop in Bloomington and was never seen again.

The authorities questioned Nowlin based on the hostess's statement and the surveillance footage. A search of Nowlin's shop made a significant discovery: Tyda's cut-up ID card, credit cards, and last-worn clothes in a dumpster behind the shop. Nowlin soon confessed to killing Tyda.

When a friend sent McNeil a newspaper clipping and Nowlin's mug shot, McNeil convinced himself there were similarities between the deaths of Linda Tyda and his daughter. There was the method: Both Tyda and Christina had died from asphyxiation, although Tyda had been strangled and Christina was smothered. (In a jailhouse letter that Nowlin wrote to Michelle after the murder, she admitted, "I started to lose control of myself too and pushed Linda away. After that, we came into a situation where we were strangling each other. I was really out of my mind.")

Then there were the victims: As McNeil saw it, Nowlin had targeted the loved ones of people she wanted revenge against. She had lured Tyda to Bloomington under false pretenses. And wasn't she planning to exact revenge on McNeil for refusing to testify in her favor at the domestic-battery sentencing when she called up her ex and asked for help in planting marijuana on him?

Now all those who had doubted him would surely listen, McNeil felt. If only he could reach them. After weeks of trying, he managed to get through to the local radio station from prison. When the host took his call, McNeil was gasping; he always seemed at the end of his breath—he had only minutes to convince listeners: "The premeditation she allegedly used in the murder of Mrs. Tyda was every bit as elaborate as the premeditation she used to murder my daughter," he panted over the airwaves.

Chris Ross and his cousin Barton McNeil had met a couple of times at family gatherings but had never been close. He knew about the sad story of McNeil's daughter from his mom and felt for him, but he hadn't thought much about it—and certainly had no desire to get involved.

But then he heard his cousin on the radio.

In December 2011, Ross wrote his first letter to McNeil: "Immediately after hearing your radio interview, I became your #1 Fan. Seriously, you were wronged and I plan to do everything in my power to get you free through legal means."

Ross started to call his cousin each day. He'd tuck the kids in at night and stay up until 2:00 or 3:00 A.M. to study thousands of pages of discovery, hoping to find something, anything, that could help him. The lawyers Ross consulted all seemed to recommend the same thing: a private investigator, specifically Kevin McClain.

McClain had been a PI for almost twenty years by that point and had worked on many capital cases. When he spoke to Ross, he was "mesmerized" by McNeil's story. He couldn't believe that McNeil, not the police, had demanded that the case be investigated as a murder: "I'd never seen it before . . . the man who'd started the homicide investigation was the one who eventually ended up accused of it," he told me over the phone.

McClain had links to the Illinois Innocence Project, which worked pro bono on wrongful convictions. He thought it might be interested in McNeil's case, so he told Ross to prepare a detailed PowerPoint presentation listing the key events and inconsistencies and send it to them. McClain would put in a good word.

It worked. On what would have been Christina's seventeenth birthday, Ross got the news that the Innocence Project had decided to represent McNeil. "There was just no evidence against Bart," John Hanlon, the former head of the organization and one of McNeil's current attorneys, told me.

More information emerged. In 2012, a former neighbor of Nowlin's reported seeing her rummaging around in a shared hallway closet at their apartment complex around 4:00 A.M. on the night Christina died, when Nowlin had told the court and police that she had been asleep.

McClain's investigators also obtained two signed affidavits, one from Michelle Nowlin and one from Dawn Nowlin, Michelle's stepmother, stating the same thing: that Nowlin's ex-husband Don Wang claimed that Nowlin had confessed to him that she'd murdered Christina. Meanwhile, in 2013, Misook Nowlin was convicted and sentenced for the murder of Linda Tyda. On McNeil's behalf, in November 2013, the Innocence Project filed a motion for additional DNA testing, arguing that only limited testing had been conducted in 1998. When the results came back, Nowlin's DNA was found on six areas of Christina's flower-patterned sheets. (Nowlin told me that of course her DNA was on Christina's sheets: She had slept on that bed many times.)

In 2018, more lawyers, these from the Exoneration Project, another nonprofit organization specializing in overturning wrongful convictions, joined the team. "There was a lot of junk science in [McNeil's] case," Karl Leonard, one of McNeil's attorneys, told me. "It was a case we knew we could win."

Momentum was building. In 2017, a defense expert, Dr. Andrew Baker, the chief medical examiner of Hennepin County, Minnesota, read the autopsy report and studied the accompanying photos and biopsy slides. He argued that there was nothing in the original pathologist's reports to suggest Christina "was smothered or that the manner of death was homicide." He also concluded that significant portions of the 1998 examinations of Christina's body were performed after a funeral director had prepared her remains, a deviation from accepted forensic procedure. His findings led him to a stunning conclusion: He believed that Christina's death was due to unexplained causes.

A second defense expert, Dr. Nancy Harper, director of the Center for Safe and Healthy Children at the University of Minnesota, also disagreed with the original pathologist. In 2019, she submitted a report in which she claimed that the area of Christina's anus and vagina, as documented in the 1998 autopsy, was "normal and without acute trauma or residua of injury." Christina had not been sexually abused, she concluded.

I felt relieved when I read these opinions—not so much for McNeil as for Christina. Suddenly it seemed possible that the little girl hadn't been murdered or abused, that perhaps she'd died without suffering.

McNeil didn't see it that way. "The natural-causes scenario leaves Misook completely off the hook," he said, his voice rising. It was the logic of it that bothered him: "You know, on the one hand, I'm innocent because Misook murdered my daughter, but on the other hand, Misook is innocent because it wasn't a murder and it was a natural cause of death. I do not sign off on that." For McNeil, there was no relief, no version of this story in which Nowlin was not the culprit.

It struck me that proving Nowlin's guilt (as well as getting the justice he wanted for Christina) was the reason he kept fighting. She was the cause, the avatar representing the otherwise inexplicable arc of his life. Someone had to be to blame for his misfortune; otherwise it was all too brutally random: His daughter died in his home, in her sleep, and he was convicted of her murder. It was too cruel to contemplate.

McNeil's legal team filed a post-conviction appeal in 2021; it included all of the newly discovered evidence not available back in 1999. They hoped to force an evidentiary hearing—to present this new evidence in court and prove to a judge that if it had been available in 1999, McNeil wouldn't have been convicted. If the judge agreed, McNeil would be granted a new trial.

But the state's attorney's office was far from receptive. (The office of the McLean County state's attorney declined to comment for this story, since the matter is still before the court.) It brushed off the presence of Nowlin's DNA on Christina's sheets, arguing that her close relationship with McNeil made finding her DNA at the scene inevitable. McNeil produced a bank statement, evidence of a laundry visit the day before Christina's death. (Forensic experts I consulted confirmed that laundering the sheets would obliterate any lingering DNA.) The state countered that, too: The laundry receipt wasn't itemized, wasn't proof of anything.

The state challenged the findings of the defense's pathologists, arguing that since the research papers they cited were published before the crime took place, they weren't "new." The state's attorney also refuted the alleged similarities between Tyda's murder and Christina's.

In 2022, following an examination of the evidence and the state's attorney's rebuttal, the judge ruled primarily in favor of the state. His decision rejected a significant portion of the defense's evidence: the DNA, Nowlin's conviction for Tyda's murder, the testimony about Nowlin and the storage space on the night of the death, and the new autopsy reviews. A public evidentiary hearing was scheduled for two days before Thanksgiving 2023. The only evidence the judge would allow to be considered that day was the affidavits related to Nowlin's confession.

Three days before the hearing, McNeil seemed exhausted. He was on edge about seeing Nowlin again. It had been twenty-four years since she testified at his pretrial hearing, in early 1999.

In the intervening years, she'd gotten remarried and divorced. (Although I've referred to her by her previous surname, her last name is now Wang.) But mostly he seemed exhausted by hope. "Back when the case was dead, there is a relief with that," he said. He felt he owed his supporters something and owed it to Christina to show the world what kind of person Nowlin was. But in truth, he just wanted it all to be over.

On November 21, a clutch of twenty or so of McNeil's supporters huddled in the lobby of the McLean County courthouse, chatting nervously. Chris Ross darted around handing out FREE BART badges and corralling the group for photos. A few of McNeil's childhood friends had gathered, along with journalists, and a man who was suing McLean County for wrongful conviction. As 9:00 A.M. approached, the onlookers filed into Courtroom 5A, where the atmosphere resembled that of a hospital—sterile and tense.

Michelle Nowlin was the first to take the stand. She called "Bart" McNeil a "father figure" and described the celebration-of-life ceremony held for Linda Tyda, where Don Wang told her something that caught her off guard. "Randomly, just out of the blue, he said, 'You know what your mom told me one time?' And I just sat there and stared at him and said, 'No, what is that?' And he said that she had killed Christina," Michelle testified.

Michelle's stepmother, Dawn Nowlin, second on the stand, corroborated Michelle's account of the conversation. "He said that he and Misook were in a big fight, and she confessed to killing Christina," she told the court.

The defense called Misook Nowlin.

Shackled and wearing a white polo shirt, she shuffled into the courtroom. Strangely, she winked at the crowd. One of McNeil's attorneys, Karl Leonard, asked: "Did you kill

Christina McNeil?" Nowlin invoked the Fifth Amendment. So Leonard instead referred to her police interview in 1998, in which Nowlin said she was still in love with McNeil. Nowlin again pleaded the Fifth.

Leonard kept going: "You told Detective Wycoff that a few days before Christina's death, you had gone over to Bart's apartment and discovered some condoms in the bathroom, so you were suspicious he had another woman. Right?"

"I plead to my Fifth," Nowlin replied.

"So you searched the trash can to see if you could find more condoms, but instead you found some printed emails that he had exchanged with an internet girlfriend, right?"

The state's attorney objected.

"Relevance, Your Honor," he murmured.

"What's the relevance, counsel?"

It went to motive, Leonard said. Sustained.

Suddenly, Nowlin seemed to burst with frustration, declaring in answer to no question at all: "I never kill Christina McNeil!"

Leonard, taken aback, asked her if she was indeed pleading the Fifth. Yes, she said, she was, and answered no more questions.

The rest happened quickly and without drama. The state called former detective Steve Fanelli, who disputed the testimony of Michelle and Dawn Nowlin about Don Wang's story. The defense and the state rested their cases. The judge would issue a written ruling soon.

McNeil was then ushered out of the courtroom, sheepishly waving to his friends in the public gallery as he disappeared behind the door.

After the hearing, I stopped by 1106 North Evans Street, where Christina died twenty-six years earlier.

McNeil's home was gone, demolished to make way for new apartments. So I looked at the photographs of the old one-story building on my phone—at its white facade, the yard with Christina's bicycle out front, the overgrown shrubbery, and the porch light.

For all the uncertainty that bedevils this story, there is one thing everyone knows to be true: The owner of the bicycle is dead. Normalcy can turn to horror at any terrible moment. In McNeil's case, he's spent most of his adult life trying to prove to anyone who will listen that his terrible moment has been interpreted all wrong.

When I talked to him by phone later that day, he said he felt the state had done its damage. In February, 2024 the judge ruled that McNeil would not be getting a new trial. He would appeal the verdict to a higher court, but an appeal in state appellate or federal court was a long way off, if his case ever reached them. The hearing was a dud, he said. In his view, the court and Nowlin had, together, ruined his life. "I'm sixty-five. The average life expectancy for males is seventy-two. I'm likely to die in prison," McNeil had told me once.

Now all McNeil had were the people who had come to see him in court two days before Thanksgiving. The people who wore the buttons. All his hard work, all his letters, his thousands of pages of notes, his hours on the phone—they had worked for that at least. There were some people out there who believed he hadn't killed Christina. That was enough for now, he said—and it might have to be enough for him forever.

Nudists Fight Off Pirate Terrorist

by Tomoki Chien

J ustice went full frontal in the Castro last week when two nudists took down a man attacking a tourist on the street.

The naked samaritans—Pete Sferra of San Jose and Lloyd Fishback of San Francisco—were letting it all hang out on a July 2 stroll through the neighborhood when they spotted a "crazy kind of pirate guy" threatening a man with a blowtorch.

A video from the scene shows an onlooker snag the blowtorch just before the attacker starts to punch the tourist. Petros Fanourgiakis, owner of the nearby Aegean Delights, said the attacker threatened to burn the tourist's face.

"My buddy Lloyd is a quiet, respectful guy," Sferra said. "But he didn't waste any time and nailed the guy with a right hook."

Fishback followed up the punch with an underhand smack to the face, after which the attacker walked away.

Shirts 0; Skins 1.

Sferra, who emphasized that Fishback is the hero, said he and at least two other people called the police as the incident unfolded. Fishback declined to comment for this story as the nudist values his privacy.

A spokesperson for the San Francisco Police Department identified the suspect as 38-year-old Zero Triball. He's suspected of assault with a deadly weapon and remains in county jail, according to official records.

Nearby business owners said Triball has a history of causing problems in the Castro.

"He's a known problem in the neighborhood," said Terry Asten Bennett, president of the Castro Merchants Association. "He's erratic and violent."

Bennett said Triball entered her store Cliffs Variety several years ago and began shouting at employees and throwing merchandise at them. She added that the nearby Castro Country Club obtained a restraining order against Triball in March 2021 but opted not to renew it because it was too costly.

Brandon Stanton, manager of the Castro Country Club, said Triball threatened to burn down the building and kill the club's executive director when they offered him support services. The club is a sober community center.

"It's completely unfair to a community when one person can hold it hostage," Bennett said.

Supervisor Rafael Mandelman, whose district includes the Castro, said business owners have every right to be frustrated that Triball continues to menace the neighborhood.

"In my view, he's a guy who'll continue committing medium violent crimes," Mandelman said. "I don't think he should be left to manage his own life. He should be in a conservatorship."

Mandelman added that he previously asked a judge to keep Triball in custody and that he has pushed to expand conservatorship authority.

"Our system is crazy," he said.

The tourist who was attacked in the video has not yet been identified but is believed to be a Brazilian man named Leo, according to Sferra.

"I hate seeing tourists experience that kind of stuff," Sferra said, adding that he wants to normalize nudity in the famously LGBTQ+ neighborhood but has been met with pushback.

"Over the years we've been doing this, we've tried to show the neighborhood that we're regular people—we just have a relaxed idea of what we're supposed to wear," he said. "We just want to be seen as good contributing members of the community."

In Plain Sight

by Adam Leith Gollner

Amateur art sleuth Clifford Schorer III has helped find works by Dürer, Rembrandt, and Rubens. Now he's embarked on his greatest discovery yet, cracking a 43-year-old cold case.

On the evening of April 7, 2021, the amateur art detective Clifford Schorer III was seated on a couch in his glass house. In silence, he opened a manila envelope that had been sent to him by a respected Massachusetts attorney. The packet contained evidence related to an unsolved crime

Schorer's midcentury-modern home, designed in 1956 by Bauhaus founder Walter Gropius, sits atop a majestic dune at the western edge of Provincetown. Its floor-to-ceiling windows offer 270-degree views of the seascape below. After dark, with the lights on, the glass house glows like a television screen. Since Schorer and his spouse, Kris, never close the front blinds, passersby can actually see into the home, as if watching a show about a sleuth who tracks down missing artworks.

Had you peered through the panes on that spring night, you might have spied Schorer, in front of the fireplace, on his Danish modern sofa, leafing through photocopied pages, seeking clues as he often does. "Your interesting package has now found its way to my hand," he would write the lawyer who had mailed the envelope. In fact, he had told that attorney some weeks earlier: "You know what I do all day long. I look for paintings."

Schorer already had a reputation for finding lost master-pieces worth millions, but this dossier contained the makings of his biggest case yet. The documents related to a 1978 home invasion in Worcester, Massachusetts, during which nine highly valuable paintings were taken, including works by several Old Masters. The stolen art, Schorer calculated, would now be worth roughly $34 million. Like the 1990 hit at Boston's Isabella Stewart Gardner Museum—in which 13 pieces, estimated at $500 million, had been swiped—the Worcester mystery ranked among America's most confounding art heists. For decades, there'd been no cracks in the case. But then again, Clifford Schorer III had never looked into it.

Schorer has quite a track record. In 2019 he uncovered an original Albrecht Dürer, today valued at eight figures; remarkably, it had wound up in a yard sale for $30. Vienna's *Der Standard* deemed this "no less than a find of the century." Schorer seemed to concur, telling *The New York Times*: "I'll never have an experience like that again." But when it comes to unearthing overlooked and underpriced art trophies, he keeps repeating that experience; his identifications and retrievals, he says, are the equivalent of being struck by a "kind of electricity" multiple times. "In Cliff's case, lightning strikes *a lot*," explains Jim Welu, director emeritus of the

Worcester Art Museum (WAM). "It's just not a fluke in his life; it's part of his DNA."

Over the past decade or so, Schorerhas stumbled across two van Dycks and "relocated" five Turners. He's been restoring an altarpiece fragment attributed to El Greco that, he suspects, was rescued from a burning church during the Spanish Civil War. He regularly identifies or reidentifies works by significant Old Masters listed as "by an unidentified artist." His specialty is the forgotten Rembrandt or Rubens that has somehow slipped between the cracks and ended up, in his words, "sleeping in plain sight."

His hunches don't always prove correct: He's been suckered by at least a few forgeries or phonies. "Sometimes you follow threads that turn into an unraveling sweater," he admits. But many filaments he's followed have led to veritable treasures: the previously unrecorded van Haarlem he spotted in New Jersey that now hangs in the Art Institute of Chicago; a Cézanne he snagged from a Campbell's Soup heiress and helped place in Ireland's National Gallery; and three possibilities he scooped up on the cheap that were subsequently reattributed to the Milanese maestro Daniele Crespi. He also owns four works from Rembrandt's studio, he claims, including "two that I believe are by the master himself."

Schorer, who does not hold a university degree in art history, is largely self-taught and makes many of his finds in his spare time. He also employs runners to scour auctions around the world in search of hidden gems. "All day and night," he says, "we send pictures back and forth by WhatsApp, going, 'Do we think *this* is *this*?'" *The Sunday Times Magazine* (UK) describes him as being "well-known in the art world for his 'eye.'" Schorer formulates it slightly differently: "I'm known in the art world for rediscovering lost things."

Despite having left high school at age 15, Schorer, 58, is
an exceptionally knowledgeable if mercurial and at times
elusive man. He is lanky, with piercing dark eyes, short-
cropped hair, and a trim white beard. "I'm no one, with no
particular education," he stated in an oral history project for
the Smithsonian's Archives of American Art. "I come to it
with an open pair of eyeballs."

The types of paintings Schorer seeks are known as
"sleepers." A sleeper is the name that the picture trade
bestows upon a work being sold below its true value because
it is mistakenly thought to be fake, specious, a probable copy,
or the work of an inconsequential artist. A sleeper hunter is
an individual like Schorer, who stalks such errors or misat-
tributions in listings at auctions. Whenever he acquires
sleepers, he joins forces with experts to reassess and properly
catalog the paintings. Then he and his team often unload
them at a profit to blue-chip institutions, using the proceeds
to procure more beauties.

Schorer's success at rousing sleepers enabled him to put
together the investment group that purchased the venerable
London gallery Agnews in 2014. He then acquired a 290-
acre forest in Vermont. Recently he became the owner of a
Gatsby-style mansion on an approximately four-acre private
island in the Long Island Sound where J. P. Morgan's great-
grandson has resided. Schorer is renovating the place to sell.

I first met him in New York City after a Christie's auction,
where he'd just won a Turner for more than $1 million. His
intent was for Agnews to offer it over the coming years at
a higher price to the European market. What moves him,
however, isn't lucrative deals. He isn't an art dealer at all.

Instead, he contends that his goals are threefold: to resurrect forsaken or neglected artworks; to repatriate pieces spoliated by the Nazis; and to die in possession of a single perfect painting, ideally an unobtainable Leonardo. This last aspiration could require selling everything else he owns, but, as he once said, "I don't mind living in a cardboard box."

When asked where he normally lives, he replies, a tad testily, "I don't really 'normally live' anywhere." He divides his time between Provincetown and homes in Boston, London, and Mashpee, Massachusetts. He attends art fairs, lectures, and meetings in Europe once or twice a month. A favorite pastime, he says, is going to symposia that end just short of "fisticuffs between scholars about attribution."

A collector and art lover, Schorer is above all a dedicated investigator. He compares the way his mind works to those wall-mounted corkboards in classic crime shows, the kind with thumbtacked photos of suspects and murder scenes and corroborating evidence, all linked together by pieces of string. Instead of a Sherlock Holmes–style magnifying glass, he uses precision binocular headband magnifiers, large bench-top microscopes, reverse-image searches in online databases, and high-tech tactics, such as MA-XRF spectroscopy or dendrochronology, that apply laboratory analytics to decode a painting's makeup and approximate age. As cutting-edge as his forensics may be, however, Schorer—upon receiving that envelope in April 2021—found himself getting pulled into a strangely old-fashioned cold case.

The dossier consisted of whatever scant information was available about the nine paintings that had vanished in

1978: 43-year-old police reports, original bills of sale, insurance documents, invoices, and—most importantly to Schorer—photocopied reproductions of the actual trove: two Pissarros, two Renoirs, a Boudin, a Turner, and some intriguing old Dutch paintings. The theft had personal implications. Several of the works had been bound for the permanent collection of WAM, where Schorer had previously served as board president and where a number of canvases he owns are currently on view. Yet despite his ties to the museum, no one had ever given him a clear description of the artworks taken in 1978—until the file arrived.

The package was mailed by Warner Fletcher, a Worcester law firm director, chairman of the $50 million Stoddard Charitable Trust, and secretary-treasurer of the $59 million Fletcher Foundation, organizations that have long supported WAM. The plundered artworks had belonged to Helen Estabrook Stoddard and Robert Stoddard, Fletcher's aunt and her husband, both now deceased, who'd intended to bequeath some of them to WAM. Fletcher wasn't holding his breath for Schorer to solve the largest private art theft in the city's history. He just thought the unassuming sleuth might find a new way into the long-moribund search. "Maybe in your wanderings," Fletcher suggested to him, "if ever you come across any of these, you might be helpful."

Scoping the inventory in the envelope, Schorer gravitated to one painting in particular, a 17th-century icescape by Hendrick Avercamp. Among the towering figures of Holland's Golden Age, Avercamp (1585–1634) is famous for his depictions of outdoor wintertime activities: Netherlanders skating and otherwise going about their business on frozen canals and waterways. In his densely peopled, somewhat freaky panoramas, figures enjoying what the Dutch call "ice fever" can be seen getting frisky in nippy haylofts, relieving themselves in subzero outhouses, hanging from dead-season gallows.

Avercamp made only 100 or so of his icy paintings. The artist, likely deaf and nonverbal, was known as "the mute of Kampen." He remains, in the view of Wim Pijbes and Earl A. Powell III, respectively the emeritus directors of the Rijksmuseum and the National Gallery of Art in Washington, DC, "the acknowledged master of the winter scene."

Schorer had owned one of Avercamp's minor watercolors, which he'd auctioned off 10 weeks prior. But the stolen composition was a much bigger deal. *Winter Sports*, as it was known, appeared to be a masterpiece. A signed 1944 attestation included in Fletcher's package qualified it as "one of the best works by this rare master." It was nearly four centuries old and in a pristine state of preservation.

The Avercamp looked "extre-e-e-emely desirable," Schorer emailed Fletcher. A winter scene of that type, he estimated, would today cost up to "$10 million if you can buy one but you can't." Per Sotheby's, the last two comparable Avercamps had sold at auction for $7.75 and $8.6 million each. Schorer considered *Winter Sports* a "sui generis rarity." He would only be able to establish a precise value after verifying its condition firsthand. He informed an astonished Fletcher, "I believe I can run it to ground in around 15 more minutes during the business day."

The trail it left behind, he felt, would likely lead to the remaining Worcester paintings. But first he needed to establish what, exactly, had happened on the night of the theft.

Worcester, the second-biggest urban center in the Commonwealth of Massachusetts, is a postindustrial city an hour west of Boston. As you drive into town, you are greeted by a WELCOME sign in the shape of an open book with blank pages, as though you're entering a story that hasn't yet been written.

Sometime after midnight on June 22, 1978, according to the police report, a vehicle containing an undetermined number of nondescript thieves cruised through the upscale neighborhood of Forest Grove. They turned onto Monmouth Road. The last home on the dead-end street was a stately blue-and-white fairy-tale mansion belonging to the art patrons Helen and Robert Stoddard. Their 36-acre property occupied one of the city's choicest private lots. The gabled 10-bedroom home, dominated by dark wood and soaring ceilings, was done in high-end Arts and Crafts style. The walls were adorned with works by Eugène Delacroix, Georgia O'Keeffe, and Marc Chagall.

In the midsummer darkness, the robbers made their way toward the Stoddards' immense backyard. Ignoring the lavish gardens and the helipad, they sought a way in through the rear sunporch.

Helen Stoddard, known locally as "the grand dame of Worcester," had attended the Sorbonne, where she'd developed a lifelong love of fine art, especially French Impressionism. At her urging, the couple had started collecting tableaux. The first piece they acquired was a small Renoir landscape; Helen couldn't imagine living without it. An ardent Francophile, she'd helped establish WAM's member council and would continue volunteering on museum committees into her 90s.

Robert Stoddard ran a lucrative metal manufacturing business and was majority owner of the Worcester *Telegram* (later to become the *Telegram & Gazette*, which *The New York Times* company eventually bought for $295 million). An amateur helicopter pilot, he enjoyed vintage automobiles and could be seen driving around town in his Bentley sporting a porkpie hat. In 1958, he cofounded the right-wing John Birch Society, the extremist group that would help give rise to the modern conservative movement. If you tried to sit to his right at a table, he'd warn you that you might fall off the edge of the world. Retrograde politically, he was a big-spending philanthropist—and a prime target for a burglary. He also happened to be a notoriously deep sleeper.

On the night of the break-in, according to news reports, only Robert was home. His wife was in the hospital undergoing jaw surgery. He finished his usual presleep milk and cookies and got into bed by 11:45 P.M.

Not long after, the thieves tried to force their way in by prying apart a jalousie window with a screwdriver. When that didn't work, they broke the glass pane on the back breezeway door. The key to the deadbolt was sitting in the lock. Turning it, the crooks walked right in.

They helped themselves to snacks in the refrigerator and booze from the liquor cabinet. Since they'd come without proper carrying cases for the artworks, they slashed open pillows from the sofa, strewing fluff all over the floor. They stuffed paintings into pillowcases, police surmised, and packed smaller ivory objets and jewel boxes into antique fire buckets. They also rifled through Stoddard's bedroom without disturbing his slumber. They placed a fire poker nearby, apparently in case he awoke and needed to be subdued. But he dozed through it all, even as the thieves ransacked the place.

Upon waking at 6 A.M., Stoddard found his glasses on the floor. His wallet was missing from the bedside bureau, as were two of his watches. The couple's beloved Pissarro port scene, which had hung above their mantelpiece, was gone. So was Helen's prized Renoir, the light of her life. Another seven paintings, including the Avercamp and the Turner, were now empty spots on the wall. A trail of footprints and pillow feathers marked the getaway route through the backyard.

"Bumblers Pull Off a Perfect Crime" read the headline in the *Telegram*. Worcester's police department called it an "amateurish job" done by "petty thieves." But for small-timers, they'd either gotten fantastically lucky or they'd known precisely which paintings were the most valuable. The Stoddards' collection had been appraised for insurance purposes 11 months prior; all the priciest pieces were the very ones that had been taken. "It was as if," officers noted, the "thieves had been given a list of paintings to steal."

Even so, the ensuing investigation went nowhere. The sergeant assigned to the case would later acknowledge that the authorities had never even come up with a suspect. Insinuations that Robert Stoddard had orchestrated it for the insurance payout were summarily dismissed. His wealth was such that the amount he stood to receive from Liberty Mutual (on whose board of directors he served) was described as "a drop in the bucket."

Perhaps the most arresting detail was that pillowcases played a part in the caper. Because a pillowcase was precisely what would end up leading Schorer to the Avercamp.

⊶⊷

The manila envelope beside him, Schorer picked up his MacBook Pro and started searching Hendrick Avercamp images online, on the off chance he might find a digital footprint of the Stoddards' winterscape. At first nothing relevant popped up. But as he scanned the Google search results, he had a thought: If I knew I had a hot painting, previously attributed to Avercamp, to whom would I attribute it if I wanted to push it through the market and get away with it? In other words, what would a fence do? The move, to any art detective, was obvious: try to sell it as something close to, but not exactly, the real thing.

Schorer retried the image search using the name of the painter's best-known disciple, his nephew Barent Avercamp. Within a few moments, a thumbnail appeared that matched the photocopied reproduction in his file. "Bingo!" he exclaimed, zooming in. As he'd suspected, the painting had been falsely ascribed to an Avercamp follower. Barent's works were inferior to his uncle's and worth substantially less—but also easier to peddle without drawing attention. Schorer clicked on the thumbnail, which brought him to a website called Pixels.com.

"That's insane," he muttered to himself, eyeing the screen. Reproductions of the pilfered Avercamp were being sold as decorative throw pillows. For $18.40, anyone could buy a pillowcase with the Stoddards' long-lost icescape printed on it. The machine-washable coverlets weren't the only products that featured the painting. The company's print-on-demand technology meant you could get the Avercamp on a yoga mat, a coffee mug, a bath towel, or an iPhone case.

The original was last seen in 1978, before digital photography existed. So how, Schorer wondered, had Pixels.com gotten access to an image that could be reproduced on products? There was only one answer: Someone must have scanned it recently.

Schorer looked closer at the onscreen pillowcase. The underlying rendering, he noticed, belonged to a collection called Bridgeman Images, a digital fine art archive. For $39, Schorer was able to license a full-resolution version of that parent file. Opening it, he checked the metadata and spotted the initials L.S.F.A.L.—which he recognized as referring to Lawrence Steigrad Fine Arts Ltd., a New York Old Masters dealer.

Schorer knew Steigrad well enough to call him. As the telephone rang, he wondered if the Avercamp was still in Steigrad's possession or if his gallery had already sold it. When Steigrad picked up, Schorer got right to the point: *Larry, why are you fucking trafficking in stolen paintings from my museum?* Steigrad was emphatic that he'd never bought *or* sold the painting; he'd simply photographed it when it had been on sale in 1995. "Where?" Schorer demanded. At the European Fine Art Foundation Fair (TEFAF), Steigrad replied, a highly reputable art market held annually in Maastricht, the Netherlands.

Every painting sold at TEFAF undergoes a rigorous vetting process overseen by experts, conservators, and academic specialists. Because this painting had been submitted as a Barent Avercamp, it did not receive the same scrutiny that a Hendrick Avercamp would have. And from what Schorer could tell by the hi-res scan, the artist's monogram-like signature, which superimposed the initial *H* over an *A*, appeared to have been forged: Someone seemed to have etched the initial *B* over the *H*.

Either way, it was the same painting that decades earlier had been purloined from the Stoddards. Unfortunately, Steigrad informed Schorer, the gallery that had represented the Avercamp at TEFAF was now defunct, and the owner had died. But through art-world connections, Schorer says he implored one of the gallery's former partners to divulge the name of the individual who'd sold them the Avercamp.

His name was Sheldon Fish.

◦━┼━◦

"What i do is I look to find lost masterpieces," explained Fish when I reached him in Lima, Peru—a proclamation not unlike those I had heard from Schorer. "I've made a lot of major discoveries." When not rooting around for sleepers, Fish is the CEO of a South American cargo shipping company that transports hazardous substances and dangerous materials, "particularly explosives and radioactive goods."

Throughout our call, Fish was adamant that he had not known the Avercamp was radioactive at the time he'd purchased it. "When you buy thousands of things, every now and then one of them ends up being stolen," he offered breezily. "Believe me, if I knew or if I thought it were"—stolen, he meant—"I would run the other way."

(Searching Fish's name online brought up reports of a theft of 18th-century artworks from a Pemvian church. Eight of the stolen paintings were allegedly consigned by Fish to an Iowa auction house, whereupon they were seized by the FBI. At the time, Fish denied knowing that the works were stolen. No charges were laid. Asked to comment, Fish noted that the sellers had given him a receipt: "You must always be careful who you are dealing with and get a signed receipt. Anyone who knowingly buys a stolen painting is an idiot.")

During our conversation, Fish had initially told me he couldn't recall where he'd found the Avercamp, though he did speak openly about having profited from it via the gallery that brought it to TEFAF. "I sold it for pretty good money: $100,000," he claimed. "I remember the painting—but I don't remember who I bought it from . . . I wish I could be more helpful, you know. It'd be great to help."

The more we talked, the less fuzzy his memories became. Upon first encountering the painting, he remembered, he could tell it was valuable. "I knew I was onto a score," Fish said. "But he didn't sell it to me as an Avercamp, obviously." Who was the "he" who'd sold it? Fish couldn't recall.

To prepare for our interview, Fish added, he'd asked his brother about the painting. The two of them often went treasure hunting together, and his brother thought they'd found it at Brimfield Antique Flea Markets, a half hour or so drive from Worcester. "You go from one booth to the other looking for the mistakes," Fish explained. "Different experts are running around all over the place, like lunatics, trying to find a lost whatever it is." By the end of our conversation, he'd concluded that he likely found it at Brimfield: "I'm fairly certain I got it from there." He told me he didn't have a receipt.

Still, Schorer now had a piece of the puzzle: Brimfield. Digging deeper into the events at the Stoddards' home and the ensuing investigation, the sleuth noticed a curious connection. The only quasi-lead from the police investigation was a call Stoddard had received not long after the burglary, during which a voice with an indeterminate foreign accent claimed to know where the paintings were. And though the cops never identified the caller, they were able to track the call to a phone booth next to the interstate, 10 minutes from Brimfield.

One of the sellers booths at Brimfield during that time, Schorer learned, had been operated by a local antique dealer named Robert Cornell and his wife, Jennifer B. Abella-Cornell. Twenty years after the 1978 Worcester heist, the two had become suspects when the Pissarro from above the Stoddards' mantel turned up at an auction house in Ohio. (Both Cornell and Abella-Cornell were questioned by the FBI; Robert Cornell denied all involvement, and no charges were ever filed.)

The artist's great-grandson Joachim Pissarro noticed the auction listing and, realizing where the painting had come from, personally alerted Helen Stoddard. (Her husband had passed away in 1984.) She informed authorities, and the FBI moved swiftly to seize the artwork before it could go under the gavel. It had been expected to fetch up to $2 million. (It might now be worth four or five times that amount.)

At the time of the raid, the FBI began investigating how the Pissarro had ended up in Ohio. But they never managed to reconstruct the painting's trajectory. Cornell and Abella-Cornell, by then divorced, had contradicted each other's statements to authorities to such an extent that the FBI described attempts to establish the truth as being "like beating a dead horse."

The couple had lived 22 miles from Brimfield in a 30-room Victorian mansion called Amesmith. Cornell ran a gallery from their home, where works by Picasso and Chagall were on offer. A specialist in coins, particularly in detecting counterfeits, he fell on hard times in the early 1980s after he was convicted of receiving stolen property. He complained that law enforcement was trying to depict him as "the biggest fence in Western Massachusetts." Initially found guilty, he was later acquitted on appeal. But the fallout from the trials and several tax audits eventually forced him to shutter his gallery.

When the Stoddards' Pissarro surfaced, Cornell denied having had anything to do with it—or the original burglary. "I've never seen that painting," he declared in the Worcester *Telegram*. "1 can say that and be lying through my teeth. But the bottom line is that painting has never been in this house."

Abella-Cornell claimed she'd found the painting in Cornell's closet, wrapped in paper. She also insisted that earlier it had been mounted on a wall in Amesmith. The couple's acrimonious breakup was compounded by Abella-Cornell's involvement in a reported love triangle. As she informed investigators, she and Cornell were working the antiques circuit when, at a Cleveland coin show, she got romantically involved with the owner of a nearby wine bar. (Abella-Cornell did not respond to requests for comment; Cornell died in 2013.)

When the couple split up, Abella-Cornell allegedly took $30,000 in gems and rare coins from Cornell. He called the police, who promptly found most of the stolen goods in her possession. Four rare coins worth $10,000, however, were missing. She was forced to reimburse Cornell that amount and serve two years probation. (Media reports at the time stated that she pleaded guilty to avoid a trial and permanent record of conviction.) Without means to pay Cornell off, she told the FBI, she turned to the owner of the wine bar. He acknowledged, in the *Telegram*, that he then raised the funds to lend her. She said she brought him the Pissarro as collateral. Cornell disputed this, contending that she was attempting to frame him. For a variety of reasons, including the fact that their dueling accounts lacked hard proof, the FBI dropped the case. In November 1998, a month after the Pissarro was seized, Helen Stoddard passed away. The work—depicting a coastal harbor in Dieppe, France—was returned to WAM shortly thereafter.

According to reporter Frank Magiera, who covered the heist for the *Telegram* and spoke with all the parties, Abella-Cornell's account sounded more credible than Cornell's. "He struck me as being a very surly, suspicious person," Magiera recalled, "a shady antique dealer." Even so, he added: "We don't have any real smoking gun that ties Cornell to this, other than Abella-Cornell." Without any strong evidence, the entire Pissarro affair seemed to dissolve into a haze—not unlike the snowy backgrounds of Avercamp's finest mid-winter scenes.

Schorer had underestimated his initial assessment of the Stoddards' Avercamp: that it would take only 15 minutes to run to ground. He chalked this up to what he called his arrogance. But he didn't stop seeking its whereabouts; its online reappearance had opened further lines of inquiry.

To begin with, Schorer tracked down Abella-Cornell. He claimed that she provided him with two addresses where the other remaining stolen paintings might have conceivably been stashed. He told me he'd hired a private investigator to poke around. He also endeavored to establish who had purchased the Avercamp at the 1995 art fair.

A breakthrough came when he tracked down the descendants of the now deceased gallery owner from TEFAF. "I come in peace," he wrote. Even so, he added that "the FBI has shown a willingness to take a heavy hand in this case." The gallerist's daughter did not answer his initial queries, but Schorer was persistent. After all, he'd been informed that the gallery's records were in her garage. Months later, she agreed to search the archives. If she could unearth the sales receipts, they would likely identify the Avercamp buyer.

Schorer was patient. He knew time was often on the side of the tenacious sleuth. Moreover, he had another case he was running down about another Dutch painter. This one was named Rembrandt Harmenszoon van Rijn.

⌐━━⌐

In the Fall of 2021, Schorer acquired one of the deepest sleepers he'd ever seen: a circa 1629 portrait of an elderly gin-nosed man, seemingly by Rembrandt. It had been put up for auction in Maryland as an "imitation in the manner of." The estimated sale price: $1,000-$1,500. After a bidding war, Schorer won it for a healthy $288,000. If real, that would be a fraction of its value. (Rembrandts rarely come to market, but a pair of plausibly authentic portraits sold for $14.2 million in 2023, and 18 months earlier, the Dutch government, in association with the Rembrandt Association and the Rijksmuseum, had paid a whopping $198 million for a bona fide self-portrait.)

Art authentication efforts move slowly; broadly accepted conclusions can remain evasive. And so, while more time is needed to determine whether Schorer had found an actual Rembrandt, he and whoever he outbid weren't alone in considering it genuine. Volker Manuth, the lead author of the artist's 2019 catalogue raisonné, wouldn't offer a categorical answer but, as he told me, "It is very likely that it has been painted by Rembrandt."

That same conclusion was reached by Manuth's esteemed predecessor, Abraham Bredius, whose landmark 1935 survey of Rembrandt's complete paintings included the portrait as *Study of a Man With a Swollen Nose*. Regardless, Schorer's putative Rembrandt hadn't been heard of since World War II.

And yet, unlike many paintings looted by the Nazis, this one, with proper papers in tow, had been smuggled to the US from Europe as the war broke out. The portrait was then sold, legally, to the chairman of Velcro Companies. In short: Its provenance appeared spotless.

The painting fell into dormancy after being donated to a Benedictine monastery in California. In the intervening decades, it nearly went up in flames in two separate forest fires. When rescued from the first blaze, one monk asked the other, who'd snatched it off the wall at the last second: "Why did you take *that*?" The brothers dismissed the idea of it being an honest-to-God Rembrandt as laughable, so they finally ended up consigning it to an auction house. (The monks had appraisers weigh in, only to be told the work couldn't possibly have been by the master.)

After his winning bid, Schorer brought a high-end 3D reproduction of the painting to the monastery as a donation. The surviving monks there were still in a state of shock over the fact that they'd unwittingly owned such a pricey work.

Schorer told them he'd found an eyelash in the impasto and was testing to see if its DNA matched Rembrandt's. (He was not, however, aware of any genetic databases he could check it against.) Either way, probing into it seemed to matter more to him than solving the problem. Working with Old Masters gets philosophical at times; attaining a clear resolution isn't always possible. In art, some questions can't be answered—as Schorer says, using a musical metaphor, they simply "hang out there in the ether as a chord unresolved." He doesn't tend to dwell on such perplexities; he just moves on to the next case. "Investigating the unseen in the twilight hour is how I enjoy spending my life," he explains. After dinner at the monastery, he confided to me that he had come to a realization: His pursuit, in effect, was a never-ending quest for some kind of religious illumination that he knew might never come.

⊙━━━⊙

The hunt for the lost Avercamp continued into Masters Week and Master Drawings New York in January 2023—auctions and gallery shows featuring old works. (More on the Avercamp saga shortly.) At that point, Schorer unveiled his Rembrandt at an invitation-only cocktail reception on the Upper East Side. Elegant guests streamed in, some wearing oversized scarves, others with glittering cufflinks. Mayfair accents could be heard over voices speaking German or Dutch. Schorer, sporting a royal blue suit with matching sneakers, winkingly and self-deprecatingly introduced himself to new arrivals as a research assistant.

For the occasion, he'd hung his recently acquired 1629 portrait next to a self-portrait made around the same time by Rembrandt's dashing friend and competitor, Jan Lievens. (Their early works can be almost impossible to tell apart.) The Lievens was on loan from Theodore Roosevelt's descendants. Schorer had been at a wedding in their home when he recognized Lievens's face on the wall. "I found it in the foyer," he told me. "I went around asking, 'Who is the proprietor?' The last time it was mentioned was decades ago. I don't think it has ever been on public view."

At the reception, a professorial man in a bowtie took in the display, rapt. "I'm having a moment," he gasped. "This Lievens hasn't been seen in over a century, and Cliff found it at someone's house." He was Lloyd DeWitt, a coauthor of

Jan Lievens: A Dutch Master Rediscovered and at the time chief curator at Virginia's Chrysler Museum of Art.

The Lievens, DeWitt added, was "very, very shocking to see. . . . This one wasn't even cataloged. Or known." By placing the supposed Rembrandt portrait next to one by Lievens, Schorer was trying to accomplish two things: first, to show an undisputed work compared to a disputed one from the same moment in time; second, to show how his ability to unearth sleepers can play a deeper role in scholarship. There was also a degree of showmanship to the scene; he was doing it, he said, "to throw meat to the wolves."

Inquisitive visitors admired Schorer's find. Whether by Rembrandt or not, it depicted a wizened man with a bulbous nose, wispy facial hair, and downcast eyes, his sad, thin lips parted in mid-sigh. He appeared to be homeless or a beggar—"a tramp," someone suggested. The brushstrokes were loose and casual, in Rembrandt's signature experimental style, but the artist still captured the sitter's essence, his burden of worries, his frailty.

Not long after the vernissage, a vetting committee designated the portrait as "attributed to Rembrandt" as opposed to simply "by Rembrandt." This meant that not everyone was convinced about its veracity. (Schorer clarifies that their decision is not permanent and can be revisited in the future; the committee may have been erring on the side of caution.) When Schorer sought to poll delegates to find out who the detractors were, some present allegedly cautioned him that he was being "strident and obnoxious." According to one witness, an attendee piped up in Schorer's defense: *He's just enthusiastic, he's not strident.*

Whatever his attitude may have been, it's hard to encapsulate an individual as singular as Schorer. During our first phone call, when I had proposed writing about his art-hound accomplishments, he responded: "I'd like to be the furniture, if I may." I laughed, not quite understanding. Then, over the course of our meetings, I came to realize what he meant: a protagonist in the background, more or less unnoticed.

The fact is, however, he is hard *not* to notice. In person, Schorer's six-foot-one frame is offset by a slight hunch, creating the impression of someone prepared to pounce at any moment. A polymath, he balances his erudition with a sardonic, arcane sense of humor. (When I told him I found a particular art historian's style to be purple, he corrected me: "Lavender is his prose; it is dancing off the poppies.")

Largely unaccustomed to publicity, Schorer seemed reluctant when I initially suggested I follow one of his ongoing cases—specifically the Worcester heist, with its alluring Avercamp. Schorer was also firmly reticent, at first, about sharing personal information. Given his keenly developed sense of sight, he struck me as both wanting—and wanting *not*—to be seen, to be the kind of furniture that's on display in a glass house. It was only after I pointed out that Arthur Conan Doyle's tales tend to start on Baker Street—the gum-shoe Holmes sitting in front of the crackling hearth, lost in thought and puffing on his pipe—that he finally agreed to have me over to the Gropius house.

⚬━✦━⚬

I arrive on a misty September Monday in Provincetown. A hurricane has just blown by, leaving charcoal-hued rain clouds in its wake. Schorer's glass home rises above the bay where the *Mayflower* first stopped in the New World. A verdigris plaque at his front gate commemorates the "Pilgrims' Landing" historical site.

He and Kris bring me into their living room, where Schorer likes to do investigative work. Birch logs lie in the marble fireplace, strictly for decor; their 60-ton geothermal system regulates the interior temperature year-round. Kris recalls the moment when Schorer first opened up about the Avercamp discovery: "He came to me and said, 'I found this painting on a pillowcase.' I was like, Okay, now he's started finding them in his mind."

"It was already in the rearview mirror 14 seconds later," Schorer adds. "I wanted to find out where the other missing paintings had gone."

The paucity of paintings on display in their home is striking, suggesting that the art is secondary to the pursuit. But there is another consideration: The walls, after all, are primarily glass panes. The house itself is the artwork, Schorer insists. Gropius and his Architects Collaborative partners had conceived of the dwelling as a "gesamtkunstwerk": a total work of art. Everything from the doorknobs and cabinets to the retractable wooden panels that conceal the TV and hi-fi were custom designed. Frank Sinatra is said to have performed on the living room's Steinway at the housewarming party six decades earlier.

Schorer's paintings, he and Kris explain, are mainly kept off-site—in storage or on loan to museums. There are, however, a number of sculptures of ancient gods scattered about. A large Song dynasty statue of a deity. A troupe of Egyptian figurines, including an Isis and a Horus. A 17th-century sculpture of Poseidon conquering the waves: a gift from FDR to Churchill. Schorer mentions nonchalantly that he'd acquired it in 2020 when he helped auction off the contents of the Waldorf Astoria.

We make our way into the dining room, where I meet the couple's two purebred rottweilers, Tyson and Nikki, whom they call their kids. Kris recommends not attempting to pet them. As we sit together, I say I'm hoping to understand how an autodidact such as Schorer has come to operate in such rarified spheres. The dogs glower in my direction. But Kris encourages Schorer to speak candidly: "Open your feelings, for the love of God, Cliff."

⊶

Schorer had a difficult childhood. His parents—neither particularly interested in art—separated when he was a boy. Their divorce litigation lasted years. Often in the care of grandparents, Schorer became precociously independent, spending much of his time alone in Boston. "I was on my own as of 11," he explains.

His father, Clifford Schorer Jr., an entrepreneur and professor at Columbia Business School, corroborates this account. "Cliff very early on decided to take care of himself," he tells me. "He didn't want the conventional kind of parenting or to be part of the family nest." His father recalls that the teenage Cliff would disappear for days on trips to Manhattan. Once, when asked where he'd been, he claimed to have spent time hanging with Andy Warhol. His father didn't believe him. But then Warhol himself called the house a few days later. "The guy is dinner and a show," Cliff Jr. says of his son.

After Schorer dropped out of high school, he started coding. Some of the software he wrote made him $27,000. When he was 17, he founded Bottom Line Exchange Company, which purchased items, mainly computing equipment and office furniture, that other companies needed to move.

To make ends meet, he drove a taxi. Branching out, he bought a soon-to-be-bankrupt database company that was selling its whole operation for the price of its only real equity: two Xerox photocopiers worth $6,000. When Schorer inspected the facility, he noticed an old 25,000-square-foot UNIVAC computer. While the owner didn't think it was worth much, Schorer, a hardware geek, knew it contained 24-karat-gold parts. The company also had 170 employees who had to be laid off; Schorer, though only a teenager, did so. He then hired a team to disassemble the UNIVAC and strip out the gold. "We ended up getting $67,000 or $70,000 from the gold," he recounts. "I was well on my way at that point."

When the computer manufacturing bubble burst in the late '80s and early '90s, Schorer found himself snapping up failing companies—and their real estate. He went on acquisition sprees, hoarding assets. At one point, by his estimate, the warehouse facilities for what he called his "crazy catastrophe of storage" took up a million square feet of space. He also invested in construction ventures and fast-food franchises, funneling his profits into a bottomless passion for art.

Schorer started becoming a serious collector in his early 20s, focusing initially on Chinese porcelain. He amassed and sold hundreds of pieces at auction. After a trip to Paris, he began getting into Baroque paintings, which he researched in Harvard's libraries. (Auction houses, before the internet, mailed listings of offerings there.) In time, one sleeper led to another, even as his entrepreneurial projects snowballed. But all of them, on some level, connected back to his childhood.

Schorer's interest in art began at age six, with a children's book called *From the Mixed-Up Files of Mrs. Basil E. Frank-weiler*. In it, two young siblings run away from home and hide in the Metropolitan Museum of Art. The book treats art as something to escape *into*, whether from loneliness, boredom, or an unhappy family life. As a child, Schorer loved the Met—and the American Museum of Natural History, which kindled an obsession with paleontology.

This obsession reached its zenith in 2008, when Schorer spent $942,797 for the nearly complete skeleton of a 23-foot-long triceratops from North Dakota's Badlands. A *New York Times* op-ed denounced the fact that a 65-million-year-old dinosaur specimen had somehow ended up in private hands. He eventually found a home for it, in a combination gift and sale, at the Boston Museum of Science, stipulating that it be listed as having come from an "anonymous donor" and that it be named Triceratops Cliff, after his grandfather, Clifford Schorer Sr. "The name is the same, unfortunately, so people know who it is," said Schorer, again wanting to have it both ways: seen and unseen.

At times, the dizzying extent of his exploits can seem to defy credulity. Even so, all the curators and insiders I have consulted for this story vouch for Schorer. Some mention a propensity for exaggeration or for conflating speculation with irrefutable fact. But Schorer merely seems to have figured out how the art business works. Frederick Ilchman, the Art of Europe chair at Boston's Museum of Fine Arts, tells me that the institution, courtesy of Schorer, acquired three major European modernist paintings from Agnews in 2023. Ilchman characterized Schorer as a brilliant, if eccentric, risk-taker, adding, "To be a good connoisseur, you have to be eccentric and take a risk."

Part of his fascination with sleepers—which are, after all, bargain-priced items—seems to stem from a constitutional frugality. Kris emphasizes how Schorer's sole overarching interest is art, which means he doesn't care much for everything else: clothing, food, even comfort. Despite his self-evident wealth, Schorer, during my Provincetown visit, suggests we meet for dinner at 4:30 P.M. to catch the early bird special. After the waitress informs us that the restaurant has stopped offering off-hours discounts, he vows never to return. Then, when we pile into his Prius, the stereo starts playing a podcast at such a rapid rate that I can scarcely make out the words. He says he likes listening to podcasts at 2.5x speed (4x speed if the speaker has a British accent and talks slowly). Kris laments Schorer's proclivity for watching films at double speed. "Why waste two hours on a movie," asks Schorer, "if you can do it in one?"

When the two of them first met, Kris thought Schorer was a spy. After their second date, at the Cheesecake Factory, they walked to Schorer's town house in downtown Boston. At the time, it contained 120 large-scale Old Masters paintings. "It was so creepy," Kris now recalls. "It was like entering the Louvre. There were four floors of paintings. Everything was *ancient*." The religious iconography on display featured a preponderance of murders and martyrdoms. "Crosses everywhere—nuns, you know?" Kris says, with a shudder. "There wasn't an inch without a painting."

Schorer still has many of those monumental canvases stored in warehouses. "I don't think I owned anything made after 1900," he adds, chuckling. "I wouldn't let anyone clean" the town house. The bathroom had original 1851 fixtures. Velvet draperies covered the windows to keep sunlight out. The lighting scheme favored gas-burning sconces and candles. The overall effect was "Welcome to old lady land," he beams, clearly proud of the anachronistic world he'd built.

"We shouldn't live in the 17th century all the time," says Kris.

Schorer disagrees. But the conversation reminds him of a line he'd written: "In the era of electric light, only the extravagant will burn tallow candles." It is derived from the narrative section of a symphony about Thomas Edison's life that Schorer co-composed for the Boston Pops Orchestra that premiered in 1997. When we settle in at the glass house, he proceeds to play us the 21-minute recording. A passage about grief, he notes, is autobiographical. "I could not let my personal pain distract me," recites the symphonic Edison. "For above all time is my enemy." These verses reflect how Schorer has transformed the tallow of his own childhood into extravagant achievements.

"Cliff cannot rest," Kris says, over swells of music as Edison proclaims his workaholic desire to continue exploring right until his funeral. "I think he always keeps working so hard because he's afraid he will be poor one day—like when he was young." ("What *psychology*," counters Schorer, who points out that working on a project-by-project basis, as he does, necessarily differs from having steady income.)

⊶

Several months later, Schorer's patience was rewarded. He received an email from the daughter of the TEFAF gallerist. Attached was the bill of sale for the Avercamp. Armed with this new lead, he determined that in 1995, the painting had gone to a prominent Dutch family that had made its fortune in footwear. They'd purchased it legally, as a work by Barent Avercamp. Schorer soon found their home on Google Earth—"a big mansion"—and started sending letters demanding the painting's return to WAM in exchange for the amount they had originally paid at the long-ago art fair. (The owners have requested anonymity.)

At first, Schorer thought he'd simply get the Avercamp back. After all, theft is illegal; missing property ought to be returned. In the fine art market, however, what's right isn't always the same as what's legal. Looted works don't necessarily get handed over to their prior or lawful owner, as the Elgin Marbles attest. "It's not fair that somebody gets to keep stolen art—but that's often how it works," says Erin Thompson, professor of art crime at the City University of New York. Certain kinds of theft were long ago legalized by colonialist powers, allowing plundered objects and resources to enrich European nations. And while some countries and jurisdictions are evolving, others are not.

Had the Avercamp been sold in America, odds are it would have already been confiscated by law enforcement. "There are huge differences between the way people in the US and in Europe approach the recovery of stolen art," notes James Ratcliffe, general counsel at the Art Loss Register, a London organization specializing in such transactions. "In the Netherlands, even a thief can get title to a stolen artwork if they have it for long enough." Conversely, American authorities have been aggressively enforcing restitution claims, even for decades-old cases. Last year, for example, New York's Antiquities Trafficking Unit seized and repatriated an ancient Anatolian bronze bust that had been in WAM's collection since 1966.

The museum's experience with that bust would lead one to assume that the inverse would also hold true: that its own stolen goods would be returned swiftly. But Schorer's and WAM's legal team's retrieval efforts soon became mired in international art-law technicalities.

First, there were the owners of the painting. Rather than acknowledge receipt of Schorer's letters, he said, the family ignored them and lawyered up. Then, as his messages continued to go unanswered, he approached Dutch authorities, trusting that the police could seize it. To no avail. He wanted to involve Interpol, Scotland Yard, the FBI's art squad—but, he says, none could help.

Growing antsy, he went public with the story. As reported in *Artnet News and Boston* magazine, Schorer threatened to initiate legal proceedings against the family if the painting was not returned within 40 days. That tactic didn't work either, but the media attention did bring another Avercampian individual out of the woodwork: Arthur Brand, a Dutch art detective who hosts a TV show in the Netherlands about tracking down and recovering hot artworks. Sometimes described in press accounts as the "Indiana Jones of the art world," he'd made his name finding objects like Oscar Wilde's ring, Hitler's horses, and a missing Van Gogh. He told Schorer he wanted to help get the Avercamp back.

Brand, having gleaned through news reports that a Dutch family had purchased the painting, contacted Schorer and offered to mediate. Because of his popular television program, he'd likely be more persuasive than Schorer. "What I do is try to get paintings back that are stolen, and which might disappear forever," Brand tells me. He contrasts this with Schorer's sleeper hunting, which, he points out, usually does not involve criminal spoils. The Avercamp overlaps between their respective areas of expertise—as well as their two continents' legal realities.

Due to his status as a Dutch TV personality, Brand managed to communicate with the family. They were concerned, above all, with keeping their name out of the press. He advised them to do the moral thing and return the painting, on the condition that they not lose money on it: "If they offer you such a deal," he counseled them, "you should accept it."

With Brand having wrangled the family to the bargaining table, Schorer and WAM's side offered to make them whole without allowing them to profit from the theft. This, despite the fact that the family, so Brand assures me, was well aware that their Avercamp was a real-deal Hendrick and therefore worth significantly more than what they bought it for. But they would likely face difficulties if they ever tried to sell it.

When the insurance company agreed to cooperate with the museum in order to get the painting returned, it seemed like a resolution might be close. Unfortunately, according to Schorer and Brand, the various sides then started haggling over taxes and other fees. Throughout the next year, as Schorer and Brand conveyed the fitful progress of the negotiations, I had to remind myself that a sleeper hunter, by definition, seeks value. Art is about beauty—but it's also a big-money game. And businesspeople don't get rich by compromising; they do so by chiseling. Developments slowed to a trickle while Schorer spoke of pushing "a very angry accelerator pedal." Seasons passed; I often thought of the forlorn-looking scrounger in his liminal Rembrandt portrait.

Then, suddenly, on Easter Sunday 2024, I received a note saying that the two sides had come to terms. "A year after originally planned," Schorer wrote. In the very next line, without pausing, he revealed that he was onto a new chase. "I've been contacted," he went on, about "a major Rubens presumed lost in WWII . . . I may drop all and go to Switzerland to see if it is real. Looks right." He was moving on to another adventure—but he was hopeful that the Avercamp would, in the end, return to Worcester.

Regarding the other missing Stoddard paintings, Schorer says there are further morsels left on the trail that might eventually lead him to that quarry. He has started to sniff them out more doggedly. At the same time, he's still trying to get his recently resurfaced tramp unanimously recognized as a Rembrandt, having cowritten a book with Simon Worrall on the subject, entitled *The Lost Rembrandt*.

He's also begun spearheading an immense art restitution case, involving a Leonardo, several Dürers, and more than 150 other foundational works of art in the Western corpus, on behalf of a Dutch Jewish bank dismantled by the Nazi regime. Schorer's efforts in the matter started coming to fruition this summer, when he brought to market a Flemish Baroque work that had belonged to the bank until its liquidation in 1940, only to be presented as a birthday gift, two years later, to Adolf Hitler. Schorer describes this latest challenge as "the first battle in the biggest war of my life."

The Incel Terrorist

by Lana Hall

Oguzhan Sert was 17 when he walked into a Toronto massage parlor and killed an employee with a sword. The Crown argued the attack wasn't just murder, but an act of terror against women. The hard part would be proving it.

T he morning of February 24, 2020, began like any other at Crown Spa. The first clients of the day began coming and going for sessions, and J. C., the manager, was upstairs in the apartment where she lived. J. C., whose full name is under a publication ban, had managed the spa for about five years, and it wasn't unusual for her to work seven days a week, greeting clients at her desk and scheduling sessions. That day, she had a dentist appointment, and a newly hired receptionist had failed to show up for work. J. C. texted a friend, 24-year-old Ashley Noelle Arzaga, to fill in. She arrived around noon.

The spa was one of Toronto's 25 licensed body-rub parlors—nondescript storefronts where attendants offer erotic massages, and that are consigned by city zoning to

semi-industrial areas. Crown Spa was in just such a neighborhood, near Dufferin Street and Wilson Avenue, just blocks
from the busy Highway 401, which ferries travelers east and
west. The spa occupied a small, two-story building on Dufferin Street, its front window obscured by frosted glass blocks,
with a sign in the window flashing "open."

A few blocks away, a 17-year-old boy named Oguzhan
Sert was getting ready for his own day, in the house he
shared with his father and stepmother. He dressed in sunglasses, a hat, and a long dark coat. He tucked his driver's
license into his coat pocket, along with a sharpening stone
and a note scrawled on lined paper: "Long Live The Incel
Rebellion." Into a black sheath attached to his belt he slid a
short sword, 17 inches long, etched with the words "THOT
SLAYER" (THOT is an acronym for That Ho Over There,
a slur sometimes used for women, especially sex workers).
Then he left home.

At about half past noon, he walked through Crown Spa's
front door into a small vestibule, then through a second
door into the lobby. He approached Arzaga at the reception
desk and, without saying a word, began stabbing her in the
neck. She collapsed to the floor as he continued slashing. As
J. C. got ready for her appointment, she heard sounds from
downstairs: banging, then a scream. She ran down and into
the lobby, where Sert stood holding his sword, blood pooling
at his feet. J. C. turned to flee, but she struggled to open the
exterior door, and Sert followed her. She slipped on the floor
as Sert stabbed her over and over, one slash cutting the flesh
on her hand to the bone, another nearly slicing off an entire
fingertip. She screamed at him to stop. "You fucking whore,"
he said as he continued his attack. "Die, die, die."

At least one attendant was with a client, oblivious to what was unfolding in the reception area. At some point, J. C.'s brother-in-law Jason, who had been waiting outside to accompany her to the dentist, tried to open the front door, but it was blocked by J. C. and Sert, who were grappling on the floor. J. C. wriggled aside to let Jason in; at the same time, she wrested the sword from Sert's grasp, struggling away as he clapped a hand over her mouth. She stabbed him in the back. Sert let out a gasp and stumbled into the parking lot. Jason leapt for him as J. C. ran, bleeding, to a neighboring business, begging the employees to call 911.

As she waited for paramedics, J. C. went back inside and found Arzaga on the floor. She had sustained 42 wounds, and J. C. could tell her friend was dead. Still, she tried to talk to her: "Everything is okay now, baby." By the time paramedics and police arrived, Sert was lying in the parking lot, bleeding onto the asphalt. His sword lay nearby. A paramedic asked him what had happened. "I wanted to kill everybody in the building," Sert said. "I'm happy I got one." Police took Sert into custody and charged him with both murder and attempted murder.

When the headlines about Arzaga's death popped up on my news feed, I began following the case intensely. My interest was not only journalistic, but personal. The streets around that part of North York are very familiar to me because, in the early and mid-2010s, I spent five years working in Toronto's massage parlors. I did it during a hiatus from university—rent was expensive, writing was economically precarious and, as I sometimes joked to clients, working a parlor job was more interesting than folding T-shirts at the Gap. For about a year, I worked at a parlor located in an office building near Highway 401, only 10 minutes from Crown

Spa. I thought of all the late nights and sleepy weekday mornings I spent with fellow attendants as we laundered towels and answered endless prank calls, as we applied each other's eyeliner before sessions and skittered around suburban strip malls on coffee or Red Bull runs.

And I thought of Ashley Arzaga, picking up a shift to make ends meet. I had never met her, but I knew plenty of young women much like her. The massage parlor economy operates on cash payments, unpredictable hours and, often, loose adherence to regulations. As a result, it attracts workers in transitional phases of life: students, single parents, women between jobs, and aspiring entrepreneurs. Violence is a risk, and a lack of trust in law enforcement makes staff more likely to handle the burden privately.

When I worked at parlors, we would occasionally get a client walking in visibly drunk or high, who wouldn't take kindly to being turned away. Sometimes, in the dimness of a session room, tensions would rise during negotiations about services, and my heart would race until I felt the smooth handle of the doorknob under my palm. Once, at gunpoint, somebody even robbed the front desk of a parlor I worked in.

But most days, it was simply a job. Contrary to stereotype—that the men who pay for sexual services are deviants, that the women who provide them are reckless or desperate—those moments were by far the exception. And the idea that anyone would walk into a massage parlor and commit an atrocity like the one at Crown Spa was unimaginable.

My interest in the case redoubled a few months later, when news broke that Sert—whose identity was then under a publication ban, since he was a minor—would be charged as a terrorist. His attack, it was alleged, was motivated by his self-identification as an incel, an "involuntary celibate," who advocated violence against women as retribution for his inability to form intimate relationships. Sert was the first person in Canada to face terror charges based on an incel-motivated crime, and he is likely the first person in the world. The charges were poised to spark a broader reckoning on what terrorism means in Canada. Violence against women has never, historically, merited such a label. Even Marc Lépine, the shooter who killed 14 people, mostly women, at Montreal's École Polytechnique in 1989, escaped that branding. A terror designation could mean a shift in how the courts treat offenders, and in how law enforcement pursues them. It could also mean that women like my former colleagues, and very much like me not very long ago, might no longer be regarded as simply the unfortunate victims of a disturbed individual—that their victimhood may come to signify something more.

As a crime recognized and punishable by Canadian law, terrorism is the new kid on the block. It didn't appear in the Criminal Code at all until 2001, when the Anti-Terrorism Act was passed in a hurried response to the 9/11 attacks in the US. The act defines terrorism as a crime intended to intimidate the public, committed "in whole or in part for a political, religious, or ideological purpose." But none of those terms—political, religious, ideological—were defined, an apparent oversight that was flagged even at the time. Robert Lanctôt, a Bloc Québécois MP, expressed reservations in a 2001 House of Commons debate, saying, "We cannot leave such a broad definition of terrorist activity in this legislation."

And yet, in the urgency of the moment, the act passed that December. Leah West is a professor of national security law at Carleton University who has written extensively about counter-terrorism and the definition of terrorism in Canadian law. She says the problem lies primarily with the most nebulous of the act's three criteria: ideology. "The term itself is fuzzy and amorphous," says West. "If you don't have a good sense of what it looks like, you don't look for it." On the other hand, if you only have a narrow sense of what it looks like, that's all you see. And, after 9/11, there was a very clear idea of what terrorism looked like. Of the roughly 60 terrorism charges laid by the Crown over the past two decades, almost all have been against extremists inspired by al-Qaeda or the Islamic State. Those include Saad Akhtar, a Toronto man who beat a woman to death with a hammer in 2020 and pledged allegiance to ISIS; and the "Toronto 18," a group of men and youth, some of whom were convicted in 2006 for planning to attack targets including Parliament Hill, CSIS, and nuclear power plants in the name of al-Qaeda.

Cases that don't fit into that narrow mold have, typically, not been prosecuted as terrorism. Consider Alexandre Bissonette, a 27-year-old man who in January of 2017 walked into a mosque in Quebec City and fired on worshippers during evening prayers, killing six. The next day, Prime Minister Justin Trudeau called the crime an act of terrorism—it felt, intuitively, like one. Yet despite outrage from Canadian Muslim groups, the Crown did not charge Bissonnette as a terrorist. In part, that's because he acted alone, without the participation of a recognized terror group, which would prove his commitment to an ideology—and possibly indicate a national security threat that extended beyond a lone-wolf incident. University of Toronto law professor Kent Roach explained as much in an interview with the Canadian Press at the time. "Inspiration alone is not enough," he said. "You would need some form of active participation or direct instruction or incitement to commit a terrorist act." Without proof of that, prosecutors would face a much steeper challenge proving that Bissonnette's motivations were ideological.

Similarly, the incel movement is, at best, loosely organized. The word itself dates back to 1997, when a Toronto university student known online as Alana coined the term "invcel" to describe both men and women struggling to form relationships. She created a web forum called "Alana's Involuntary Celibacy Project," a sort of online support group. Eventually, she started dating and stopped maintaining the forum, and it was only then that the term began to acquire its darker connotations.

In 2014, Elliot Rodger, a 22-year-old self-described incel, killed six people and injured 14 others in Isla Vista, California, shooting some and ramming others with his car. He then shot himself dead, leaving behind a manifesto expressing frustration over his loneliness, his hatred of women, and the plans for his crimes. Rodger died by his own hand, so the debate that followed over whether he was a terrorist or not was academic—there was no one to prosecute. But his crimes were a watershed moment for the incel movement: a burst of mainstream notoriety, and a fallen hero to rally around.

And rally they did. In 2015, 26-year-old Chris Harper-Mercer killed nine people at a college in Oregon; he had previously written a manifesto describing how Rodger had inspired him. In 2018, a man named Scott Beierle murdered two women at a yoga studio in Florida. He, too, had expressed admiration for Rodger in videos he uploaded to YouTube.

That same year, 25-year-old Alek Minassian drove a rented van onto a sidewalk near Toronto's North York Centre subway station, killing 11 people. Minutes after committing the crime, Minassian posted on Facebook, "The Incel Rebellion has already begun!" and "All hail the Supreme Gentleman Elliot Rodger!" In spite of his professed allegiance to Rodger and the "incel rebellion," police did not lay terror charges. Just as in the Bissonnette shooting, there appeared to be no organized threat to public safety. The judge in the case found that Minassian was motivated by the potential for notoriety, not by ideology—whatever his social media posts said.

Oguzhan Sert idolized Elliot Rodger too. He was born in Toronto to a mother from Mexico and a father from Turkey. They divorced when he was young, which devastated him. By all accounts, he was a lonely and depressed teen, bullied relentlessly in school. In Grade 9 he told his parents he no longer wanted to attend classes. He left school, effectively ending his education. At some point, Sert's mother looked for professional help for her son, and mental health practitioners suggested medication. That never came to pass. Instead, Sert moved to his father's house, where he spent his days alone in his basement bedroom, spiraling deeper into a network of fringe websites and YouTube channels promoting alt-right and anti-Semitic conspiracy theories—and the incel subculture.

Sert sought out incel-themed videos on YouTube and discussed incel themes on social media and on Steam, a gaming platform. Without in-person social contact and the structure of secondary school education, Sert found his feelings of abandonment reinforced online. He began describing himself as a "proud incel," and a "Seeker of Martyrdom" on Steam, declaring in his profile that he hated feminists.

After Sert was arrested in February 2020, he told police that he regretted what he'd done, but only because he'd assumed police would kill him at the scene of the crime. Left alive to face the consequences, his life was ruined. He said he believed people like him deserved a country of their own and that he couldn't advocate for those rights without hurting women. "Nobody would take us seriously," he said.

Sert was charged with murder and attempted murder, but as the depth of his ideological motivations became obvious to Toronto police, they tapped the RCMP's Integrated National Security Enforcement Teams, a federal counterterrorism unit. In May 2020, Crown attorneys charged him with terrorism during a remote court appearance, where Sert appeared via video link from a youth detention facility. He was only 17 years old. As a minor, he was facing a maximum 10-year sentence for the murder. But if he was convicted of terrorism, he could be sentenced as an adult, with the possibility of a life term.

Two federal Crown prosecutors—Lisa Mathews and Amber Pashuk—were brought aboard to assist with the case. Mathews is a 23-year veteran of the Public Prosecution Service of Canada, while Pashuk had already prosecuted a handful of domestic terrorism cases. To get a terrorism conviction, they would have to prove something that had never before been argued in a Canadian courtroom: that the incel subculture constitutes a real ideology and therefore a terrorist threat, and that Sert himself intended to intimidate the public, or at least a segment of it, with his crimes.

Maurice Mattis, who was once Jamaica's superintendent of police before studying law and setting up practice in Toronto, took on Sert's defense. For assistance he tapped Monte MacGregor, a former corporate finance lawyer turned criminal defender with experience in homicide cases. They knew that a first-degree murder charge would be basically impossible to defend against. Sert had already implicated himself, and admitted his premeditation, in his police interview. Mattis and MacGregor knew their best chance would be to try to fight the terrorism charge and have Sert sentenced as a youth—likely his only chance to avoid a life sentence.

The case came at a time when the perception of the incel movement, and of the crimes committed by its adherents, was changing fast among lawmakers. In February 2020, the International Centre for Counter-Terrorism at The Hague retroactively described Elliot Rodger's murders as acts of misogynist terrorism. That same year, a domestic terrorism threat assessment produced by the Texas Department of Public Safety described incel violence as a serious risk. "Once viewed as a criminal threat by many law enforcement authorities," it read, "incels are now seen as a growing domestic terrorism concern due to the ideological nature of recent incel attacks internationally, nationwide, and in Texas." It said the threat could potentially eclipse other domestic terrorism threats.

Still, no one, anywhere, had ever been convicted of terrorism based on incel ideology. Such a conviction, says Leah West, could help prevent such crimes in the future: law enforcement might allocate counter-terrorism resources to the incel threat and improve data collection and tracking of incel-related crimes. It could also begin to shift public perception of the perpetrators. "It helps the public understand that these are terrorist movements," says West, "not just wacky things that people are saying online." Mathews and Pashuk would need to put that argument to a judge, however, with little precedent, domestically or otherwise.

⚬━✦━⚬

Sert pleaded guilty in September 2022 to charges of murder and attempted murder. But the court still needed to determine if his crimes met the threshold for terrorism. That month, the prosecution and defense began arguing their cases at the Superior Court of Justice in Toronto, before Justice Suhail Akhtar. Silent and downcast, Sert sat in the prisoner's dock, dressed in a burgundy sweatsuit issued by the William E. Hay Centre in Ottawa, where he'd been in custody. He was alone, save for a court official who sat a few feet away. Neither of his parents were there—they had, according to MacGregor, washed their hands of him.

Behind the counsel table, Mathews and Pashuk launched into their case. To prove the first part of their argument—that Sert was motivated by ideology and an overarching set of shared beliefs, just as jihadists or political extremists might be—they brought forward an expert witness, known as T. E., an academic who has researched the incel subculture for almost a decade. T. E., whose name is under a publication ban, told the court that incel culture revolves around a consistent theory of hypergamy: the belief that women are more sexually selective than men and seek to "marry up" into higher social status. A key incel belief, said T. E., is that as women have gained greater sexual and financial independence, they rely less on men for physical and financial security. But men, their attractiveness determined at birth, are more or less powerless to change their romantic prospects. The least attractive are denied sex and intimate partnerships and, as revenge for being denied what they're entitled to, they feel violence is justified.

Incels especially loathe sex workers, who they see as exploiting and profiting from their inability to access sex or intimacy, at least without paying for it. That's very close to what Sert told police during his interview in 2020. "I was thinking about this incel ideology," he'd said, adding, "I guess that's why I chose that spot. Some incels say prostitutes are taking advantage of their bodies and gaining money as a result." (There's no evidence that the services offered at Crown Spa went beyond erotic massages, but Sert apparently didn't make that distinction.)

That quote addressed the prosecution's second challenge: to prove that Sert chose Crown Spa to target and intimidate a certain group. Sert's choice of weapon—a sword inscribed with a misogynist slur—was further evidence. "Mr. Sert here," said Mathews, "by showing up with his THOT Slayer sword, dressed in his *Matrix* costume, with the incel rebellion note in his pocket, his Steam profile, declaring himself to be a proud incel and a killer and a seeker of martyrdom—these are messages to the world."

The defense strategy took an opposite tack: that Sert was a confused child who had no friends and little parental guidance. In custody, he was diagnosed with autism spectrum disorder, social anxiety disorder, and a tendency toward major depressive episodes, one of which he'd endured shortly before the attack in February 2020. Yet he'd received essentially no support before committing his crimes. He appeared to have a limited intellect, said MacGregor, and the rigid, categorical thinking often associated with people on the autism spectrum made him vulnerable to the nihilistic thinking of conspiracy theorists. This argument was all too easy to believe when observing Sert, who often seemed overwhelmed by the formality of court proceedings. At his sentencing hearing, I watched Sert stare into space, looking as if he could scarcely believe where he was. I found it hard not to imagine his life playing out differently, had he found the psychological supports his mother had hoped for, and had he not spent hours online in that basement bedroom.

He seemed hopelessly alone, and his aloneness was also part of the defense. "That's who he is," said MacGregor, delivering his argument with the cadence and hushed melodrama of a radio host, which he had been before becoming a lawyer. It was in these tones that he painted a decidedly unflattering picture of his own client. "Not loved enough, friendless, bullied, uneducated, ignorant to the world, and choosing to lash out for no reason but because other introverts hidden in the dark share their conspiracy theories about why they are mistreated."

When lone actors have faced terror charges in Canadian courts, the results have been mixed, even when their crimes and motivations closely align with the post-9/11 spirit of the Anti-Terrorism Act. In 2019, Crown prosecutors failed to convince a judge that Ayanle Hassan Ali—who had gone on a knife rampage at a Canadian Forces recruiting center in Toronto, injuring two people and claiming that Allah had sent him to kill people—was a terrorist. He was acquitted on terror charges, and an appeals court upholding the ruling later said that a person cannot commit a crime of terror on behalf of a cause or group and be the only member of that group.

But here, too, perceptions are changing. In 2022, the Standing Committee on Public Safety and National Security delivered a report to Parliament on the rise of "ideologically motivated violent extremism." It explicitly described the growing threat of lone actors, radicalized by social media and affiliated with shaggier, less-coherent ideologies than traditional terror groups. "Terrorist groups whose credo, membership, command structure and tactics are known and relatively stable have not disappeared," read the report. "Rather, these long-standing national security threats have been joined by a new breed of violent extremists, lone actors and leaderless movements."

The report cited, as examples, far-right extremists, lone-wolf jihadists—and incels. This interpretation is similar to the argument Mathews and Pashuk made for the prosecution. They said that the attacks at Crown Spa were not being prosecuted as a terrorist group offense, so no organization or communication with a larger group was required.

Closing arguments didn't wrap up until October 2023. Mathews stood up to read victim impact statements from Arzaga's two sisters and her best friend. Arzaga's older sister's letter detailed the devastation her family had endured. She talked about watching Arzaga's five-year-old daughter observe Mother's Day at a cemetery. She talked about the anxiety and hypervigilance she felt, wondering which men in a crowd might harbour violent thoughts about her. She talked about arguing with Ashley and never having a chance to resolve it. Arzaga's younger sister's letter described the agony of watching the casket close on one of the people she loved most in the world: "Ashley was one of the toughest people I knew, and not once did I think I would ever lose her."

Mathews, who had until then delivered her arguments in precise, methodical fashion, became clearly emotional; Pashuk quickly took over. In the prisoner's dock, Sert stared into the distance, periodically tugging at his short black beard. Provincial Crown attorney Chikeziri Igwe asked the judge to sentence Sert as an adult. Later that day, Sert also delivered a statement, standing up to face J. C. and Arzaga's family in the gallery as he read, stiltedly, from a piece of lined paper. He asked for forgiveness, claiming to not understand why he'd committed the attacks. He said that he'd matured and no longer hated women. "I wish I could travel back in time and talk some sense into my former self," he said. "That way Ashley would still be alive and none of this would have ever happened."

In the end, Justice Akhtar accepted the Crown's case: that Sert's crimes were motivated by a poisonous and virulent ideology, one that would require "the entire might" of correctional programming to rehabilitate. He cited Sert's meticulous planning, suggesting it required a degree of maturity. He noted that Sert intentionally sought out web forums, online videos, and other information and took little responsibility for the attacks. The crime, said Akhtar, "reflects the evils of that ideology."

Sert's sentence is life in prison, although he will be eligible for parole in 10 years. His lawyers wanted to ask for a lighter sentence under the Youth Criminal Justice Act, in which he would complete an intense rehab program in a provincial facility. But that would have required Sert to serve out his sentence in a shared cell, which he was terrified of doing. He refused.

Leah West thinks the decision has the potential to change how the justice system—from local law enforcement to lawyers to judges—deals with terrorism and, ultimately, what the public at large considers to *be* terrorism. Lisa Mathews also recently prosecuted the case of Nathaniel Veltman, a young man who in 2021 ran over and killed members of a Muslim family in London, Ontario, with a pickup truck. That too is a high-profile terror case, involving a lone actor radicalized online with a loosely defined ideology. This February, Veltman too was convicted of terrorism, another sign that the legal and public perception of the word is expanding.

In October, shortly after both sides had delivered their closing arguments, I returned to Dufferin and Wilson on a Sunday afternoon to walk the stretch where Crown Spa was located. The spa now operates under a different name, but it otherwise looked the same as it would have in 2020: the late autumn sun dappling the hard industrial landscape, the highway stretching into oblivion. I thought about J. C. and Arzaga, fighting for their lives behind its frosted-glass window—in a place, J. C. said, where "we love everybody."

Sex workers, like those in the massage parlor community, are familiar with precarious employment and public judgment. The spa business particularly can feel insular; many are located in the same part of the city, and attendants, who are independent contractors, often swap parlors regularly in search of more clients or a better environment. Anyone in this small community could have ended up as one of Sert's targets that day.

Yet I was struck when reporting this story by how many people—including lawyers and legal experts—were surprised that the case resulted in the watershed conviction it did.

Some felt it would open the door to an overly liberal definition of terrorism, while others thought that a case resulting in only one homicide lacked the notoriety normally associated with terror convictions.

Sert's case expands not only the definition of a terrorist, but that of a victim. The perception that sex work is intrinsically seedy or undesirable often lends itself to the idea that the people who do the work perhaps deserve that violence. Or at least that it's inevitable. The Sert case blows up those assumptions, demanding that both perpetrators and victims receive more attention and effort from law enforcement and courts. For now, his conviction looks like the beginning of a change.

The Devil Went Down to Georgia

by Hallie Lieberman

For years, a mysterious figure preyed on gay men in Atlanta. People on the streets called him the Handcuff Man—but the police knew his real name.

"STAY AWAY FROM HIM."

In May 1991, Michael Jordan visited Atlanta, Georgia, to revel in the city's social scene. Jordan, who was 21 and lived in Florida, came on vacation and ended up in a neighborhood called Midtown. If the Deep South had a gay mecca, Midtown was it. The bars there were legendary; among the busiest were the Phoenix, a brick-walled dive, and the Gallus, a sprawling three-floor property transformed from a private home into a piano bar, restaurant, and hustler haunt. Piedmont Park, situated in Midtown's northeast, was a popular cruising spot, thanks to the privacy offered by its dense vegetation. Cars lined up in droves there, bearing license plates from as far away as California and Michigan. Local residents complained about the traffic, and arborists put up fences to "protect" the trees. A cop once told a reporter that the park was "so busy" with gay men, "you'd think they were having a drive-in movie."

But Midtown's freedoms and pleasures had limits. Sodomy was illegal in Georgia, and cops routinely detained gay men, sometimes by going undercover and posing as hustlers. "One of the television stations would scroll the names of all the people who had been arrested for soliciting sodomy," recalled Cliff Bostock, a longtime journalist in Atlanta. The HIV/AIDS crisis was approaching its zenith, and testing positive was a near certain death sentence that some Americans, especially in the South, believed gay men deserved. Prominent Atlanta preacher Charles Stanley had made national headlines in 1986 when he declared that the epidemic was a way of "God indicating his displeasure" with homosexuality.

On the evening of May 12, his first day in the city, Jordan was milling around Midtown when he was approached by a man in a white Lincoln Town Car who asked if he wanted to make some money. "What do I have to do?" Jordan replied. The man said he was conducting a study and would pay Jordan $50 to drink vodka. "I'm going to watch as you become more and more inebriated, and I'll take notes," the man said. Jordan jumped at the chance to earn some easy cash and agreed to meet the man at the corner of Fifth and Juniper Streets.

Jordan was already there when the man arrived. The man motioned for Jordan to get into his car, handed him a fifth of vodka, and told him to drink it fast. Jordan downed about half the bottle, at which point the man left the car for a few minutes to get something to mix the alcohol with. When he came back, the man asked Jordan to get hard because he wanted to see him masturbate. Jordan said he was too drunk to get hard quickly. Then he drank more and blacked out.

Early the next morning, a man named David Atkins found someone curled up in the fetal position on the ground of the parking lot behind the Ponce de Leon Hotel, where Atkins worked as a clerk. "At first I thought he was 30 to 35 and very dirty. I nudged him with my foot, told him to wake up," Atkins told *Southern Voice*, a gay newspaper in Atlanta. "Then I realized it was blisters all over his body and he was just a kid."

The person on the ground was Jordan. He was naked, and his genitals had been wrapped in a rubber band and set on fire. Burns extended to his buttocks and legs, and his nose and mouth were filled with blood.

Atkins called 911, and Jordan was rushed in an ambulance to the hospital, where he would remain for a month. When the police were slow to respond to the scene, Atkins reached out to Cathy Woolard, a gay-rights advocate working with Georgia's chapter of the ACLU. Woolard sprang into action and contacted the police investigator assigned to the case. In her words, she got "nothing but runaround." Because of the victim's profile, the police had designated the attack a bias crime. For the same reason, Woolard sensed, they weren't taking the incident seriously.

Woolard urged law enforcement to talk to a potential witness: Bill Adamson, a bartender at the Phoenix. Adamson said that Jordan had come into the bar before going to Fifth and Juniper and had described his conversation with the stranger in the Town Car. Adamson issued a warning: "Stay away from him. He's dangerous."

Adamson didn't know the driver's name, only that people around Midtown called him the Handcuff Man. He was a serial predator who approached gay men, offered to pay them to drink liquor, then beat or burned them and left them for dead. Sometimes he handcuffed his victims to poles—hence his sinister nickname.

There were men who said they'd narrowly escaped the Handcuff Man, and rumors that some of his victims hadn't survived. But there were also people who thought that he was nothing more than an urban legend. Jordan's assault would bring the truth to light: Not only did the Handcuff Man exist, but there were people in Atlanta who knew his name, including members of the police force. He hadn't been caught because, it seemed, no one was trying in earnest to catch him.

That was about to change.

"I'M GOING TO SUE YOU."

No one could be certain when the Handcuff Man had staged his first attack. Adamson claimed that he'd been terrorizing Midtown since the late 1960s, that he drove a white Lincoln, was about five foot ten, and had black hair and glasses. A sex worker said that the Handcuff Man had picked him up in Piedmont Park in 1977, asked him to take shots of liquor, then assaulted him. The victim managed to flee with a stab wound to the shoulder, and later saw the man again at the park eyeing other male hustlers. He didn't report the crime because he was afraid of being outed to loved ones.

In 1984, Susan Faludi, then a twentysomething reporter a few years out from becoming a Pulitzer Prize–winning author, wrote a front-page story about gay hustlers for the *Atlanta Journal-Constitution*. She asked her sources about the dangers of their lifestyle and learned that "the greatest fear on the street right now is invoked by the specter of 'The Handcuff Man,' a man who reportedly picks up hustlers, offers them a pint of vodka spiked with sleeping pills and then handcuffs and beats them."

The following year, in April 1985, a thin man rolled down his car window on Ponce de Leon Avenue and asked Max Shrader if he wanted to make some money. Shrader, 21, had been hustling since he was 13, turning tricks for out and closeted men alike, including a married Baptist preacher. He knew that what he did was dangerous; someone had pulled a gun on him, and a female sex worker who was his friend had been killed. "They found her head in one dumpster, her arms in another," Shrader said. "She was a nice person." Shrader knew about the Handcuff Man, who had attacked another of his friends. But the man in the car on Ponce, as the thoroughfare is commonly known, didn't come off like a predator. He wore glasses and a pressed shirt; he seemed normal.

The man asked Shrader to drink some alcohol with him, and Shrader obliged. But after a little while he started to feel funny. Had the man slipped him something? Shrader collapsed to the ground. "Don't hurt me!" he begged, as the man pulled him into his car.

The man drove to a wooded area, parked, and dragged an intoxicated Shrader into a patch of kudzu. He then poured a liquid onto Shrader's groin and lit a match, illuminating his face in a ghoulish way Shrader would never forget. When the man dropped the match, Shrader caught fire.

Shrader lay in the woods for hours, drifting in and out of consciousness. He cried out for help when he had the energy. Around 9:30 P.M., a man who happened to be a nurse was driving home with his girlfriend when he spotted a naked figure on the side of the road. The nurse stopped, saw Shrader's condition, and rushed home to call the police and to get some blankets to wrap Shrader in. "I guess God sent him," Shrader said.

Shrader was taken to Grady Memorial Hospital, the same place Michael Jordan would go six years later. He stayed there six weeks, during which the police came to see him once. They left a business card and said to call if he wanted to talk. He misplaced the card and never heard from the cops again.

Shrader wasn't surprised. Atlanta cops seemed more interested in harassing and arresting gay men than in protecting them. Sometimes they wrote down the numbers on license plates in Piedmont Park and blackmailed drivers terrified of having their sexual orientation exposed—it could cost them their families, their jobs, possibly their lives. Incidents of gay bashing often went unsolved, if they were investigated at all. *Etcetera*, a gay and lesbian magazine in Atlanta, reported that between 1984 and 1986, at least 18 gay men died at the hands of unidentified perpetrators. The publication noted with frustration that police had "little understanding" of homophobic crimes. The Atlanta Gay Center began offering sensitivity training for cops, but feedback was mixed. "I think what you told us will be helpful in the longrun and should be expressed more often in police work," one participant wrote in an evaluation of the training, "but I still think gays are disgusting and a disgrace to our country." George Napper, Atlanta's public safety commissioner, refused to make a statement condemning crimes against the gay community because it might be construed as favoritism.

After healing for two years, Shrader went back to hustling, scars and all. He'd grown up poor, and selling sex was one of the only ways he'd ever made money. At least now he knew what the Handcuff Man looked like and could steer clear of him.

J. D. Kirkland suspected that he'd seen the Handcuff Man's face, too. Kirkland, an Atlanta cop, worked security a few nights a week at the Gallus. According to Don Hunnewell, one of the owners of the Gallus, Kirkland was a combination of Dirty Harry and the sheriff from *Gunsmoke*—a "kick-ass, cowboy type of tough cop." In his free time, he trained horses on a large piece of property outside the city and worked on a novel about a time-traveling cop. Kirkland was married with kids; he wasn't gay, but he was compassionate toward the Gallus's clientele. "He really cared," Hunnewell said. "I don't think he was judgmental at all on what they were doing." (Kirkland died in 1996.)

Patrons had told Kirkland about the Handcuff Man, including what he looked like, and on November 4, 1983, a man came into the Gallus who matched the description. Kirkland wrote a trespass notice, then snapped a polaroid of the man. The Gallus had a "barred book" filled with photos of people who weren't allowed on the premises; bartenders were supposed to check it at the start of their shifts so they could eject any banned patrons. Kirkland put the man's photo in the book.

Before kicking him out for good, Kirkland asked for his name. The man said he was Robert Lee Bennett Jr. "I'm an attorney," he added, "and I'm going to sue you."

"WHAT HAVE YOU DONE?"

Robert Lee Bennett Jr. was indeed an attorney, like his father before him. He had been adopted as a baby by Annabelle Maxwell Bennett and Robert Lee Bennett Sr., of Towanda, Pennsylvania, a small town perched on the Susquehanna River. Annabelle was a socialite and the daughter of a wealthy judge; in addition to practicing law, Robert Sr. was the president of a bank.

Robert Sr. was originally from the South but moved to Towanda for his bride. They lived with their son, their only child, in a Victorian mansion nicknamed Nirvana. It had five bedrooms, a white marble fireplace, and a pool house; a Steinway grand piano, Tiffany sterling silver, and plush oriental rugs. The local paper chronicled the family's every move: vacations to Africa, charity dinners. They were the Kennedys of Towanda.

Ellie Harden Smith, who knew Bennett in high school, said that he was charming, fashionable, and quirky. Most of his friends were girls, and he liked to cross-stitch and garden. He was devoted to his mother. As far as Smith knew, he was never bullied or mocked for his feminine tendencies. Bennett sang in the glee club in high school, was active in the Boy Scouts, and worked at the student newspaper.

After graduating from high school in 1965, he moved to Colorado to attend the University of Denver. Smith visited him there, and he took her out to gay bars. "I guess I sort of knew, but that was the first I realized that he was really into that stuff," she said.

Bennett's first run-in with the law appears to have happened in 1971, when he was arrested in Virginia for indecent exposure during a homosexual act. At the time, he was pursuing a master's degree in political science. According to legal documents, he was arrested two years later, this time in Atlanta, for assault with an automobile. A year on, soon after graduating from law school at Emory University, he was arrested again. It happened in Midtown, when he was cruising near the Gallus. Bennett tried to pull a man into his car—a man who happened to be an undercover cop. Bennett was charged with kidnapping a police officer, but he ended up pleading no contest to simple battery and paying a $75 fine.

Once he'd finished his law degree, Bennett moved back to Towanda, where he lived a double life. By day he worked at a law firm and claimed to be looking for a wife; in his free time, he paid poor local boys to take their clothes off and drink or have sex with him. Eventually, he quit the firm and bought a plant and flower business called the Tree Stump.

On April 16, 1976, Bennett met a young man at Leonard's, a beer garden in Towanda, and suggested that they go to a lake cottage his parents had bought him as a gift. The men had sex in Bennett's car, then drove to the cottage. According to Francis Panuccio, a police captain quoted in a local newspaper, "something occurred that frightened" the young man, who fled the cottage in Bennett's car and drove it into an embankment. When police arrived at the scene, they arrested the young man, but Bennett deflected scrutiny thanks to Robert Sr. "Nobody wanted to press charges against him because of the influence of his father," a retired state police investigator later told the press. "His father was gold."

Still, Robert Sr. feared that his son would keep getting into more trouble if he remained in Towanda. Two months after the incident at the lake, Bennett moved back to Atlanta. He was 29.

Bennett was hired by a law firm, which is where he met Sandra Powell, 34, a secretary and bookkeeper. She was small and demure, a junior-college graduate who wore her dark hair in bangs. They started dating, and Bennett told Powell that he was impotent. She said it didn't bother her; they talked about adopting a child. In 1978, on a trip to the lake cottage in Towanda, Bennett proposed and Powell said yes. They were married at Rock Springs Presbyterian Church in Atlanta. Powell wore an ivory gown decorated with pearls and lace, and carried a bouquet of burgundy roses. Bennett wore a tuxedo with a white bow tie. They honeymooned in South America.

His hometown friends were surprised that Bennett got married. Irma Henson, who had known him since his early twenties, said that he likely did it for his parents, especially his mother, with whom he was still close. "He probably gathered from his mother that who he was wasn't fitting her picture of who he should be," Henson said.

Shortly after the wedding, Bennett quit the law firm. He worked for a while behind the jewelry counter at Davison's department store, but mostly he lived off dividends from stocks his father had gifted him. "He would just hang around the house all day, and he would be in his robe when I got home," Powell later said in court. She was unhappy, but "kept it inside."

Then one day in the fall of 1982, Powell was getting off the bus she rode home from work when she saw police placing her husband in handcuffs. "What is it?" she asked. "What have you done?"

Over Labor Day weekend, James Lee Johnson, 24, had been found shot to death with a .25-caliber pistol in the middle of the street close to his apartment. His wallet was missing. Police learned that Johnson may have been a sex worker, and that he'd last been seen with a man who looked like Bennett. According to friends, Johnson was in a relationship with a man named Robert whom he'd met at the jewelry store where Bennett once worked. A few weeks before his death, Johnson had expressed fear of this man, telling friends, "Robert's gonna get me." When investigators examined the contents of Johnson's stomach during his autopsy, they found roast beef and potatoes. They searched Bennett's home and, discovering those items in his refrigerator, arrested him for murder.

Bennett was released on a $25,000 bond and was never tried, because the prosecution's case was entirely circumstantial. His arrest marked the end of his marriage—Powell soon filed for divorce—but not of his comfortable lifestyle. When he wasn't in Atlanta, Bennett spent time in Clearwater, Florida, where his mother, widowed in the mid-1980s, kept a home. He vacationed in Nassau, Mexico, and China. He hosted lavish parties, and when he and his mother attended an annual lobster boil at a club in Towanda, an otherwise casual affair, he made sure their table was set with linens, porcelain plates, and a silver candelabra.

Meanwhile, in Midtown, the Handcuff Man's reputation was mounting. Max Shrader was attacked in the spring of 1985. That August, a man named Charles Gallows was assaulted and robbed. The following June, Anthony Charles Poppilia got in the car of a man who offered to pay him $50 to drink vodka, then pushed Poppilia from the moving vehicle. The stories continued until May 1991, when Michael Jordan turned up maimed behind the Ponce de Leon Hotel. Midtown denizens would later report that, in the hours leading up to Jordan's assault, the Handcuff Man had approached at least one other man in the area.

"A SADISTIC WOODY ALLEN LOOKALIKE."

When word of Jordan's assault reached Richard Greer, he immediately thought of the Handcuff Man. Greer, 32, worked the 5 P.M. to 1 A.M. cop beat at the *Journal-Constitution*. A few months prior, he'd overheard a Midtown patrol officer casually mention the Handcuff Man to some colleagues. Greer asked around and gleaned that a lot of cops thought the attacker might be "folklore." Jordan's assault seemed to be confirmation that he was not.

Greer went to gay bars in Midtown to speak with employees and customers. He heard a rumor that the Handcuff Man had either removed the door handles inside his car or covered them with duct tape to trap his victims. People were upset that authorities seemed to be doing nothing to stop the violence. "The victims were people that most people either wanted to ignore or didn't know existed," Greer said.

Greer left his business card with patrons of the Gallus and told them to get in touch if they ever saw the person they believed to be the Handcuff Man. "I started getting calls at one in the morning saying 'He just drove by' or 'He's on the corner of X street and X street,'" Greer said. If he thought the information was reliable, Greer would jump in his car and drive to Midtown, but by the time he arrived, the suspect was always long gone.

Then Greer was given a name: Robert Bennett Jr. But the tip didn't come from a hustler or a bartender—it came from a cop. Greer was surprised. In his experience, it was unusual for a cop to be so candid. More importantly, if people on the force believed that they knew who the Handcuff Man was, why hadn't Bennett been investigated and arrested?

Greer spoke with Kirkland, the cop who moonlighted at the Gallus, and Kirkland said that he was never able to do anything about Bennett except ban him from the bar back in 1983, because it was difficult to persuade survivors and witnesses of the Handcuff Man's attacks to come forward. But if that were true, law enforcement bore at least some responsibility for people's reluctance: Victims of homophobic crimes in Atlanta feared that if they spoke to the police, they might be blackmailed or arrested, or simply not believed. "The police say if you don't report the crime, we can't do anything about it," Bill Gripp, an activist with the Atlanta Gay Center, told Greer. "We say if we don't have confidence in them, we won't report it."

On May 28, two weeks after Jordan was assaulted, Greer published a front-page story about the Handcuff Man. "Gay prostitutes in fear of sadist," the headline read. Greer wrote that the Handcuff Man may have attacked up to 100 men during his "reign of terror," and that gay Atlantans were "angered" that the police were "indifferent" to his crimes. Greer quoted Kirkland, who said that it was possible the Handcuff Man was responsible for several unsolved murders.

Greer characterized the Handcuff Man as "a sadistic Woody Allen lookalike . . . scrawny and peering with eyeglasses through his car window." He wrote that Kirkland believed the predator was a "DeKalb County professional." But Greer didn't name Bennett. He couldn't. Doing so would have risked a defamation suit against the newspaper; Bennett hadn't been arrested or charged with a crime, and he was a wealthy lawyer with his own wealthy lawyer on call. To finger Bennett, Greer needed to keep digging.

Greer began combing through public records and police files. He read documents pertaining to Bennett's prior arrests. He learned that Bennett had briefly been a suspect in one of Atlanta's most high-profile crime sprees: From 1979 to 1981, a serial killer murdered 30 people in the city, most of whom were young boys. As pressure mounted to find the perpetrator, the FBI arrived to help. Based on various records, law enforcement came up with a list of 65 suspects. Bennet was among them, perhaps because of his previous arrests. He was also a known fixture in Midtown, and the FBI thought that the killer might be gay. Agents were assigned to surveil "homosexual bars and areas frequented by male prostitutes," and to pursue the "development of informants with knowledge of child prostitution," according to a February 1981 memo. Bennett was eliminated as a suspect after three months. (In late 1981, a man named Wayne Williams was arrested in connection with the slayings. He was convicted of two of the murders and is presumed to have committed the others.)

Greer also found the transcripts from Bennett's contentious divorce proceedings in 1984. Astoundingly, the Handcuff Man was mentioned. Powell's counsel called three male sex workers to the stand, all of whom testified that they believed Bennett to be the Handcuff Man. Frank Sheridan, a local gay-rights advocate who liaised with the police, testified that he had been "working with the street prostitute community . . . to build up information on this gentleman regarding his sexual habits and picking up of young men from the street." Powell herself claimed that her estranged husband was "violent" and a homosexual.

Bennett denied being gay, then admitted that he was. However, he was adamant that he wasn't the Handcuff Man. Attorney Guy Notte, who represented Bennett, chastised the authorities for not identifying the real threat. "The Handcuff Man is still down there somewhere," Notte said. "Could you please tell me why this man hasn't been caught?" The court ended up ordering Bennett to pay Powell a divorce settlement of $40,000.

On May 29 and 30, 1991, Greer published two additional articles about the Handcuff Man. There were still concerns about naming Bennett, so Greer didn't. By then Jordan had picked a photo of Bennett out of a lineup. Greer reported that Jordan had identified his attacker, but that police hadn't issued a warrant for the suspect's arrest. "I'm sure we will call him," the chief of the sex-crimes unit told Greer.

Greer grew increasingly worried that Bennett might attack another man soon; naming him seemed like a matter of public safety. There was a heated debate in the newsroom about what to do. One editor told Greer that he hoped never to be an uncharged suspect in Atlanta, lest his name show up in the paper. Another editor, Pam Fine, was on Greer's side. "Heinous crimes were involved," Fine later said, "and we recognized that police had waited two decades to actively pursue the case."

On May 31, Greer published an article naming Bennett as the man Jordan identified as the last person he saw before losing consciousness during his attack. The piece indicated that the police still hadn't spoken to Bennett, much less detained him. "I would certainly love to interview him," Bobby Ford, a sex-crimes detective, told Greer. The article went on to state: "For 20 years, police officials and members of the gay community say, a man fitting Mr. Bennett's description has been involved in cases of brutality against young white male prostitutes. The perpetrator of these crimes has come to be known as the Handcuff Man."

After the article was published, Greer reached Bennett on the phone at his lake cottage in Towanda, and Bennett denied being the Handcuff Man. "No attorney in his right mind is going to make a comment one way or the other on something the police are investigating," Bennett continued. "You know as well as I do that that is not an indication of guilt or innocence." In a separate interview, attorney Guy Notte, who was still representing Bennett, said that his client would be flying down to Atlanta the following week "to defend every allegation."

"I LITERALLY WENT NUTS."

Atlanta police didn't immediately issue a warrant for Bennett's arrest. "There's just more work that needs to be done to make this thing stick," Detective Ford told Greer. But the department did send out a dispatch to law enforcement agencies around the country describing the Handcuff Man's crimes. When the message arrived in Tampa, Bob Holland, a local police detective, recognized similarities with a case his department had been investigating for a few months.

On February 22, 1991, 35-year-old Gary Clapp was standing outside a Salvation Army shelter, waiting for it to open. Clapp, who hung drywall for a living, was broke and struggling to feed his family; he also had a severe alcohol problem. When a white Town Car pulled up and the driver said that he was conducting a survey on how alcohol affected people's moods, Clapp hopped into the vehicle. In between chugs of vodka from a plastic cup, Clapp asked the man his name, but he wouldn't answer. Eventually, Clapp passed out.

Around 10:30 P.M. that night, police officer Jimmy Caplinger was driving on the frontage road along the mangrove-lined Courtney Campbell Causeway, which connects Tampa and Clearwater, when he noticed what he thought was a bonfire. He parked, got out, and saw a person engulfed in flames. It was Clapp. Caplinger grabbed an extinguisher from his car and put out the fire, then called for emergency services. When Clapp arrived at the hospital, his blood-alcohol level was "so high they could not get a reading," according to a police report. He had fourth-degree burns on nearly half his body and was suffering from smoke inhalation.

Holland went to the hospital to conduct an interview. He wrote in his report that Clapp "was able to answer certain questions by either shaking his head or nodding his head." Holland discerned that someone had deliberately set Clapp on fire.

Clapp's injuries were so severe that doctors had to amputate his legs. When he regained consciousness after surgery, he began thrashing around. "I kept pulling out all my IVs," Clapp told the *Tampa Tribune*. "I literally went nuts and they had to tie me down in the hospital bed."

Holland spoke to Clapp's ex-girlfriend, who said that she'd broken up with him because of his alcoholism. She also said that Clapp had previously been in a "homosexual relationship," but that it "was an isolated incident." There were only a few possible clues at the scene of the crime, including a Riva vodka bottle and a container of lighter fluid. Nearby were bags containing decapitated chickens and a headless goat. A dead body had recently turned up just 500 feet from where Clapp was found, which made police wonder if the two crimes were connected.

In early March, Holland interviewed Clapp more extensively. Clapp said that the man who'd attacked him drove a Lincoln Town Car made sometime between 1977 and 1984, with a brown leather interior. He worked with a sketch artist to produce a picture of the suspect, who Clapp said was between 40 and 45 years old, stood a little under six feet tall, and weighed 160 to 170 pounds. Clapp also described the man as having dark hair, a mustache, and glasses. The sketch was published in the *Tampa Bay Times* on April 9.

Two months later, when Holland saw the dispatch about the Handcuff Man, he quickly picked up the phone and called the Atlanta police. They sent him a photo of Bennett, which Holland then showed to Clapp in a lineup. Clapp, who had only recently been released from a hospital burn unit, identified Bennett as his attacker. Holland pointed out that in his photo Bennett was clean-shaven, and that Clapp had said his attacker had a mustache. Clapp said he was certain that the man in the photo was the one who'd set him on fire. "It's hard to forget someone that's done you wrong like that," he told a reporter.

Authorities in Tampa connected more dots. Bennett's mother's home in Clearwater, a seventh-floor condo, wasn't far from the area where Clapp was found. Bennett had been visiting her in February; in fact, a few days after Clapp's assault, Bennett and his mother embarked on a Caribbean cruise together. Bennett also owned a Town Car, which he'd recently driven up to Towanda.

It was enough to bring him in. On June 5, Tampa police issued a warrant for Bennett's arrest. They alerted their counterparts in Atlanta, who were expecting Bennett that very afternoon for questioning about the Handcuff Man attacks in Midtown. Just after 3 P.M., he was taken into custody based on the Tampa warrant.

Speaking to reporters, a shaking Bennett proclaimed his innocence. "I am here to tell the Atlanta police and the city of Atlanta I am not the Handcuff Man," he said. He later complained that he wasn't served breakfast in jail, and that he had to wait five hours to get a blanket, pillow, and cigarettes.

"IT STRUCK A BELL."

In Midtown, people were relieved that the Handcuff Man may have been caught, but they were also frustrated that Bennett had only been charged with the attack on Clapp, not the crimes in Atlanta. District Attorney Lewis Slaton assured the public that his office was developing a case against Bennett, but also noted that it would be deferring to Tampa authorities. "Since Florida has asked for him, we're going to let them have him," Slaton said. "That case is obviously worse." But worse by what measure, and for whom? "My life will never be the same," Jordan told Greer at the *Journal-Constitution*. Jordan was upset at the way police had handled his ordeal. "It wasn't until it was in the news that they seemed to care," he said.

Bennett was extradited to Florida on June 11. He pleaded not guilty and was freed on a $200,000 bond. His mother helped him get the money together by putting up her condo as collateral.

By then, other men had started coming forward to accuse Bennett of attacking them. One of the men was Max Shrader. He'd been sitting at home one day in May when his dad called and told him to turn on the news. "There's another guy who just got burnt the same way," his dad said. Shrader saw the report about Jordan and called the police to say that he'd suffered a similar attack six years earlier. They asked him to come to the station, where he was shown a lineup of men's photos. "That's him," Shrader said, pointing at Bennett's face.

On June 21, an Atlanta grand jury indicted Bennett on two counts of aggravated assault and two counts of aggravated battery for the attacks on Jordan and Shrader.

Investigators noted that Bennett was suspected of commit-ting similar crimes going back two decades. Bennett again pleaded not guilty and was released on bond—an additional $100,000.

For Dale Sisco and Chip Purcell, who were prosecuting Bennett in Florida, the Atlanta indictment was good news. Their case against Bennett was proving delicate. Clapp had identified his attacker, but because he'd been drunk when he was set on fire, the defense would almost certainly argue that he was an unreliable witness. The defense would also likely argue that evidence found at the scene—the lighter fluid and vodka bottle—wasn't necessarily connected to the case. Locals called the area where Clapp was found "the redneck Riviera," because people liked to grill, drink, and party in the mangroves. "There was no videotape of him doing the act," Sisco said of Bennett. "We had no photographs of him. There were still many circumstantial aspects of the proof that were going to be challenging." The prosecutors didn't even have fingerprints connecting Bennett to Clapp's attack.

So Sisco and Purcell decided to rely on the Williams Rule, a legal precedent in Florida that allows prosecutors to present evidence from other cases or incidents that indicate a pattern of criminal behavior. They identified a handful of recent instances in which men had endured injuries similar to Clapp's, hoping to find other witnesses willing to testify against Bennett. For instance, there was an unsolved case from 1989 in Detective Holland's jurisdiction involving a man who was found unconscious outside a gay bar with his genitals burned. But survivors were wary of telling their stories in court. "We talked to several guys who were not excited about coming to Tampa and testifying to what their sexual activities were," Purcell said.

The Atlanta indictments expanded the pool of potential witnesses. If the Florida case went to trial, Jordan could testify under the Williams Rule. So could Shrader. The same went for a hustler named Shane, who asked to be identified by his first name in this story. Shane was the man in Atlanta who claimed that the Handcuff Man had tried to pick him up in the hours just before Jordan was attacked.

At the time, Shane was in his mid-thirties; he had a wife and a kid he supported with sex work. When a man in a white Lincoln pulled up one day and asked him to drink vodka for $50, Shane was suspicious. He told the driver that if he wanted to drink, they could go to a bar, but the man insisted they imbibe in the car. Shane declined and went about his night. When he heard about the attack on Jordan, "it struck a bell," he said. Shane got in touch with the police and later identified Bennett in a photo lineup as the man who'd tried to give him vodka. The experience shook him up. "It put a kibosh on me for a while from hustling," he said.

As Sisco and Purcell built their case, a shocking news story seized headlines: In July 1991, Jeffrey Dahmer was arrested in Milwaukee and confessed to murdering more than a dozen gay men over the course of 13 years. Some journalists made the connection to the Handcuff Man's crimes. "As in the case of Jeffrey Dahmer," Mary T. Schmich wrote in the *Chicago Tribune* on August 3, "Bennett's arrest has raised questions about the speed and sensitivity with which police handle crimes involving homosexual activity." Schmich quoted Cathy Woolard, the activist who months before had asked the Atlanta police to take the threat of the Handcuff Man seriously. "A lot of people don't care that much if gay people get killed," Woolard said. "It doesn't seem to matter that much that someone is savagely burning male hustlers, because they're not the cream of the crop."

The article ended with an update on Bennett's whereabouts. "Bennett, who was released on bond, is spending the summer with his 85-year-old mother in Towanda," Schmich wrote, "where he reportedly indulges a passion for gardening."

"YOU DON'T COUNT."

To work alongside Guy Notte in the Tampa case, Bennett hired a defense attorney based in Florida. Rochelle Reback had spent the previous decade representing all sorts of clients, but none quite like Bennett. "Usually people involved in crimes of violence don't have a lot of money," Reback said in an interview for this story. Bennett was different. "We had an investigator. We had a jury-selection expert. We had a lot of resources that a lot of clients can't afford," Reback said.

When Reback visited Bennett's mother in Clearwater, there were photos of Bennett everywhere. Many of them were from his childhood, when his mother had dressed him to the nines. "One was like Little Lord Fauntleroy looking, with his long, curly hair," Reback said. Between how his mother viewed him and his wealth, it was clear to Reback that Bennett had led a cosseted life. And now he seemed sure that his privilege would protect him. "He really just felt like this was just one more case that was going to go by the wayside and he would suffer no ongoing consequences," Reback said.

Bennett's arrogance grated on her. "He was the most unpleasant client I ever had," Reback said. When they clashed about strategy, Notte stepped in to smooth things over. He had a long history of appeasing Bennett. "Notte wanted to keep Bob happy because Bob was a wealthy client," Reback said. Together, Notte and Reback tried to find character witnesses willing to testify on Bennett's behalf, but according to Reback they found none. (Notte did not respond to a request for comment.)

In October 1991, Clapp was interviewed for a front-page story in the *St. Petersburg Times*. The picture accompanying the article showed him in his government-funded concrete-block apartment, seated in a wheelchair and cradling a black kitten. "There's times I forget I don't have legs and I want to get up and go take a walk, you know?" Clapp said. He told the reporter that he couldn't stop thinking about Bennett. "Truthfully, I'd like to see the same thing happen to him that happened to me," Clapp said.

When they spoke to the press, Bennett's legal team tried to use what Reback called the SODDI defense ("some other dude did it"). Notte told a reporter that Clapp's assault "smacks of the cult [of] Santeria," because decapitated animals were found near the crime scene. As for the accusations against Bennett in Atlanta, Notte called them "stupid lies."

Behind the scenes, however, it was becoming clear that Bennett was likely to lose in court. Sisco and Purcell had obtained a five-minute video, shot by the Tampa fire department, that showed Clapp burning in the mangroves; his cries of pain were audible. The prosecution upgraded the attempted murder charge to include use of a deadly weapon, which meant that, if convicted, Bennett could get a life sentence. This wasn't an outside possibility: The judge assigned to the case was known for tough rulings.

Bennett's lawyers persuaded him to take a deal. On February 13, 1992, he appeared in court in Florida to plead guilty; he planned to do the same in Atlanta several days later. At least three of his victims—Clapp, Jordan, and Shrader—were in the courtroom. Shrader wanted to lunge at Bennett as soon as he laid eyes on him. "But I knew if I hit him right there," Shrader said, "I'd get hell."

Bennett, who stood with his arms crossed, was sentenced to 17 years in prison followed by 13 years of probation. Under Florida law, he would be eligible for parole in five years. Clapp considered the sentence too light. "I don't think he'll ever feel sorry for anything he's done," he told the court. "He's a sick puppy."

Bennett's attorneys requested that he be allowed some time to make arrangements for his aging mother's care. He was told to turn himself in on March 9. "I trust you as a man and as a lawyer," the judge told Bennett. The prosecution was stunned by the three-week reprieve. "This is clearly one of the most heinous crimes I've ever prosecuted," Purcell told the *St. Petersburg Times*.

Frustration mounted further when it was announced that Bennett might get a deal that would allow him to serve his sentences in the Florida and Georgia cases concurrently rather than back-to-back. The *Journal-Constitution* argued in an editorial that this would effectively mean "no prison time" for the crimes he'd committed in Atlanta. "The full force of the legal system should be used to show that such acts will not be tolerated and to prevent them from happening again," the editorial said. Had Bennett's victims "been women or straight men . . . it is hard to believe the Florida sentence and the Fulton plea bargain would even be discussed." (Atlanta is the seat of Fulton County.)

Gay-rights advocates agreed with the paper. Larry Pellegrini of the ACLU called the deal "horrendous." Jeff Graham of Atlanta's chapter of ACT UP told a reporter, "I think that clearly you've got a prejudiced judicial system in Atlanta."

On February 24, Bennett appeared in an Atlanta courtroom for sentencing. It was packed, with cameras everywhere. Shrader was nervous, and when he got nervous he smiled; a lawyer told him to stop smiling.

The plaintiffs' counsel argued against the plea deal. Jordan's attorney said that her client "wants this man to serve life." Shrader's lawyer said that "this child of affluence has developed into a sadistic sociopath" for whom "the concurrent sentence is not adequate."

When the judge asked if Bennett wished to say anything, he said no.

"Did you, in fact, pick up those two fellows?" the judge then inquired, referring to Jordan and Shrader.

"I'm pleading guilty to the charge, Your Honor, on the advice of my counsel," Bennett said.

"I asked you, did you pick up those two fellows?"

Notte interjected. "Your Honor, he would rather not answer that question."

"I want to hear from him. You don't want to say so, say you don't want to say so," the judge said.

"Yes," Bennett responded.

Ultimately, the judge ruled in favor of the plea deal. In addition to the concurrent prison sentences, Bennett was banned from Fulton County for life, instructed to see a psychiatrist, and ordered to pay restitution of more than $100,000 to his victims. When asked where the money would come from, Notte said that Bennett would use his mother's trust fund.

Gay activists who had come to see the sentencing shouted "shame" repeatedly at the judge. In an article for *Southern Voice*, reporter K. C. Wildmoon wrote that the court sent "a message to the lesbian and gay community, to the hustler community, that these things will happen. It says 'you don't count.'"

"A DANGER TO SOCIETY."

There are lingering questions in the story of the Handcuff Man. Chief among them is how many victims there actually were, and whether any of them died from the attacks. But no further indictments were ever brought against Bennett. "What upsets me the most is how many Max Shraders there are that maybe nobody even knows about," said Don Hunnewell, the Gallus's owner. "Maybe nobody even knows they died." (The Gallus closed in 1993.)

Greer, who now lives in Virginia, wonders what lessons were learned from the whole affair—by the police, the media, and the wider Atlanta community. "The Handcuff Man was the perpetrator, but in a sense we're all accomplices. I'm certain a dead hustler on the south side today would be all but ignored, while a crime against a wealthy family in Buckhead would get a lot of ink and cameras," he said, referring to one of Atlanta's poshest neighborhoods.

Then there's the question of why Bennett committed his crimes, what motive he had. Was it a combination of rage and self-loathing? Shrader thinks so. "He was gay and he hated that," Shrader said. "Then he decided that he'd get rid of [who he considered] the lowest of the gays, the slime on the totem pole, which were gay hustlers, and unfortunately I just happened to be in his path." For her part, Reback said that she gleaned from her conversations with Notte that Bennett was "deeply repressed" and couldn't "function sexually in any way." (After his convictions, Bennett filed a court motion claiming that Reback had provided ineffective counsel; it was dismissed.)

An old friend of Bennett's in Towanda, quoted in the local paper, placed some of the blame for Bennett's crimes on the people who'd helped him evade the consequences of his actions as a young man. "He should have had some help earlier in his life when he got into some of the minor scraps in Pennsylvania," the friend said. "If some of that was not covered up, he might have gotten some sort of help."

The Handcuff Man himself never offered any insight. Two days after the contentious Atlanta hearing, the judge in Florida revoked the bond he'd released Bennett on so that he could sort out his mother's care. After his sentencing, Bennett had been seen cruising a red convertible through an area of Tampa known to be popular with gay hustlers. The judge called him "a danger to society."

Once in prison, Bennett was placed in solitary confinement at his own request. Eventually, he was moved to the general population because, as Notte told a reporter, he was "going buggy" in isolation. His mother died in 1993. Bennett would receive a $1.5 million inheritance upon his release from prison.

But that never happened: On April 1, 1998, just one year before he was supposed to get out, Bennett had a stroke and died behind bars. "He got the life sentence that he probably deserved," Reback said.

The bulk of Bennett's estate went to Towanda's historical society and to the Boy Scouts. He left $25,000 to the son of his friend Ellie Harden Smith and $15,000 to the local country club, with the condition "that this bequest be acknowledged and established as a memorial to my grandfather, the Honorable William Maxwell, my mother, Annabelle Maxwell Bennett, and myself, Robert Lee Bennett Jr." He also requested the erection of a memorial to himself and his mother as a condition of a gift to the county library. There was no mention of honoring his father.

As for his personal effects, namely his clothing and photographs, he issued an unusual directive: Bennett said he wanted them burned.

Death and The Masque

by Joe Pompeo

In Hollywood in 1977, punk rock was exploding and a small band of scene makers were flourishing in a dingy basement club. Little did they know a pair of serial killers would soon claim one of their own.

J ane King sat down at the bus stop on Franklin Avenue and stretched out her legs, crossing them at the ankles as she inhaled the nighttime air. Class had ended, and King was waiting to board an 89 for the roughly four-and-a-half-mile ride home. Across the way, the old Château Élysée loomed over her. A palatial seven stories of Norman revival architecture, the building had begun its journey in November 1924, when the filmmaker Thomas Ince was stricken with chest pains during a party on William Randolph Hearst's yacht. Days later, Ince died of heart failure, leaving behind $1.6 million for his widow, the actor Elinor Kershaw, who used a portion of her inheritance to construct the Château Élysée. (Gossipmongers whispered that she'd financed the Château with hush money from Hearst, rumored to have murdered her husband, but that's another story.)

Over the next two decades, before it was sold and converted into an upscale retirement community that fell into disrepair, the Château served as a luxury hotel and apartment complex for Hollywood stars. Now, revitalized amid the towering palms, it belonged to the Church of Scientology, which hosted a weekly acting class in the basement.

Like so many young women in Hollywood, King wanted to be an actor, and she looked the part too. Tall and slender with shimmering blond hair that fell to her shoulders, she had brown eyes, thin lips, and a face that turned heads. She'd arrived at class that Wednesday in a fitted sweater and tight jeans folded into cuffs above shiny silver heels, which matched the small purse she carried.

After class finished around 11 P.M., a friend had asked King if she needed a lift back to her apartment in West Hollywood. In what would turn out to be the most fateful decision of her 28-year-old life, King had declined the offer, saying she would take the bus instead. And so there she sat on the corner of Franklin and Bronson, waiting for the 89 in front of a Mayfair supermarket—alone, but not for long.

Three days later, on the morning of Saturday, November 12, King's roommate called the Los Angeles County Sheriff's Department to let the authorities know she had never returned home. A sheriff's deputy, after making inquiries with the church, King's mother, and Cedars-Sinai Medical Center, began to prepare a missing person's report. Twenty minutes before noon, he typed out the following words: "ASSIGNED: HOMICIDE BUREAU."

⚬━━⚬

That night, about a mile west of the Château, a cavernous basement boomed with the furious din of punk rock, which had taken London by storm, torn through downtown

Manhattan, and was now spreading like wildfire in Los Angeles. Here, in the seedy heart of the city, just off Hollywood Boulevard, a community of misfits had begun congregating in an underground—figuratively and literally—venue called the Masque.

Headlining the evening's four-act bill was a new band called X, which would become one of the most influential and longest-running punk bands of all time. Tonight was their first time playing the Masque, Hollywood's answer to CBGB. "Response from the front was unanimous," one attendee raved. "X is a good way to go."

To get to the Masque from Hollywood Boulevard, you had to walk down North Cherokee and hang a right into an alleyway where there was no obvious indication that you had arrived, as the *Los Angeles Times* rock journalist Kristine McKenna put it back then, at "the hottest punk nightclub in town." (In fact the only punk nightclub at the time.)

Through a prison-like doorway, concrete stairs descended into the underworld of a five-story Art Deco building, which in the 1930s housed Hollywood's newly minted labor unions. A second stairwell (the "Stairway to Nowhere"), located at the other end of the 10,000-square-foot space, dead-ended at the floor of the Pussycat Theater, where *Deep Throat* earned as much as $11,000 a week.

On a typical night, the Masque reeked of sweat, beer, and cigarette smoke, illuminated by dim lights hanging from a ceiling dotted with splotches of dried glue. (The tiles were long gone.) Graffiti covered the walls, displaying catchphrases and band names. "The Whisky and Starwood *may* showcase the big punk acts," wrote McKenna, "but the Masque is the only spot with authentic underground ambiance."

Sartorially, the Masque was a bit of a hodgepodge, with a heavy dose of retro thrift-store finds. The eclectic LA punk style that would take hold over the next few years was beginning to rear its head: slim jeans, skinny neckties, thin-striped T-shirts, snug greaser jackets and blazers, torn fishnets, heavy eyeliner, sunglasses after dark, leopard print, the occasional black trash bag fashioned into a dress. "We knew something really special was going on," recalls Belinda Carlisle of the Go-Go's. "You could feel it in the air."

Bands that emerged at the Masque became the stuff of legend. Carlisle and her fellow Go-Go's were inducted into the Rock & Roll Hall of Fame in 2021, celebrated for their "well-crafted songs" that "formed a bridge between the brash urgency of LA punk and the dark melodies of new wave pop." That same year, the Screamers received a belated *New York Times* profile, pegged to the first and only official release, after more than four decades, of their avant-garde synth punk. The Germs, whose guitarist, Pat Smear, broke into the mainstream as a member of Nirvana and the Foo Fighters, were immortalized in Rodger Grossman's 2007 biopic, *What We Do Is Secret*, starring Shane West as doomed singer Darby Crash and Bijou Phillips as celebrated bassist Lorna Doom.

Some habitués of the Masque found their own success in film and TV. Penelope Spheeris directed box office hits like *Wayne's World* and *The Little Rascals* after chronicling the early days of LA punk in her landmark 1981 documentary, *The Decline of Western Civilization*. Screamers drummer K. K. Barrett became an Academy Award–nominated production designer, known for his work with Spike Jonze and Sofia Coppola. Kira Roessler, who went on to play bass in Black Flag, made her name as an Emmy Award–winning dialogue editor with credits on the *Twilight* saga and *Game of Thrones*. Fear frontman Lee Ving has an IMDb page that includes appearances in *Flashdance*, *Clue* (as the menacing Mr. Boddy), and an infamous 1981 episode of *Saturday Night Live*, during which Fear—thanks to a bit of string pulling by John Belushi—wreaked havoc as the evening's musical guest.

The Masque's unlikely impresario was Brendan Mullen, a skinny Scottish expat who lived at the bottom of the main staircase in a room that doubled as his office. In the coming years, Mullen would give the Red Hot Chili Peppers their first gig, book shows for a prefame Guns N' Roses, and help launch the Viper Room with Johnny Depp. For now, at 28, he was simply an affable, music-loving UK transplant who'd stumbled into a career promoting shows. As Mullen wrote in 2007, "No big plans to open up a punk palace; no entrepreneurial impulse inspired me to start a business. . . . Only dumb luck compelled me."

A former newspaper reporter and a drummer, Mullen had come upon the basement by chance in the spring of 1977 while looking for somewhere to jam without having to worry about neighbors calling the cops. He struck a deal for an $850 monthly lease, cleaned the place up, partitioned off some rooms, and advertised it as a spot for bands to rent rehearsal space. "We were literally dead center in the bowels of Hollywood," Mullen later recalled. "I agreed to take it as is—thrashed to hell—and got a free month's rent to clear out 15 years of debris."

Almost in the blink of an eye, Mullen's humble rehearsal studio transformed into an all-hours playground for the first generation of LA's punk rock and new wave cognoscenti. "It was more of a clubhouse than a club or a venue per se," says Marina Muhlfriedel, better known as Marina del Rey, whose band Backstage Pass was among the first to shack up in one of the Masque's practice rooms. (Muhlfriedel's salary as an editor at *Teen* magazine enabled her to cosign the lease when Mullen ran into trouble with the landlord.) "We were all in it together."

Another early visitor was the performance artist and Andy Warhol star Bibbe Hansen, who frequented the Masque with her father, the Fluxus artist Al Hansen. Bibbe could often be found taking photographs of the Controllers, another early Masque band, during their rehearsals; she would sometimes bring along her seven-year-old son, a future Grammy Award–winning musician named Beck. "I'm from New York, so I'm used to alternative spaces and dark places," she says, "but for LA, it was pretty raw."

In late August, with the addition of a stage that couldn't have been more than a foot high, Mullen started booking shows. Through the end of summer and into the fall, hundreds of young punk fans and other miscellaneous oddballs packed the Masque to see bands like the Dickies and the Zeros, the Avengers and the Bags, the Weirdos and the Eyes and the Alleycats. "No two bands born or bred at the Masque were alike," the *LA Times*' McKenna later recalled, also observing: "The mix of people . . . was incredibly diverse: rich kids, poor kids, drug addicts, alcoholic art students. On the surface nobody had much in common, yet all were unmistakably members of the same tribe."

In the popular imagination, late-'70s LA was a sun-kissed Xanadu of disco and yacht rock. The Masque nurtured a dark and irreverent alternative, creating a space where an influential subculture could thrive. It was a heady atmosphere of vice, debauchery, art, rebellion, and the requisite dash of danger. "To a punk rocker," recalls Kid Congo Powers, who went from Masque regular to guitarist for the Cramps, the Gun Club, and Nick Cave & the Bad Seeds, "few things were more alluring than danger." Danger, indeed, was closing in.

An era had dawned that would become known as the "golden age of serial killers," and Los Angeles was on its way to earning the unfortunate designation of Serial Killer Capital of America. The latest serial killings were now unfolding in the hillsides around Hollywood, where the corpses of young women had been turning up with ligature marks around the necks, victims of an anonymous perpetrator dubbed the Hillside Strangler.

The seventh identification of a Strangler victim came on the evening of Wednesday, November 23, as the Masque filled up for a show headlined by the Germs. Authorities were able to get an ID on the body using fingerprints and dental charts. As it turned out, she was a familiar face at the Masque, a blond beauty who had celebrated her 28th birthday just a month earlier. She lived in an apartment at 8530 Holloway Drive, West Hollywood, and she'd been reported missing by her roommate on November 12 after failing to return home from an acting class at the Scientology center on Franklin Avenue.

Her name was Jane King.

⚬━━⚬

King's body was discovered on the outskirts of Griffith Park beside an off-ramp of the Golden State Freeway. A cowboy-boot-wearing homicide detective named Dudley Varney arrived to inspect the crime scene, determining the body had been "thrown or tossed . . . from the area of the roadway."

Varney had been appointed to oversee the field investigations of the cross-agency Hillside Strangler Task Force, which set out to probe the killings. Yolanda Washington, a 19-year-old sex worker, mother of a two-year-old daughter, and the sole Black woman on a growing list of victims, had been found near Griffith Park on October 16. The body of Judith Miller, a 15-year-old runaway and former Hollywood High School student, turned up on November 1 in a residential neighborhood in La Crescenta. Lissa Kastin, 21, a waitress from North Hollywood and member of an all-female dance troupe called the LA Knockers, was found on a highway embankment near the Chevy Chase Country Club in Glendale on November 6. Kristina Weckler, a 20-year-old honors student at Pasadena's Art Center College of Design, was found dead in Highland Park by a group of hikers on November 20. Later that same day came the discovery of Dolores Cepeda and Sonja Johnson, just 12 and 14 years old, last seen at the Eagle Rock Plaza shopping center; a nine-year-old boy hunting for treasure in a trash heap near Dodger Stadium happened upon their remains.

And then there was King, identified in newspaper reports as a "beautiful" aspiring actor and model sometimes known to "accept hitchhiking rides in the Hollywood area."

"She was trying to break into famous Hollywood," the roommate who had reported King missing on November 12 told the *LA Times*. She was always on the go, running around, always out someplace. . . . She was just in the wrong place at the wrong time."

The director of Scientology's Celebrity Centre International told the *Times* King had studied there. "She was currently working as a model and was into music," he said. "She had a definite interest in acting and had hoped to pursue that line." Overall, he sensed that King was "trying to find herself."

Born in Arizona on October 20, 1949, King grew up in Arcadia, California, just outside LA's northeast city limits. "She was quiet and shy," says Bill Pauley, a childhood classmate.

Cecilia Joder befriended King at Arcadia High School, where they were members of the class of 1967, one year behind Stevie Nicks. "We sat next to each other in arts and crafts and we just had a ball," says Joder. "She was a run-of-the-mill girl like me. I didn't expect her to be running around Hollywood. When I heard that she'd been killed, I was shocked."

A brief inscription in one of Joder's high school yearbooks was the only trace of King's voice that I could find. "Cecilia," she wrote. "It was fun this year in psychology and last year in artcrafts. Be happy. Love, Jane King."

King's younger sister, Judy King, told me about their childhood being raised by a single working mother, Abra King, in Arcadia, where the family lived with Abra's parents. There were vacations at the national parks and at the beaches near San Diego. Occasionally, letters and gifts arrived from the girls' absent father, a ranch hand in New Mexico. After high school, Jane found jobs as a candy striper and a massage therapist. She discovered Scientology, drawn to its promise, as Judy recalls, of helping practitioners "remove hindrances that might keep you from being your best self." And she gave birth to a daughter in 1968, fathered by a young man Jane had met while celebrating Mardi Gras in New Orleans. Jane, not yet 20, decided that an adoption was in the baby's best interest. Before saying goodbye, she settled on the name she would have given her: Goldberry, in homage to a character from the works of J. R. R. Tolkien.

After Judy graduated from high school two years behind Jane, she moved to Oregon with a man who lured her into what she described as a cultlike community. Sometime in 1973 or 1974, Jane visited Judy and tried to bring her back home. It was the last time that Judy, who eventually did break away from her communal "family," saw or spoke to her sister. "She realized I was being deceived," Judy says. "She was trying to rescue me."

Jane's love of rock and roll, especially the Rolling Stones, blossomed in her teenage years. So it made sense later when she began dating a fellow Stones enthusiast named Rick Wilder, who would be described in the *LA Times* as "a Mick Jagger–Johnny Rotten clone created by some mad punk scientist."

Wilder can't recall exactly when he met King, but it had to have been sometime in the mid-1970s. Back then, Wilder was the singer of the Berlin Brats, once dubbed "LA's first homegrown glam rock band."

His parents were the opera singers Giovanni Millo and Margherita Girosi. One of his two sisters, Aprile Millo, became a luminary of the Metropolitan Opera. The other, Grace Millo, became a singer-songwriter. They had a peripatetic childhood traveling around as their parents toured small opera houses and concert halls in Italy and the US. When a heart condition forced Giovanni to give up his singing career, the family settled in Los Angeles, where Wilder attended Hollywood High School, Fairfax High School, and the now defunct Hollywood Professional School, whose alumni include John Drew Barrymore, Judy Garland, Melanie Griffith, Val Kilmer, Mickey Rooney, and Natalie Wood.

King entered Wilder's orbit when she started dating his childhood friend and bandmate Matt Campbell. As King and Campbell's relationship went south, King and Wilder hit it off. "He would have fights with her," Wilder recalls. "After one of those fights, we ended up in a closet making love."

King showed Wilder her headshots. Wilder offered to give King singing lessons. They became an item, on and off, and shared an apartment for a period of time, according to Wilder, who still has photos of his former sweetheart. "I used to have one of her holding my Hamlet skull," he says, "which she thought was maybe a good picture."

King frequented Berlin Brats performances. In the summer of 1977, as Wilder was falling under the spell of punk rock and Mullen was getting his new rehearsal space off the ground, the Brats rented a room, becoming one of the earliest bands to inhabit the basement, alongside Backstage Pass, the Controllers, and the Skulls (some of whose members went on to form Wall of Voodoo, which scored an early MTV hit with the 1982 single "Mexican Radio"). King was a regular at the Brats' practices, hanging around and sipping Rainier Ale through a straw. "She was a sweet-natured, goofily naive Stevie Nicks fan," Mullen would later recall, "who danced around her apartment to 'Rhiannon' rather than the Sex Pistols or Ramones."

King worked in a clothing shop on Sunset Boulevard while pursuing her Hollywood aspirations. Her sister told me she appeared briefly as part of a photographic montage in the opening credits of Richard Brooks's *Looking for Mr. Goodbar*, starring Diane Keaton and Richard Gere, a 1977 crime drama that would garner two Oscar nominations. (The film, inspired by the 1973 murder of a New York City schoolteacher, premiered just weeks before King's disappearance.) "She wanted to be famous," says Wilder.

To some of the Masque's more bedraggled patrons, King seemed out of their league. "She looked a little out of place," says Johnny Stingray, guitarist for the Controllers. "I was a little too shy to say anything to her." Skulls frontman Steven

Fortuna, aka Billy Bones, remembers King as a more conventionally fashionable figure than the rest of the Masque crowd. "She always had style," he says. "Just a really nice person."

Liz Winchell first encountered King at Wilder's Hollywood party pad on the corner of Franklin and Whitley in a 1920s building designed by the same architects responsible for the Beverly Wilshire Hotel. "I remember the day I met her," says Winchell (whose grandfather was the legendary gossip columnist Walter Winchell). "We were playing the Stones, and that's what she and I first started talking about. We both loved the music. She was not a typical punk girl at all. She was very beautiful and put together in a way that we were not. She was on a different level."

Winchell and King would go shopping together on Hollywood Boulevard and run around looking to score quaaludes. "I just remember her being really kind to me," says Winchell, now a licensed marriage and family therapist, "and because I was younger, it was like, she didn't have to be kind. She didn't have to take me under her wing. In some way, I looked up to her."

By the fall of 1977, King had moved into the apartment in West Hollywood, which she shared with an architect named Steven Moskowitz, whom she'd met through a roommate service. King remained close with Wilder, but she was going out with someone else, a chauffeur named Steve Rockne.

On Monday, October 31, Mullen had booked the Berlin Brats for a show billed as an "Anti-Disco Hallow'een." King asked Rockne if he wanted to accompany her, but he said he'd meet up afterward. The Berlin Brats didn't end up playing, and when King arrived, she found the place more sparsely attended than usual. She stayed for a couple of hours and left the Masque around 10 to call Rockne for a ride back to his place.

Wilder couldn't have known it at the time, but he would never see her again.

———

After King's missing persons report was filed on November 12, Abra King started calling her daughter's friends. *Were they with Jane? Had they seen her? Did they have any idea at all where she might be?*

"That was the minute I knew she was gone," Wilder recalls of his conversation with Abra. "I had a sixth sense."

Winchell, who was living with her mother at the time, came home after being away for a couple of nights. Winchell's mother burst out crying and pulled her daughter close. "Were you with Jane today?" she wailed. "*Where's Jane?*" Winchell listened as her mother called Abra King. "I'll never forget hearing my mom talk to her mom after she told her I was home," Winchell recalled, choking up. "I remember them crying so hard together. I remember her saying what it must be like to be Jane's mom right now. I felt guilty. It could have been me."

By the morning of Thursday, November 24, King's whereabouts ceased to be a mystery. An article in the *LA Times* reported that the Hillside Strangler Task Force, created two days earlier, had identified her as "the seventh body found since October 15 in a six-mile radius including Glendale, Highland Park, La Crescenta, Griffith Park, and Elysian Park."

When Wilder learned about King's murder on the news, it was too much for him. "I just didn't want to even think about it," he says. "She was so harmless, and so sweet."

As the number of murders ticked up, investigators developed a theory that there was not one killer but two, luring victims by posing as police. The suspected duo claimed another two lives in the coming weeks. First, police found the body of 18-year-old college student Lauren Wagner on November 29 in the hills around Mount Washington; she'd been abducted the previous night, just steps from the house where she lived with her parents. Then, on December 14, after 17-year-old sex worker Kimberly Martin was reported missing by a call-girl agency she had joined, her body was found on a hillside within view of Los Angeles City Hall.

"Prostitutes on Sunset Boulevard and suburban mothers in southern California," *The New York Times* reported, "are sharing something this Christmas season: fear of a multiple murderer."

Firearms sales ticked up. Self-defense classes sold out. Streetwalkers clustered in groups of six or more. "The Strangler case makes a grim fact vividly clear," said a young Geraldo Rivera, reporting for ABC News. "People can never totally protect themselves from a madman who apparently chooses his victims at random."

The sheer number of women who populated the Masque helped define it as a scene. For some, Rivera's observation was all too real. (A number of them would soon move into an apartment complex up the street called the Canterbury, which was essentially becoming a dormitory for punks—it stood just a few doors from one of the last known residences of Elizabeth Short, better known as the Black Dahlia.) These were bold young women who played in bands and published zines and obliterated any notion of punk as a boys club. But they were nonetheless vulnerable, and King's death brought the Strangler case close to home.

"I remember how horrifying it was when we found out she'd been murdered," says Pleasant Gehman, who went on to become an accomplished writer, burlesque performer, and singer of the Screamin' Sirens. "We had never known anyone that was murdered. That was something you read in a newspaper." One night, after leaving the Whisky without a walking companion, Gehman was apprehended by two cops—actual cops, thankfully—who searched her leather jacket and demanded to know why she was carrying a switchblade. "I just looked at them and I was like, the *Hillside Strangler!*"

Alice Bag, aka Alicia Armendariz, front woman of the Bags, got an eerie feeling about an incident relayed to her by a friend earlier that fall. Her friend, nicknamed Pearl Harbor, had been walking near the Whisky in October when two men claiming to be cops stopped her. They put Pearl in the back of a car and drove around "just abusing her, telling her she's a whore, she's disgusting, threatening her," recalls Armendariz, now a retired teacher who still has an active music career. "To this day, I believe Pearl had an experience with the Hillside Stranglers, and that she lived to tell the tale." (Pearl died several years ago.)

Writing about the murders around the 30th anniversary of the first killing, the photographer and former Masque-goer Theresa Kereakes observed, "The Hillside Strangler provided the tense undercurrent during this character building period of LA punk rock. Punk rock girls stood up in defiance about being paranoid and went out anyway, dressed the way they wanted to . . . not so much to spit in the face of authority but to assert themselves and claim responsibility for their actions."

King's murder weighed heavily on Mullen. "How would anybody be able to hear anything," he worried, "a girl's screams, if somebody was strangling her in one of the many dark corners at the Masque?" Mullen hired a 350-pound, six-foot-four uniformed security guard nicknamed Tiny "to

keep antennae out for sickos and to walk girls to their cars."
Detectives interviewed people who knew King from the
Masque, where the band F-Word began to perform a song
that would become its anthem: "Hillside Strangler." During
a meeting in his office at the bottom of the basement stairs,
Mullen gave the task force "what little information I could."

Mullen would soon have a different sort of encounter with
the law. He had obtained a police permit for "cafe entertain-
ment/shows" at the Masque, which was drawing ever bigger
crowds as punk's siren call blared across the Los Angeles sprawl.
What Mullen didn't possess were occupancy permits. The oversight caught up with him on January 17, 1978, when the Los
Angeles Fire Department ordered the Masque to stop operating
as a live music venue, at least until Mullen addressed a list of
issues such as poor ventilation and a lack of sufficient egress.

"Owner Brendan Mullen says to bring the theater up to
specifications would require expensive changes including
soundproofing and re-wiring," the *LA Times* reported.

One month later, a few days before a 20-band "Save the
Masque" benefit at the Elks Lodge No. 99 near MacAr-
thur Park, a 10th name was added to the death toll. Police
found 20-year-old Silver Lake resident Cindy Hudspeth
on February 17 in the trunk of her orange Datsun, which
had tumbled 50 feet down an embankment off the Angeles
Crest Highway. "We can see she is a Strangler victim," an
investigator told the press.

After that, something unexpected happened. March came
and went without another body. Then April. Then May. As
the year drew to a close, police had yet to encounter another
murder that fit the profile.

Had something spooked the killers? Were they simply
biding their time before striking again? The Hillside

Strangler Task Force still didn't have any suspects. It was beginning to look as though they might never figure out who was behind the slayings. Then they got a phone call.

⊙━━━○

In January 1979, the police chief of Bellingham, Washington, a waterfront city 21 miles south of the Canadian border, contacted the task force with some crucial information. The bodies of two young women, Karen Mandic and Diane Wilder, had been found in the trunk of Mandic's car, deep ligature marks around their necks. Police already had a suspect in custody. He'd been a security guard at the grocery store where Mandic worked, and he'd offered the women $100 each for a supposed house-sitting job from which they'd never returned. Notably, he'd lived in Los Angeles until the previous year.

The suspect's name was Kenneth Bianchi, a handsome and charismatic 27-year-old originally from Rochester, New York, where he'd been born to a 17-year-old alcoholic sex worker and raised by adoptive working-class Italian Catholics. A variety of behavioral issues were evident from a young age: compulsive lying, incontinence, passive-aggressive personality disorder, and poor academic performance belied by above-average intelligence. After high school, he'd bounced around between menial jobs while trying, unsuccessfully, to break into law enforcement. With no career prospects and a history of petty theft, Bianchi had sought a new beginning in the mid-'70s in Los Angeles, where he used fake credentials to pose as a psychologist and began relationships with two women. One of them became pregnant with Bianchi's son but spurned his marriage proposal and moved north to

be near her family in Bellingham, which is what brought
Bianchi there in 1978.

After learning about Bianchi from his counterparts in
Washington State, Dudley Varney picked up the phone and
called his boss. "We're going to Bellingham," he said.

Connections to the LA victims became apparent. Bianchi
had lived for six months in the same Glendale apartment
complex as Kristina Weckler. He'd also lived at 1950 Tama-
rind Avenue, the apartment complex to which Kimberly
Martin had been dispatched by her call-girl agency. Around
the corner stood the bus stop where King had waited after
her acting class.

Members of the task force took Bianchi's fingerprints.
Back in LA, Varney was waiting for an elevator when a colleague bounded up to him with the news that they'd matched
the prints to one of their crime scenes: "We got him!"

As Varney suspected, Bianchi had not been working alone
during the killing spree. He confessed he'd committed the
crimes with his adoptive older cousin, Angelo Buono, a
minor crook with a record of abusive behavior toward women
who ran a car upholstery business in Glendale. To nail
Buono, prosecutors offered Bianchi life with the possibility
of parole, no death penalty. He agreed to testify against his
cousin, who maintained he was innocent and that Bianchi
was a pathological liar. Evidence gathered by detectives
suggested otherwise—they found fibers on two victims that
matched those in Buono's home.

Interrogations of Bianchi unspooled the stories of 10 young
women in and around LA who'd shared the misfortune of
encountering a pair of twisted men between October 1977 and
February 1978. It turned out there'd almost been 11. Posing
as undercover vice cops, Bianchi and Buono had stopped

Catharine Lorre one evening near the former Max Factor building just off Hollywood Boulevard. Bianchi aborted the plan after rifling through his intended target's wallet and realizing she was the daughter of the late actor Peter Lorre (who himself played a serial killer in Fritz Lang's *M*). "I had two photographs depicting my father and myself together," Lorre later testified, recalling that one of her would-be captors had remarked, "Hey, this really is Peter Lorre's kid!"

Buono wasn't wrong in depicting his cousin as a liar who couldn't be trusted. Bianchi had led a double life, after all. He'd even conjured supposed alternate personalities during his psychiatric evaluations. It's impossible to know how honestly Bianchi described each victim's abduction, rape, and murder. (He would later claim to have invented details under pressure from interrogators.) But his accounts are the closest we have to the truth about how these young women came to lose their lives.

In King's case, the story Bianchi initially told goes like this: He and Buono were joyriding in Bianchi's 1972 Cadillac when they saw King, solitary and stunning in her shiny silver heels, at the bus stop on Franklin Avenue. They pulled into the parking lot of the Mayfair supermarket. Bianchi exited the car, walked over to the bus stop, and struck up a conversation. He and King were chatting when Bianchi feigned surprise at spotting his cousin, as if he just happened to be driving by. He waved at the car as Buono slowed down with a friendly honk and pressed on the brakes. *Did King need a lift home?* It was no trouble at all, they said. For reassurance, Bianchi flashed a fake badge and told her they were members of the LA Police Reserve. He opened the front passenger-side door and, against her better judgment, King stepped in.

The Cadillac cruised west on Franklin, past the Scientology center, past Wilder's apartment, before pulling into a

Hughes Market on the corner of Highland. King waited in the car while Bianchi and Buono went inside to buy cigarettes. When they returned, Bianchi told King that Buono was in a hurry to get home. Would she mind if they dropped him off first, and then Bianchi could take Buono's car and drive King back to her place? Not at all, King replied.

They drove up Highland Avenue, and then Barham Boulevard, and east onto Forest Lawn Drive before catching the freeway. King looked straight ahead as the Cadillac came to a stop in the driveway of Buono's yellow bungalow in Glendale. Everything happened so fast. Bianchi and Buono grabbed King's arms. She struggled to break free. They slapped handcuffs on her wrists and forced her into the house. The scene that unfolded from there is too graphic for these pages, but it ended with twine around King's neck and the life leaving her body. As King's roommate had said, "She was just in the wrong place at the wrong time."

Buono's murder trial, the longest in American history, began in November 1981. Two years later, on October 31, 1983, the bailiff announced that the jury had reached its first of 10 verdicts. Roger Boren, the lead prosecutor in the case, felt his heart pounding as he awaited the jury's decision. He breathed a sigh of relief upon hearing the crucial word: *guilty*. "It was like heaven opening up when that first verdict came in," Boren recalls.

In the coming days, Buono was convicted of all but one of the killings. "We, the jury," the foreman declared on November 10, "find the defendant, Angelo Buono, guilty of the murder of Jane King." A reporter informed Abra King of the outcome. "I got to the point where I didn't care," she said through tears. "The thing you care about is losing your daughter."

On November 18, Buono, aged 49, was sentenced to life without the possibility of parole. According to a reporter in the courtroom, he stared straight ahead and "swallowed hard but took the verdict with no other show of emotion."

Bianchi is serving out his life sentence at the Washington State Penitentiary in Walla Walla. He was denied parole in 2010 and will be eligible to apply again in 2025, at the age of 74. Buono died of natural causes in 2002, at the age of 67, alone in his cell at California's State Prison at Calipatria. The following year, fronting a new lineup of the Skulls, Billy Bones recorded a song in memory of his former acquaintance:

"Jane hitched a ride on the Hollywood stars one night / Up to the hillside, that's where they took her life / Glad he now lies in his own death bed / Yeah yeah, the Hillside Strangler's dead."

⊶⊷

After his run-in with the fire department in January 1978, Mullen found creative ways to circumvent the show stoppage at the Masque, like acquiring a film permit for a TV crew to tape a performance, or hosting quasi-legal word-of-mouth parties where bands would just happen to play. At one such shindig, in May 1978, the Go-Go's made their world debut, opening for the Weirdos and the Germs. "Everybody in the scene was at that show," recalls Carlisle. "We played a song called 'Overrun' twice, and we played a song called 'Robert Hilburn.' He was the music critic at the *LA Times*. That was our set list."

With the scene rallying around him, Mullen tried to raise money to bring the Masque up to code. But the modest funds he amassed from benefit shows got eaten up by legal costs, and discussions with potential investors didn't pan out. For a brief stretch, Mullen operated a space on Santa Monica Boulevard called the Other Masque, which overlapped with his stealth gigs at the original Masque. The final nail in the coffin came on July 13, 1979. That night, Rick Wilder had put together a party with several bands, including Wilder's new act, the Mau-Mau's; a pre–Henry Rollins Black Flag; and a group called the Blackhearts, members of which would go on to perform under the same name as the backing band for Joan Jett (herself a scene fixture). Not long before the Mau-Mau's were set to take the stage, a fire marshal entered the basement with members of the LAPD. This time, two years after first opening its doors, Mullen accepted the venue's fate. The Masque may have come to an end, but as Mullen later put it, "The new indigenous punk spirit was already too rooted, too strong to just go away."

LA punk had snowballed into a force that 10 Masques couldn't contain. Bands could now sell out traditional venues like the Whisky. The scene was spreading to new stomping grounds, places like the Hong Kong Cafe in Chinatown, Club 88 on Pico Boulevard, and the Fleetwood in Redondo Beach. For some bands, the road ahead was paved with record deals, world tours, and MTV. By 1980, as the *LA Times* suggested, punk had "turned Los Angeles into arguably the most exciting live music center in America."

Mullen went on to enjoy a fruitful career as a show promoter, music journalist, and author. His works include 2001's *We Got the Neutron Bomb*, an oral history of LA punk co-authored with Marc Spitz, and *Live at the Masque: Nightmare in Punk Alley*, a 2007 coffee-table book.

In 2009, Mullen was working on a book with the Red Hot Chili Peppers when he died from a stroke, suffered the day after celebrating his 60th birthday with his longtime partner, writer and researcher Kateri Butler. In a *New York Times* obituary that heralded Mullen as a "Pillar of Los Angeles Punk," Ben Sisario wrote: "Although the Los Angeles punk scene has generally been less celebrated than those of London or New York, it was extensive. With the Masque as their incubator, the city's bands began to develop a distinct style that reflected the disaffection of young people in a sprawling, glittery megalopolis."

In November, I made a pilgrimage to the Masque, which is now used for storage and video shoots by World of Wonder Productions (the company behind *RuPaul's Drag Race*, head-quartered in the building above). WoW cofounder Randy Barbato—who knew Mullen, coincidentally—took me down to the legendary basement to have a look around. I brought along three esteemed tour guides from the Masque's heyday: Pleasant Gehman, K. K. Barrett, and Trudie Arguelles-Barrett (famously christened "LA's most popular punk" in a 1978 issue of *New York Rocker*).

As we pored over ancient graffiti that still decorates the walls, Barrett pointed to a name scrawled on a yellow beam in thick black marker: "Rick Wilder." He never became as well-known as some of the other Masque alumni, but he's an underground legend nonetheless. (Fans of The Weeknd will recognize Wilder as the haunting figure who appears in three of the Grammy-winning pop star's music videos.) In a cruel and eerie twist, King was not Wilder's only former girlfriend to fall prey to a serial killer. In the early '90s, while living in Manhattan at the storied Whitby apartments on West 45th Street, Wilder dated a young woman named Tiffany Bresciani. Like King, Bresciani was an aspiring actor who'd found her way into the punk scene. Her relationship with Wilder deteriorated and Bresciani spiraled into heroin addiction and prostitution, a path that ended in 1993 when she became the 17th and final victim of Joel Rifkin. "She didn't deserve any of that," Wilder laments.

Wilder told me King was his first love. I thought of her when I was down in the Masque, where King had watched Wilder perform 46 years earlier. You might say King's story echoes that of the Black Dahlia: two striking young women trying to make it in Hollywood, who ended up brutally murdered by elusive killers, their bodies left nude and desecrated for strangers to find. The difference is that Elizabeth Short became famous in death, while King was essentially forgotten to time.

At the Masque, King inhabited the same social space as people who would become stars, some in the most conventional sense of the word, others in their capacity as subcultural icons. Whether King herself actually had a chance of making it is beside the point; the killers took more than her life—they took her dreams.

Right before our visit to the Masque, Gehman and I strolled past the old Château Élysée and stood for a few minutes at the bus stop where King disappeared. Gehman, whose apartment is a short walk from there, mused thoughtfully about the paradox of Hollywood. It's a sparkly wonderland of ambition, bright and sunny and beautiful, but its sinister underbelly is always just a tragedy away. King may not have attained the fame she sought in life, but in death, she became a part of this haunted legacy.

Standing beside the bus stop, Gehman turned to me and said, "There's something about Hollywood that people who aren't from Los Angeles don't understand. The energy here is so hopeful but also so doomed."

Anatomy of a Murder

by John Rosengren

How a shocking crime divided a small Minnesota town.

Grand Marais is a quiet outpost on Lake Superior's North Shore, set among boreal forest in the easternmost corner of Minnesota. The town of roughly 1,300 is home to a mix of artists and outdoor enthusiasts, working-class people and professionals, liberals and diehard Trump supporters. In the summer, Grand Marais's art galleries, shops, and restaurants swell with tourists drawn to what the website *Budget Travel* once dubbed "America's Coolest Small Town." The wait for a table at the Angry Trout Café, which serves locally sourced cuisine in an old fishing shanty, can run to more than an hour. When summer is over, the town retreats into itself again, which suits full-time residents just fine. "Even though we're a tourism economy, most of us live a life where we just don't want to be bothered," said Steve Fernlund, who published the *Cook County News Herald* in the 1990s and now writes a weekly column for *The North Shore Journal*. "I'm at the end of a road, and I've got 12 acres of land. My closest neighbors are probably about 600 feet away through the woods. So, you know, we appreciate being hermits."

Yet privacy only extends so far here. Gossip travels fast while having breakfast at the South of the Border café, or in chance encounters along Wisconsin Street. Everybody knows everybody else's business—or thinks they do. "Even though there are differences of opinion—we have an eclectic collection of opinions—this is a close-knit community," said Dennis Waldrop, who manages the Cook County Historical Museum. "Anything that happens here is discussed extensively."

The residents of Grand Marais have had a lot to discuss in recent years. A suspicious fire that destroyed the historic Lutsen Lodge. The suicide of their neighbor Mark Pavelich, a star on the 1980 US Olympic hockey team that defeated the Soviet Union. Plans for the 40 acres near town owned by convicted sex offender Warren Jeff's fundamentalist clan. All those events stirred plenty of talk.

But nothing has captivated local conversation quite like what happened between Larry Scully and Levi Axtell in March 2023. A shocking act of violence attracted international attention and split the town over questions of truth and justice. Grand Marais is still trying to piece itself back together.

Every small town has its cast of offbeat characters. Larry Scully was one of Grand Marais's. Larry, who was 77 in 2023, dwelled on the fringe of town, where Fifth Street meets Highway 61, and on the fringe of reality. His two-bedroom house, which used to belong to his parents, was crowded with items he'd hoarded over the years. The mess spilled into his front yard, which was cluttered with satellite dishes, a statue of the Virgin Mary, and a wood-frame sign advertising "antler bone art." The sign was decorated with several of Larry's scrimshaw carvings, which he hawked at art fairs. In addition to carving, he'd tried his hand at an array of other pursuits: refurbishing broken electronics, selling solar-powered generators that could run home appliances in the event of an emergency, and even fashioning leather lingerie that he peddled to women. Larry had had no stable career to speak of since he arrived in town in the early 1980s.

Larry was a conspiracy theorist. On his Facebook page, he posted videos and articles declaring that the federal government controlled the weather, that Sandy Hook was a hoax, that Timothy McVeigh was a "CIA patsy," that the totalitarian New World Order was real. Around Grand Marais, Larry was also known to be exceedingly religious. He attended Mass on Saturday evenings at St. John's Catholic Church, always sitting in the front row, and he believed that the statues there cried actual tears—sometimes of blood. He carried a lock of hair that he said once belonged to Father Mark Hollenhorst, a priest at St. John's who died in 1993, in a leather pouch around his neck; he claimed that it could effect miraculous cures.

Larry referred to himself as a prophet and would often appear around town dressed in a cloak and sandals and carrying a wooden staff. He once showed up on the courthouse steps for the National Day of Prayer clad all in black, his head covered by a medieval-type chain mail hood, and fell to his knees screaming. Another time he berated a group of gay people who'd gathered in downtown Grand Marais, shouting through a bullhorn that God didn't approve of them.

Many locals found Larry's zeal exhausting. "When I'd see him, I'd know I was going to be there for a long time, because he'd go on and on," said Laura Laky, a Grand Marais resident. "He'd talk about the end-times, the Book of Revelation, Christ coming again."

Other people were scared of Larry. Rumors that he abused children circulated around Grand Marais for years. People whispered about him watching kids from his parked car. There were claims that he'd videotaped girls' volleyball games and children at Sven and Ole's, the local pizzeria. A member of the nearby Chippewa tribe told me that Larry had been banned from the Grand Portage powwow after parents complained about him passing out candy to their children.

Larry once approached a man named Gary Nesgoda at a gas station and asked if he had kids. When Nesgoda said that he did, Larry showed him pictures of a fairy garden he'd built behind his house. There were miniature staircases and doors, and little figurines set amid tree roots. Larry insisted that Nesgoda, who had recently moved to Grand Marais, should bring his kids over to see it. "Everything he was telling me sounded pretty neat," Nesgoda told me. Then, in the gas station parking lot, someone who'd overheard the conversation stopped Nesgoda. "Do not bring your children over there," they warned.

This was a common theme. "Larry was the boogeyman," said Brian Larsen, editor and publisher of the *Cook County News Herald*, who is a father of four children. "You'd tell your kids to stay the heck away from him."

In 2014, Larry decided to run for mayor of Grand Marais. In a candidate forum broadcast on WTIP, a community radio station, he ranted about Christianity. "We can't sit by and let our government stop us from having the Bible in the military, taking out the crucifixes, taking out the Ten Commandments in our federal buildings and establishments," he said. Then, just before election day, the *Cook County News Herald* ran a front-page article that seemed to confirm the longstanding speculation about Larry. The piece detailed his criminal conviction for the sexual assault of a six-year-old girl.

Before he became an object of fear and fascination in Grand Marais, Larry was married—twice. For a time he lived with his second wife, Sheila, in Ramsey, about 25 miles outside Minneapolis. On Ash Wednesday in 1979, Sheila went to evening Mass and then to bowl in her weekly league, leaving Larry home alone with their five children: three young boys from his first marriage and six-year-old twins, a boy and a girl, from hers. While the other children slept, according to police and court records, Larry invited his stepdaughter into his bedroom.

The little girl later told a police investigator that he showed her "pictures of naked people," touched her "potty area" with a vibrator, then stuck his tongue and finger into her vagina. She said it wasn't the only time he'd touched her, and that he'd warned her not to tell anyone, but she went to her mother anyway. Sheila reported the incident to child welfare services, who notified law enforcement. She told the police investigator that her husband had also recently become violent and suicidal.

The police arrested Larry. In a recorded statement with investigators, he admitted that he'd had sexual contact with his stepdaughter on two Wednesday evenings while his wife was bowling. A psychiatrist determined that he was competent to stand trial, finding no evidence of "any kind of psychiatric disorder." Rather than face a jury, Larry confessed to second-degree criminal sexual conduct, and the prosecution recommended a sentence of five years. Two court psychologists submitted reports indicating that Larry wasn't open to receiving treatment. At an October 1979 hearing, the judge urged Larry to reconsider. "Take whatever treatment is available to you," the judge said, "because this type of conduct, of course, is just wholly unacceptable."

Larry was incarcerated in Minnesota's Stillwater prison, and in records from his time there, there's no mention of him receiving counseling or treatment, though he did join a Bible study. Soon, changes to the state's sentencing guidelines allowed Larry to seek early release. Since the state did not provide evidence that doing so would "present a danger to the public," the court approved Larry's request. He left prison on January 19, 1982, after serving a little more than two years for his crime.

In those days, there was no sex offender registry in Minnesota, or in most states. Larry was at liberty to go where he liked. Sheila had divorced him by then, and his three sons were living with their mother. Larry, who was 36 at the time, hitchhiked to Grand Marais to move in with his parents.

Three decades later, Larry lost the town's mayoral election, 345 votes to 42. Many locals were surprised that he'd gotten any votes at all, especially after the story broke about his criminal record. "Forty-something people voted for him," said Amber Waldrop, who lived down the street from Larry.

"They knew about this guy. For anybody to even think that someone like that should become mayor of this town is sickening."

Some of those votes came from Larry's friends, many of whom shared his belief in conspiracy theories. Perhaps it's no surprise that they also believed what Larry told them: that the accusations against him were made up, that his ex-wife had encouraged her daughter to lie to the police, that he only took the plea deal to avoid a long prison sentence.

Larry's friends knew that he tended to hijack conversations and go on at length about topics ranging from the Rapture to homeopathic cures, and that he engaged strangers in ways many people found uncomfortable. But being an oddball, they said, isn't a crime. Some of his friends thought Larry was on the autism spectrum, which made it hard for him to read social cues and show empathy. "This man has been persecuted all of his life," said Bob Stangler, a Vietnam veteran who knew Larry for years. "The citizens of the area have labeled him a pervert, and he's not a pervert at all. He's a genius with Asperger's who's overcaring of people."

A woman I'll call Carol, who asked that her real name not be used, said she was so close with Larry that she spoke to him almost daily for 12 years. She knew him to visit sick people, distribute food to the needy, and take care of his ailing mother, who died in 2013. At her memorial service, Larry displayed his mother's ashes in a cookie jar resembling the Star Wars character R2-D2, saying that it was what she wanted. (His father passed away in 1997.) "As long as I've known him, he never hurt anybody," Carol told me.

She knows that hers is a minority opinion, that for many people in town Larry was foremost a convicted sex offender. "You can never get rid of that label," she said.

Once they learned about his 1979 conviction, many parents in Grand Marais were more worried than ever that Larry posed a threat to their children. It's a common enough fear. On the far right, popular conspiracy theories such as QAnon decry a global cabal of child molesters, but even among the general population, concern about the danger posed by pedophiles is widespread. In a Lynn University poll, 75 percent of roughly 200 Florida adults said they believed that sex offenders would reoffend. Yet according to a meta-study conducted by researchers at Public Safety Canada in 2004, one of the most comprehensive available, only 23 percent of people convicted of child sexual abuse were charged or convicted of a similar crime within the next 15 years. (The study's authors concede that many victims never come forward.) In interviews for this story, researchers noted that recidivism rates have declined even more in recent years.

No one came forward to accuse Larry of more recent abuse after his 1979 conviction. Still, perception alone was enough to put many Grand Marais parents on edge. For one young man, that concern became an obsession.

⊙━━◆━━◦

If you were passing through Grand Marais a few years back and stopped for gas at the Holiday station on the corner of Broadway and Highway 61, you might have met a stocky cashier with a round, friendly face. While making change, he might have told you one of his homespun puns or signature dad jokes: *Why does Paul Bunyan trip in the woods? Because he's always felling.*

That cashier was Levi Axtell. He was raised by his parents, Denise and Treg, in Hovland, a small community located 18 miles from Grand Marais. The Axtells were devout Christians and widely respected in Grand Marais, where they both worked. Denise was a nurse, Treg a physical therapist. The couple had three children: daughters Karlee and Katrina, and Levi, the youngest.

Levi grew up in a picturesque log cabin in a clearing among birch and pine trees. The woods were his playground. He spent hours there as a child, often with his friend and neighbor Cedar Adams. They roasted marshmallows over campfires, tried to catch fish barehanded, and played make-believe, running through the trees as if an attacker were pursuing them.

But Levi couldn't outrun his demons. There was a history of addiction on Denise's side of the family, and Levi seemed to have inherited a predisposition to substance abuse. At Cook County High School, he played football, ran track, and drank. Brad Wilson, a carpenter in Grand Marais who was a few years behind him in school, recalled Levi getting caught with liquor bottles in his locker and running from the cops.

Levi's parents sent him to finish school in Duluth, but he was cited twice within two months for underage drinking. The first time was at Duluth East High School. On the morning of May 29, 2014, when a resource officer tried to restrain him, an inebriated Levi pulled away. The officer wrestled Levi to the ground, but he pushed himself up and army-crawled—with the officer on top of him—down the hallway, until he wore himself out. Levi spent two days in jail and was charged with disorderly conduct and obstructing the legal process with force. "I didn't know it made the charges worse if you resisted arrest," he later told Cedar Adams.

Not long after, a law enforcement officer stopped Levi as he walked along the shoulder of Interstate 35. The officer

smelled booze on his breath, and Levi admitted that he'd
been drinking. The officer cited him and let him go after Levi
dumped out a container of alcohol he was carrying.

Three days later, Levi was given a year of probation for
his disorderly conduct at Duluth East. (The obstruction
charge was dropped.) A judge also ordered him to obtain a
chemical-dependency assessment and follow any recommendations. Levi satisfied the terms of his probation, including
a stint in treatment.

By 2015, Levi had started dating Anna Ross, who was
from Duluth. Their daughter was born on June 17, 2016.
Anna had just turned 19; Levi was 20. At first they didn't
live together—Anna stayed in Duluth, while Levi lived with
his parents in Hovland. He adored his daughter and beamed
when she was in his arms.

Despite the new light in his life, Levi remained burdened
at times by darkness. About a year after his daughter's
birth, on the Sunday evening of Memorial Day weekend,
Levi got drunk, taped a vacuum hose to the exhaust pipe
of his car, ran the other end through the back window, and
started the engine. When he texted Anna about what he'd
done, she called the sheriff's department. While she was on
the phone with them, Levi called her, and she talked him
into turning off the car. Deputies arrived at his home and
transported Levi to the hospital. It appears that he received
some psychiatric treatment after the incident; a year later he
indicated in a court document that he'd been a patient in a
mental hospital and had seen a psychiatrist.

Despite his troubles, Levi was by all accounts goofy and
lovable. Christina Conroy, a friend who worked with Levi
briefly at the Holiday station, described him as "a beautiful
soul." Cedar Adams said, "He's the best person you'll ever

meet. He's joyful." Michael Farnum, another friend, told me, "Levi is very kind and caring. He'd give you the shirt off his back." His mother, Denise, described Levi as "a sweet, thoughtful boy." (Levi's family otherwise declined to talk to me.)

People who knew him casually from encounters at Holiday or Grand Marais's Whole Foods Co-op, where he also briefly worked, described Levi as personable and a hard worker. Pat Eliasen, the Cook County sheriff and a former assistant coach for the varsity football team at the local high school, coached Levi, who played nose tackle and offensive guard. "You'd tell Levi to do a technique or something and he would just go do it," Eliasen told me. "You couldn't find a better football player than that."

A photo posted on Facebook in 2023 shows Levi with his daughter climbing on his shoulders. According to friends, she was his everything. He was often her primary caregiver while Anna completed a social work degree and later held down two jobs. In the winter, Levi built his daughter snow forts that were so solid he could light a campfire inside. He and his daughter cooked together, drew pictures, and took walks. "She's his life," Adams told me.

Levi could not bear the thought of anything bad happening to his little girl. Like any parent, he was on the lookout for any threat to his child. At some point, his attention came to rest squarely on Larry Scully.

By 2018, Anna was working as a day care provider at the YMCA in Grand Marais, which was adjacent to an elementary school. People in town had seen Larry in his van across the street; they claimed that he was watching kids. Anna told Levi that the day care staff opted not to take the kids, which included her and Levi's daughter, on outings when they knew that Larry was in the vicinity. (Sara Cole, who oversaw the Grand Marais day care operation as CEO of the Duluth Area Family YMCA, disputed this in an email to me.)

But while Anna and other local parents were wary of Larry, Levi became fixated on him—intensely so. On April 5, 2018, when his daughter was 21 months old, Levi filed for a protective court order to keep Larry away from her. In his petition, Levi wrote that Larry "was stalking" his daughter "by waiting in his van by the YMCA," where he'd said hello to the little girl. "He has been there many times stalking children in his van. I have seen him parked right next to the school," Levi noted.

On April 12, just a week after filing for the protective order, Levi went for an afternoon run. Even though he'd been attending 12-step meetings, he wound up drunk after buying a handle of whiskey and draining it in half an hour. Levi and Anna had an agreement that he couldn't be around their daughter if he was intoxicated. He knew he had to tell Anna not to bring their daughter over that night, so he stopped in at Trinity Lutheran Church in Hovland to call her—either because he didn't have a cell phone on him or because his service in the area was spotty.

Around 4:30 P.M., pastor Kris Garey encountered Levi at the church. He told her that he was drunk and needed to use the phone, which she'd let him do in the past. They sat down to talk in the sanctuary, then Levi tipped out of his chair, which triggered an outburst of anger. "I'm getting the fuck out of here," he yelled. "I'm killing the fucking bastard."

Garey followed Levi outside to the church's parking lot, which was empty except for her gray Nissan Rogue. Levi circled the car and climbed inside. When he couldn't find the keys, he got out and yelled so loudly about killing someone that neighbors of the church heard him. Then he grabbed a snow shovel and punched out the Nissan's headlights and pounded its hood. Garey quietly called 911.

Levi kept going: He picked up a wrought iron table and heaved it at the Nissan's windshield. He removed the car's gas cap and sparked a lighter next to the opening. Garey, trying to remain calm while waiting for the police to arrive, implored him to give her the lighter. Levi sparked it again. She approached him, holding out her hand and asking for the lighter. Finally he let it fall to the ground.

When deputy Christopher Schrupp pulled into the Trinity parking lot, Levi dropped to his knees, placed his hands on his head, and let Schrupp handcuff him. Levi would later plead guilty to first-degree criminal damage, a felony, and receive four years of supervised probation. The judge would also order him to complete an additional chemical-dependency assessment and submit to more treatment.

In his report about the incident, Schrupp wrote that Levi had screamed the same thing repeatedly. He did it inside the squad car, during the 15-minute drive to the hospital, and in the emergency room, even after hospital staff had placed him in restraints. Over and over, Levi screamed that he hated pedophiles and wanted to kill Larry Scully.

—

None of this came up six weeks later, on May 25, 2018, when Levi appeared before Judge Michael Cuzzo in the

Cook County courthouse to argue that Larry should not be allowed anywhere near his daughter. Cuzzo, a grandfatherly type with a close-cropped gray beard, told Levi to provide "evidence of specific facts and circumstances" supporting his petition for a protective order. Levi was unable to do so. Indeed, he seemed confused and overwhelmed by the proceedings. He even backtracked on his charge that Larry had spoken to his daughter and to other children, saying that he'd merely waved. "You were expected to have come prepared," Cuzzo admonished Levi.

The most Levi could do was describe his worry. "I fear for my daughter's safety and well-being knowing that Larry's out there stalking and grooming children, like giving them gifts and stuff, while I'm at work and unable to watch out for her," he told the judge. "It's very distressing for me."

When it was Larry's turn to speak, he told the court, "I have never had any words of disagreement, or arguments, or anything to incite Mr. Axtell. And as far as I know, I've never done anything that would upset him. And in the past, he has been very gracious and pleasant to me at his place of employment, even going so far as giving me stuff that was going to be discarded. "

Larry called two witnesses, his friend Jerome Brandt and Jerome's wife, Patricia. The couple lived across from the YMCA, and Larry explained that when he parked his van on the street next to the facility, it was to visit the Brandts. He said that he waved at children when they waved at him. Jerome confirmed in his testimony that Larry visited the Brandt house "several times a week." Patricia, addressing Larry directly, said, "You've always been good to us, and our family, and my granddaughter, too. I trust you with children. I've never seen you abuse one of them."

Cuzzo needed only six minutes in his chambers to consider the situation. When he returned, he said that Levi had not provided sufficient evidence that Larry had harassed his daughter or was a threat to her. "I can't just issue a harassment restraining order because you believe Mr. Scully has performed acts against other people," Cuzzo said. But before he adjourned the court, Cuzzo issued a directive to Larry. "Take notice from the filing of this petition that Mr. Axtell does not want you to have contact with his daughter," Cuzzo said. "Take heed of that so we don't end up back here at some point in the future."

A few weeks later, Larry came into the Holiday gas station to buy lunch, and Levi refused to ring him up. Larry left in a huff. He drove to the sheriff's office and reported the matter to a deputy, demanding that she make Levi serve him. The deputy pointed out that this wasn't a criminal matter, and she suggested that Larry speak to the Holiday manager.

Larry complained that he was being harassed, and not for the first time. It seemed like people were trying to make his life miserable, maybe even run him out of town. That included members of his own family.

<hr />

Larry, born in 1945, was the eldest of eight children. His parents, Marge and Al Scully, raised their kids in Minnetonka, now a Minneapolis suburb. Patrick, the youngest, was a sophomore in high school and the only one still living at home when his parents relocated to Grand Marais in 1975. He stayed in town after finishing school, working as a first responder and an ambulance driver. Patrick didn't like it when Larry got out of prison and moved in with their parents, and he didn't like it when Larry stayed in the family home after their parents died. Nor did their brother Jon, who visited regularly from his home in suburban Minneapolis. (Jon eventually retired and moved to Grand Marais in 2019.)

Patrick and Jon kept close tabs on Larry. They tracked him on Facebook, scoured the newspaper for items about him, confronted him in town, and frequently reported perceived legal infractions to the sheriff's department. Patrick and his siblings showed people around Grand Marais photocopied court documents pertaining to Larry's 1979 conviction. In 2015, shortly after Larry's conviction had been detailed in the newspaper and he'd lost the mayoral election, Patrick obtained a restraining order against his brother. He applied for another one to protect himself, his wife, and his brother Jon in 2019. At the hearing, Judge Cuzzo, who'd denied Levi Axtell's request for a restraining order a year prior, was again on the bench.

Around town, Larry complained to anyone who'd listen that he was the real victim in the situation. He accused his brothers of slashing the tires on his car, torching his motor home, and stealing a crucifix from outside his house. He claimed Jon once pointed a pistol at his head in Patrick's presence. "Don't shoot him here," Larry claimed Patrick said. "If you shoot him here, I'll go to prison as an accessory." When a sheriff's deputy questioned Jon, he said the incident never happened. The brothers also said they had nothing to do with any damage to Larry's property and were able to provide alibis when questioned by law enforcement.

Patrick told his pastor, Dale McIntire, that he was worried about Larry's mental state and thought Larry needed medical treatment. Patrick and Jon insisted that by monitoring their brother and publicizing information about his criminal record, they were only trying to keep the citizens of Grand Marais safe. They had the support of their other siblings, who were scattered about Minnesota and Colorado, and details from court records and subsequent interviews with six of the siblings indicate why.

According to the Scully siblings, when they were growing up in Minnetonka, Larry molested all seven of them. "We're all in one large bedroom, and I'm up in my bed, listening to my sisters trying to fight off my brother," Terry, the fourth-eldest child, told me. "This happens repeatedly. It was so tormenting for me. I wanted to protect my sisters, but I felt so weak." Patrick stated under oath that Larry molested him on a family vacation, when Patrick was just five years old. Jon testified that Larry once suspended him by his wrists from the rafters in a cellar and abused him. "The torture Larry did to Jon was medieval," said Beth, the second youngest, who also claimed that Larry raped her many times. If she fought back, she said, he smothered her mouth and nose with his hand or clamped down on her carotid artery until she passed out. If she stayed still, he rewarded her with candy or a trip to Queen Anne Kiddieland, a small amusement park not far from their home. "He's the devil," Beth told me, bursting into tears.

Patrick remembered Larry killing chickens and decapitating a cat. "He'd tell us, 'If you tell Mom and Dad what's going on, you're next,'" Patrick said. That mostly kept them quiet, but when they did speak up, according to the siblings, their parents didn't believe them, even when presented with direct evidence. Jane told me that Larry raped and impregnated her when she was 12, and when their mother noticed that Jane had stopped using menstrual pads and confronted her about being pregnant, Jane snapped, "If I am, it's your asshole son's baby." She said that Marge knocked her down a set of steep steps, causing Jane to bloody her head against a wall. Jon said that he watched it happen. According to the siblings, their parents borrowed money to pay for an abortion and gave Larry condoms.

In another instance, Mike, the Scullys' second son, came home one night when he was 17 and found Larry assaulting Mary, the eldest girl. Mike blackened Larry's eyes, then carried him into his parents' room and heaved his naked brother onto their bed, waking them up. "I said, 'Larry, you tell them what you were doing,'" Mike said. Larry wouldn't, so Mike did. "My mother said to me, 'Pack up your stuff and get the hell out of here, you little lying son of a bitch!'" Mike left and moved to Colorado.

Much of this was detailed at the 2019 court hearing to consider Patrick's application for a restraining order. When it was Larry's turn to speak, he didn't deny the accusations against him. Instead, he focused on an anecdote Jon had shared about a time when Larry had held him down in the front pew during Mass and wouldn't let him go until the priest, Father Seamus Walsh, halted the communion service to intervene. "I wish Father Seamus was here as a witness," Jon said, to which Larry responded, "Being that Father Seamus isn't here, then you don't have any[thing] other than your word against mine on what took place."

Larry argued that his siblings had no evidence of what they claimed he'd done to them as children, or of the threat he now posed—to them or to anyone else. "I have never done anything to hurt anybody," Larry told Judge Cuzzo. "There was no proven stuff of me being a person going around trying to groom people, or going around in town, assaulting children, and doing all this stuff. So it was false accusations, just hearsay." Still, Cuzzo found the siblings and their concerns credible and granted the restraining order Patrick had requested. The judge set it for 50 years.

Larry's friends dismissed his siblings' accounts of abuse. "That's all false," Carol told me. "There were no facts, no evidence to prove it." She said that Larry's brothers and sisters resented that he'd been given the family home after their mother died and were motivated by greed. The siblings maintained that Larry was squatting in the house, though they never took any legal action to remove him.

Jerome Brandt recounted a time when, in July 2015, he drove Larry over to Patrick's house so that Larry could give his brother a Bible. As they walked up the driveway, Patrick saw them through the screen door. "He was shouting, 'Get off my property, you blankety-blank,'" Brandt said. "'I've got you in my crosshairs.'" Brandt did not see a gun. Still, afraid that they might be shot, he persuaded Larry to leave the Bible in the driveway and retreat to his car.

According to Patrick, he met Larry and Brandt ten feet from the door and told them to go away. He recalled Larry saying, "I'm praying for you. I forgive you." Patrick insisted that he never threatened to shoot the two men. He said that he wasn't even armed. He told a sheriff's deputy who questioned him about the encounter that if he'd wanted to shoot his brother, he would have done it.

Brad Wilson, who lived next door to Larry, told me that he sometimes saw Patrick and Jon slow down when driving by. They'd shout nasty things or throw objects to provoke Larry to come outside. They'd yell that he needed to get out of their parents' house. Larry would tell them to leave or he'd call the police. Wilson thought that the brothers picked on

Larry. "I believe the guy was trying to mind his own fucking business for a long time," he said.

Paul Scully, the eldest of Larry's three sons, told me that he didn't believe his father had ever molested anyone—not in the family, and not outside of it. He blamed his father's siblings, especially Patrick and Jon, for tension in the family. "They hated my father," Paul told me. "It's almost like they made it a full-time job to harass him. They wanted that house ever since my grandma died."

"My father always said if anything ever happened to him," Paul added, "my uncles had something to do with it."

⁘

Following their encounter at the gas station, when Levi Axtell refused to ring Larry up, the two men had a few more run-ins. The Holiday's owner ended up banning Larry from the premises because of something he'd said to a female cashier that made her uncomfortable, but almost a year later he came back anyway and purchased a prepaid Verizon card. Levi was at the register. When the phone card didn't work, Larry demanded a refund, and Levi told him to take up the matter with Verizon. Larry returned the next day and confronted Levi, and the owner, Courtney Quaife, told him that he had to leave. Quaife then reported Larry to the police, and he was charged with misdemeanor trespassing.

On November 13, 2020, a court determined that Larry was not competent to stand trial for the misdemeanor charge; according to two court-appointed psychologists, he met the criteria for civil commitment, in which individuals are placed in a secure facility for treatment, most often for mental illness. One of the psychologists diagnosed Larry with "substantial psychiatric disorders of thought, mood, perception, and orientation that grossly impair [his] judgment, behavior, capacity to recognize reality, and to reason or understand." The psychologist concluded that Larry posed a danger to other people, based on "recent alleged threats that he made toward his family members," and that there was a "substantial likelihood" of him causing "physical harm to himself," because he seemed to have difficulty with self-care.

In recent years, Larry's house had become practically unlivable. His hoarding was so out of hand that there was almost nowhere to move inside. Four-foot-high piles of debris clogged the rooms. "Nobody could go in there," one of his friends told me. "Same with his car—you couldn't even get in it." Larry had grown a long, unkempt white beard. His teeth were rotting. He told his son Paul that he'd stopped taking his diabetes medication because he'd "cured" it by losing weight.

Patrick and Jon managed to enter the house at one point, and what Patrick saw stirred his compassion for his brother. Larry had moved a microwave and toaster into the bathroom, because it was the only place with any space for him to live. "I saw he'd been reduced to this, eating and sleeping in the bathroom," Patrick said. "I saw him as a victim at this time. Even a pig doesn't have to live like that."

At first, Larry contested that he met the criteria for civil commitment. At a court hearing on March 19, 2021, Judge Cuzzo agreed to stay a mandated commitment for six months, in part based on Larry's willingness to meet with a primary care physician, follow any recommendations for therapy, and take any prescribed medications. The court also informed Larry that he'd be required to allow representatives from the Cook County Public Health and Human Services

Department to inspect his home. Grand Marais being a small town, one of the social workers who would attempt to visit Larry's home was Anna Ross, the mother of Levi's daughter. But neither Ross nor any other social workers were able to reach Larry or gain access to his house, prompting the county attorney's office to ask Cuzzo to lift the stay and commit him to a facility. Larry failed to appear at a court hearing on April 21, and sheriff's deputies detained him three days later. Cuzzo signed an order for him to be treated for six months at the Community Behavioral Health Hospital in Baxter.

At the hearing regarding a restraining order two years prior, Patrick had requested that his brother receive a psychiatric evaluation so that he could "get the long-overdue help that I believe he desperately needs." Now Patrick believed Larry might finally get that help, at the age of 75. For the other Scully siblings, the overwhelming feeling was one of relief in seeing the man they claimed had abused them locked up; they hoped that he would remain so for the rest of his life. When Jane saw him in court before he was sent to Baxter, Larry was wearing an orange jumpsuit and shackles. "That was wonderful," Jane told me. "It was good to see him like that. He could hardly walk. Being restrained where he couldn't get you, you know?"

The feeling of relief didn't last. After Larry's mandated stay at Baxter, the court ruled that he had "substantially complied with all items outlined in the discharge treatment plan." He was released and went home to Grand Marais. The county and court would intervene again only as a result of a precipitating event: another arrest, a family member expressing concern, or a physician who'd treated him saying he could no longer take care of himself. None of that happened.

Larry remained at home, where his physical condition, and that of his house, declined over the next two years. The mounds of junk grew. They blocked the path to the bathroom, so Larry started using an outdoor toilet. Sympathetic observers were concerned. "Law enforcement could've done more in getting him help for his problems and him away from his community," Grand Marais resident Laura Laky told me.

But there are limits to how long the state can hold someone. In Minnesota, individuals can only be committed for up to six months at a stretch unless someone is deemed to be mentally ill and dangerous, to have a sexual psychopathic personality, or to be sexually dangerous. Larry didn't qualify as any of those. "We did what we could when we could," Cook County attorney Molly Hicken told me. "Our commitment laws are such that people maintain their own authority over themselves and their bodies up until a certain point. It's all about the balancing of people's rights. That's what our system is set up to do."

Some people in Grand Marais believe that the system was to blame for what happened next—and not only to Larry. "I believe if Levi would've gotten more help," said Amber Lovaasen, Larry's niece, "that probably wouldn't have gone the way it did."

<hr/>

Levi and Anna got married in late 2018, but they filed for divorce less than two years later, signing legal paperwork that said "the marriage cannot be saved" due to "an irretrievable breakdown of our marriage relationship." Levi's mental health no doubt played at least some role in this.

The following winter, Levi staged a one-man protest urging a boycott of the Whole Foods Co-op, where he'd recently been employed. He'd earned $14 an hour stocking produce and ringing up groceries, but he didn't think it was enough to provide for his daughter. Her day care alone cost $760 a month. After wrangling with the store's management over a personal tip jar he propped up at the register, Levi lost his job. Soon after that, he set up a table and chair outside the store's entrance along with a sign demanding that the co-op pay living wages.

Levi sat alone in the bitter cold for days—some locals remember it as weeks. He collected a few donations that he split with other co-op employees, but on the whole his campaign garnered scant sympathy. For a lot of people, it was a sign that something might not be quite right with Levi. "That was an indicator to me that perhaps he was struggling with his mental health," his friend Christina Conroy told me.

After that, to make ends meet, Levi did odd jobs: clearing snow from roofs, picking weeds, cutting down trees, cleaning apartments, building shelves. By the end of 2022, he and Anna had reconciled enough that they agreed to live together for their daughter's sake. They shared a split-level home on the edge of Grand Marais, and their property backed up against the woods behind Larry's house. That meant Levi was now neighbors with the man who, over the previous five years, he'd come to consider his worst nightmare.

According to friends, Levi generally kept his fears about Larry to himself following the outburst at Trinity Lutheran. He didn't bring up Larry in casual conversation, though it seemed that Larry was on his mind. He once posted a meme on Facebook depicting a person holding a gun, with a caption that read, "Only cure for pedophiles. A bullet." In a comment below the image, Levi wrote, "People always ask me why I hate pedophiles. They assume I've been abused. But really I think being protective is just an Axtell trait."

His friend Amber Waldrop knew that trait well. She'd met Levi in an outpatient treatment program for addiction, and she found that despite his personal struggles—or maybe because of them—he looked out for other people. Once, they were walking on the lakeshore together and stumbled upon a hornets' nest. Waldrop thought that she'd been stung and panicked because she was allergic and didn't have an EpiPen with her. Levi rushed her home in his car. In another instance, when Waldrop was in a dark place, Levi talked her through it. "He has a really big heart," Waldrop told me.

Many people in Grand Marais knew that Levi had issues and that he could be aggressive when he was drunk. But those close to him didn't imagine that he would commit brutal violence against another person. On March 8, 2023, Brad Wilson, the carpenter who lived next to Larry Scully, learned that they were wrong.

As the light drained from the sky that afternoon, Wilson was in his garage putting away some tools when he heard a loud crash, like the sound of a car accident. It came from Larry's driveway. Wilson raced over and saw that Levi had slammed his white Dodge Caravan into Larry's car. Levi had then jumped out of the van, grabbed a garden shovel from the deck, and barged inside the house. Wilson arrived on the scene in time to hear Larry's screams.

Wilson stopped short of going inside. He heard the thud of the shovel hitting something, then hitting it again. "Help! Help!" Larry cried out.

Wilson, who had mowed Larry's lawn the previous summer without pay and generally felt sorry for the man, wanted to intervene, but he feared for his own safety. From his vantage at the front door, he could tell that Levi was in a drunken rage. And Wilson knew from watching Levi play football when they were in high school that although he was only five foot eight and 185 pounds, he was strong. Wilson also feared that Levi might have a gun.

Wilson went around the back of the house to look through an open window. He saw that Levi had trapped Larry in a corner of the kitchen. Hemmed in by stacks of hoarded junk, 77-year-old Larry had nowhere to go. Wilson saw Levi swing the shovel at Larry, who raised his arms as a frail shield against the blows.

Wilson ducked beneath the window and called the sheriff's department. He then heard a different kind of smash and what was "almost like gurgling." Wilson said, "It sounded like he was choking on his own blood." The screaming stopped; Wilson knew that Larry was dead.

Levi bolted out of the house, got into his van, and peeled away. But he wasn't fleeing. Instead, spattered with his victim's blood, he drove four blocks to the sheriff's department, walked inside, and announced that he had just killed Larry Scully. He confessed that he had hit Larry between 15 and 20 times with a shovel, then "finished him off" with a large moose antler.

⊙━━⚬

At Levi's arraignment, Cook County attorney Molly Hicken successfully argued that bail should be set at $1 million. She told Judge Cuzzo, who was again presiding, "This was a brutal attack without provocation on an elderly man." People close to Larry thought the attack *was* provoked—by his brothers Patrick and Jon. "They basically got the whole town against him," his son Paul told me. "They created the environment where my father could be lynched."

It was a sentiment that Larry himself had voiced at the hearing three years prior, when Patrick sought a restraining order. "He's talked to other people and had Levi Axtell say I was trying to groom his daughter," Larry said. "This shows the vindictiveness of my brother Patrick. He's trying to establish that I'm a predator."

According to a report from Mischelle Vietanen, the court-appointed psychologist who evaluated him, Levi considered himself a hero for killing Larry. "[He] believes that others are likely 'relieved this was taken care of,'" Vietanen wrote. She determined that Levi was "impacted by hallucinations, delusions, and paranoia," and that he was "unable or unwilling to take responsibility for making decisions to interrupt a repeat of impulsive, harmful behaviors."

Based on Vietanen's recommendation, Cuzzo found Levi incompetent to stand trial and suspended the criminal charges against him. Should he regain competency, prosecutors could proceed with trying him for second-degree murder.

In a separate and parallel proceeding before a different judge, the Cook County Public Health and Human Services Department pursued a civil commitment of Levi on the grounds—supported by Vietanen's report—that he was mentally ill and dangerous as well as chemically dependent. At a hearing held via Zoom on June 23, 2023, Levi sat at a table inside the Lake County jail in Two Harbors, 80 miles down Highway 61 from Grand Marais. He wore a black-and-white-striped uniform. He picked at his hands while answering a series of questions, agreeing that he met the criteria for civil commitment. He appeared docile, almost childlike. The judge, David M. Johnson, ordered that Levi be committed, "for an initial period not to exceed 90 days," to a secure treatment facility.

Levi would remain in the Two Harbors jail for nearly a year, waiting for a bed to open up at a psychiatric facility. When I spoke to him briefly on the phone in late September 2023, he couldn't discuss the particulars of his case, but he told me a story about a time when he was working at the Holiday gas station and a customer—a man who drove a snowplow for the city—reached across the counter and slapped him in the face. Levi said that he reported the incident to the sheriff's department, but "they were saying since he didn't slap me very hard, I shouldn't have called about it. I was feeling like the cops didn't care about anything that happened."

Levi told me that he didn't know Larry was arrested for trespassing at the gas station, or that the arrest had led to his civil commitment. It seemed as though Levi mostly felt that law enforcement had failed to find a permanent solution—meaning a way to keep Larry away from his daughter and other kids forever.

While he awaited transfer, Levi was able to see visitors, including his daughter. He passed the time drawing pictures that he intended for his daughter and others to color. He sent them to his sister Katrina, dozens every week, and she posted the pictures on Facebook with the invitation, "Please consider mailing him your colored version of his artwork, a letter, photos, and/or a piece of art of your own creation."

Levi also sent drawings to his friends. One of them went to Amber Waldrop. It depicted a bird's wings spread wide.

"To my dear friend Amber," Levi wrote. "Remember to . . . celebrate every victory. To not give up . . . To leave the past behind . . . And on your darkest days I hope you learn to dance in the rain."

When Waldrop showed the drawing to me, she said, "It's almost like he's giving himself advice."

It didn't take long for a substantial cohort of people in Grand Marais to elevate Levi to the status of folk hero. In their view, what he did was in service of the greater good. Brandy Aldrighetti, a sexual-abuse survivor who lived near Larry, told the *Star Tribune*, "To me, Levi is like St. George who slayed the dragon—he killed a monster." Kelsey Valento, a Grand Marais resident and mother, posted an article about the murder on her Facebook page with a comment addressing Levi directly: "I stand by you for removing a horrible nasty pedophile from this community."

Within days of the crime, his sister Katrina had started a crowdfunding campaign, "to ease the financial burden of the family." As of this writing, it had raised more than $7,000. When Katrina saw that Amber Lovaasen, Larry's niece, had posted on Facebook that she and her family had nothing against Levi, she reached out. Soon Lovaasen had designed T-shirts featuring the words, "Our Connection Is Our Strength. Two Families. One Goal. Stop Childhood Sexual Abuse." She told me that "my family and Levi's family are coming together pretty much as one family now."

She does not speak for Larry's three sons. "I feel sorry for this poor Levi guy," Paul told me. "He's obviously got mental issues. I just hope my father gets some justice, that his name is cleared, and he can be seen as the kind, gentle, loving person he was." Paul and his brothers also hoped to inherit Larry's house, but a district court judge ruled in March 2024 that a photocopy of their grandmother's will appointing Larry the sole inheritor of the property was not valid. That placed the home in the possession of Larry's seven siblings.

His siblings had mixed reactions to Larry's death. His sister Beth told me that she was worried when she heard the news. "I wanted to make sure that none of my siblings had done anything," she said. "When I realized that everybody I loved was okay and they all had alibis and it was not them, then I felt relief, kind of lighter and bouncier." His sister Jane said, "Nobody has the right take anybody else's life, but when Larry was beating me up and doing things to me as a kid, I wish I would have had access to something to kill him." Patrick told me that he feels Larry's death was preventable, if the court system had only listened to him and his siblings. "The sad thing is we tried to warn authorities something like this was going to happen," he said. "We were afraid some kid's dad would go over and kill him when they found out about him."

Within a week of the murder, someone created an online petition asking people to sign "if you agree that Levi Axtell should not be charged with any crimes and immediately be released from jail." As of mid-May 2024, it had drawn nearly 900 signatures. The petition asks people to "stand by this father, who tried to seek relief via the justice system which failed him." People who signed the petition noted various reasons for doing so: "I would've done exactly what he did if the court system failed me" (Dmitri Birmingham); "Anyone with children understands how this man felt and why he acted" (Joan Folmer); "The world is better off without a child molester!" (Grace Koopman).

Paisley Howard-Larsen, a local mother, told me that she believes Levi did the community a service by killing Larry. "I think this should have been done a long time ago, and I feel bad that it had to be Levi doing it," she said. "I don't even see Larry as a human. I think he's just a monster. It makes me really sad that Levi is going to do any sort of time, whether it's in a prison or a mental institution. I don't think that's right. I think he should have got off free."

"Even though he actually murdered somebody?" I asked.

"Yeah. I think he did the right thing."

Others in town, while not condoning murder, nevertheless welcomed the news of Larry's death. One mother of four young children said, "What Levi did wasn't justified, but that's not to say I'm not thankful for it." Others felt that Levi had been treated unfairly by the state. "Levi tried to go the legal route, he tried to do what he was supposed to do," his longtime friend Cedar Adams said, citing Levi's effort to get a protective order against Larry. "They say, 'Don't corner a wild animal, because if you do it will attack.' I feel he felt he was backed into a corner and had no other choice. I feel he's a victim more than anything."

Adams's boyfriend, Nick Swenson, who works at Buck's Hardware, never met Larry but had heard rumors about him. "You can't go around killing people," Swenson told me, "but Levi couldn't have picked a better person."

❦

There's another side to public opinion, and its defining feature is dismay. The *Cook County News Herald* published a letter from Jim Boyd, a Grand Marais resident and retired newspaper editor, that argued against vigilante justice. "Scully had not been arrested, charged, jailed, tried, or convicted of any recent crime," Boyd wrote, referring to the fact that no one had come forward to accuse Larry of abuse since 1979. "You can't go around killing people just because they are horrible. (The dead would be stacked up like cord wood.)" Similarly, on Facebook threads about the case that mostly lionize Levi and disparage pedophiles, an occasional voice of dissent pops up. For example: "You can't just murder people because you 'think' they might do something" (Penelope Orl). And: "Child molestation is horrible and wrong. Murdering someone by butchery is also wrong" (Don Croker).

For Larry's friends and sons, much of the discourse about his death is chilling. "He did not deserve to die the way he did," Carol told me. "I hate the way Levi's family and Pat and Jon are going after Larry as a monster, and Levi's a hero." She conveyed that the main reason she didn't want her real name used in this story was that she feared repercussions from Larry's brothers.

She wasn't the only person to request anonymity. People on both sides of the Levi–Larry divide told me that they were concerned about their reputations. Two sources said the situation is so polarizing that having their names attached to their opinions might hurt their businesses.

On March 7, 2024, Levi was finally moved to the Forensic Mental Health Program, a locked facility in St. Peter, Minnesota. Where his life goes from here, and how the dust of his crime will settle in Grand Marais, is an open question. During my visit to Grand Marais last August, I spent the better part of an hour talking to Amber Waldrop and her father, Dennis, a thoughtful man with a thick gray beard.

We met in a building downtown overlooking Lake Superior's seemingly infinite horizon. When it came to this story, the Waldrops saw no happy ending in sight.

"It's just a series of people being hurt: Larry's family, Levi's ex-wife and daughter, Levi's parents," Dennis told me. "There are a lot of victims here. And being in a small town, there's a conflict going on with what happened and what should've happened. It's a tough line to walk. This is sensational news to the rest of the world, but we're living it."

The Forever Cure

by Jordan Michael Smith

Is civil commitment rehabilitating sex offenders—or punishing them?

On Taisa Carvalho Mick's first day as a psychotherapist with Larned State Hospital's Sexual Predator Treatment Program (SPTP), her co-workers warned her to be careful around her patients. She shouldn't get close to them or believe a word they said, other staffers told her. They were untrustworthy predators, liable to manipulate her—or worse. Mick was suprised. She didn't hear anything about empathy or treating patients with respect, even though the ostensible goal of the program was to provide therapy.

Larned, Kansas, is a city of 3,700 people surrounded by wheat fields and cattle farms. Like nineteen other states, the District of Columbia, and the federal government, Kansas detains many former inmates convicted of sex offenses after they finish serving their criminal sentences. They remain confined in treatment facilities until an evaluator deems them unlikely to reoffend and a judge agrees to their release. Supporters of this practice, which is called civil commitment, defend it as a form of medical treatment necessary for public safety. The handbook provided to those detained at Larned puts it this way: "It is the vision of the SPTP to provide residents with the knowledge and tools needed for their reintegration back into society." For Mick, the residents were simply people in need of care. They had committed crimes, but they had completed their sentences. "No human being is beyond redemption," she told me.

Mick is a mother of two, has tattoos and nose rings, and wears purple braids in her hair. She emigrated from Senegal as a teenager in 2012, joining her older sister in Waco, Texas. When Mick arrived, she spoke Portuguese and French but hardly any English. She learned the language quickly, though, and excelled academically. After graduating from college at Fort Hays State University, in Kansas, she earned a graduate degree there in clinical psychology. She soon obtained a temporary therapist's license and, in July 2023, began working at the SPTP.

Although her family worried for her safety around convicted sex offenders, Mick was excited to start her new job. As a graduate student, she had done clinical work testing people for personality disorders, and was fascinated by the complexity of their cases. Her clinic's director suggested she consider a job with the SPTP, where many patients have personality disorders. Even though Mick had heard that the SPTP was an awful place to work, she decided to apply. "I like working with unpopular populations," she told me.

But upon her arrival, Mick found that the SPTP resembled a prison more than it did a place for therapy.* A perimeter of sharp wire ringed the four buildings to which SPTP residents were confined, and security guards roamed the grounds. Residents—almost all of whom were men, though a few identified as nonbinary or transgender—reported substandard medical treatment, terrible food, and little time outdoors. Their telephone calls were monitored, as were their conversations with one another. Outside of a sparse weekly schedule of group therapy sessions, classes, and menial labor at the facility, residents mostly spent their days watching TV or simply sitting around.

According to the Association for the Treatment and Prevention of Sexual Abuse, sexual abusers vary widely in both their treatment needs and the level of risk they pose to society. As such, the organization recommends that they receive dignified, individualized therapy and clear benchmarks of progress. At the SPTP, however, Mick discovered that treatment seemed directionless and outdated. Her patients didn't appear to understand what personality disorders even were. They told her that staff members sometimes shamed them, and that when they complained about their confinement or the treatment they received, they were often reprimanded and had their meager privileges revoked. They could be punished for countless minor infractions: swearing,

---

* A fact checker from *Harper's Magazine* sent the Kansas Department for Aging and Disability Services, the agency that oversees Larned State Hospital, an extensive list of this article's claims about the SPTP and its employees. In response, a spokesperson confirmed Mick's employment and declined to comment further, citing privacy law, and concluded: "The Kansas Department for Aging and Disability Services will not be entertaining any further discussion on the matter as her claims are categorically false."

smoking, getting tattoos, sharing food. Unlike in prison, where some over-the-counter medications are available for sale, accessing something like throat lozenges at the SPTP required getting a doctor's order; residents sometimes had to beg for medical attention. Their use of the internet was severely restricted, and they were obliged to disclose their assets, their credit and debit card numbers, and an annual credit report. Those who made more than $127 per month were required to pay half their earnings to Larned.

Despite the severity of these measures, however, Mick found that her patients rarely resembled the monstrous criminals her colleagues had warned her about. A few residents she met did seem to pose a threat to public safety, but they struck her as outliers. Most of her patients seemed relatively harmless, and she never felt unsafe around them. Some had developmental or intellectual disabilities. Many had been there for years, even decades—a number of them were in their seventies or eighties. They clearly weren't progressing through any genuine treatment program. In fact, Mick believed, some had received improper diagnoses after leaving prison. She told me about one such patient, who had been committed at nineteen, and who had admitted a decade later that he still had sexual fantasies about his ex-girlfriend, whom he had dated when they were both teenagers; this became the basis for a diagnosis of hebephilia (a sexual attraction to children in early adolescence), which made him unlikely to ever be released. And there were others who had been confined on the basis of crimes they'd committed as juveniles, and who lacked lengthy criminal records that might suggest a propensity for recidivism. "They've already served prison sentences, and they would have been fine doing outpatient treatment," Mick told me.

She came to believe that the SPTP would never release most of these people, no matter how eagerly they participated in treatment and kept up good behavior; her job wasn't to treat these patients but to perpetuate the illusion of treatment. Whatever the program claimed, Mick grew convinced that it was designed to lock people up indefinitely, not to rehabilitate them.

⚬─✦─⚬

In 1989, following public outcry over a string of high-profile murder and sexual-assault cases, Booth Gardner, then the governor of Washington, appointed a task force to consider how the state might strengthen its laws against violent crimes. In the course of its work, the task force coined a legal term: "sexually violent predator." SVPs were defined as people charged with or convicted of a sexually violent crime, who have also been determined by psychological evaluators to be likely to reoffend because of a "mental abnormality" or personality disorder. The task force recommended using this term to adopt a new statute enabling the state to confine sex offenders indefinitely under civil commitment—a procedure that has historically also been used for treating mental illness in other contexts, such as when patients pose a danger to themselves. The legislation, which passed in 1990, became the nation's first modern law authorizing civil commitment for sex offenders. To its architects, the practice seemed poised to prevent violent crimes by keeping sex offenders—who might otherwise have reentered society—off the streets. Other states across the country soon followed suit.

Kansas passed its civil-commitment law in 1994, after a Pittsburg State University student and waitress named Stephanie Schmidt was raped and murdered by a co-worker on conditional release from prison, where he had served time for rape and aggravated sodomy. "It is for those extremely dangerous people that we can prove in court are predatory and will likely strike again," one Kansas district attorney explained after the law's passage. While some protested that accurately predicting who would commit crimes was impossible, he told the *Kansas City Star* that doing so was easy: "If you want to be able to predict the future in just about anything, look at the past."

This law established the SPTP at Larned as the state's sole facility for civilly committed sex offenders. Shortly after the SPTP's founding, the program's director at the time, Janet McClellan, told a reporter that program residents would become eligible for release once administrators had "reliable, valid, scientific assurances" that they wouldn't commit further crimes. But the details of how one might meet such a burden of proof were left to the discretion of evaluators. "I can't deny that there may be some people who could end up here for a very long time," McClellan acknowledged. "Some might even be here for life."

As a wave of civil-commitment laws passed in the '90s and '00s, many critics questioned how effective they would be at curtailing sexual abuse. More recently, a growing body of research has borne out their concerns: as a 2013 *Brooklyn Law Review* article put it, "SVP laws have had no discernible deterrent or incapacitation effects." Some opponents have argued that civil commitment diverts resources from more effective programs such as structured therapy and education and risk-management programs. In 2024, for instance, the SPTP's budget was $33.7 million, which works out to nearly $130,000 per resident. Rather than spending billions on a "regime that has continued to fail to adequately protect children," a 2023 Johns Hopkins University–led study concluded, states should invest in programs that can better "prevent child sexual abuse in the first place."

Even some who oversee long-established civil-commitment programs have questioned their efficacy. Robin Wilson, the clinical director of Florida's civil-commitment program from 2007 to 2011, believes that treatment should begin at the outset of a prison sentence, not after it has ended, and that most programs start treatment too late to be psychologically helpful. "You end up having people who potentially end up going to treatment long after the treatment would have been most effective, and ultimately for much longer and more intensively than their risk profile suggests," he told me. "There are better, more efficient, more scientifically defensible, more ethical ways to do this." In 2014, the research director of Minnesota's Department of Corrections, Grant Duwe, called on states to consider more intermediate, community-based alternatives to civil commitment, such as intensive parole.

The admissions processes for civil-commitment programs vary from state to state, but in most cases, when a person incarcerated for a sex offense approaches the end of his sentence, prosecutors can appoint a psychological evaluator to assess whether he should be classified as an SVP. The findings of this evaluation are then sent to a judge—or, in some states, a jury—who will determine whether the person meets the legal criteria of that state's SVP statute. Many experts argue that these evaluations are arbitrary, biased, and scientifically flimsy; the American Psychiatric Association's Task Force on Sexually Dangerous Offenders urges psychiatrists to oppose SVP laws, viewing civil commitment as a violation of civil rights and a misuse of psychiatric methods. A 2020 report by the Williams Institute at the UCLA School of Law found that black sex offenders were twice as likely as their white counterparts to be civilly committed. One common evaluation tool is a ten-item questionnaire that asks, among other things, whether an offender had any male victims; if the answer is yes, he is deemed more likely to reoffend. Such apparent pretensions to precision exasperate critics, who often point out that "sexually violent predator" is a legal designation, not a medical one. "Overly broad terms like 'mental disorder' and 'abnormality' have no medical meaning," said Ilan H. Meyer, one of the report's authors. And in some states, SVP evaluations are so likely to result in civil commitment as to make precision seem beside the point. In Kansas, for example, the portion of those evaluated who are then designated as SVPs has at times reached as high as 94 percent, according to a *Lawrence Journal-World* investigation.

No state has adopted civil commitment since New York did so in 2007—a sign, perhaps, that many have come to recognize the inefficacy and exorbitant cost of such programs. But in states where such programs have long existed, few politicians, if any, have shown interest in dismantling them. "It's become a political third rail," Eric Janus, the director of the Sex Offense Litigation and Policy Resource Center at the Mitchell Hamline School of Law, told me. That's not only because of the bad optics of shuttering a program meant to protect the public, he explained, but also because the facilities provide jobs. Larned State Hospital, for instance—where the SPTP is the largest program—is one of the biggest employers in town. "You've got a lot of people in the community who are just dependent on those jobs," Rick Cagan, the former executive director of the Kansas chapter of the National Alliance on Mental Illness, told me. "It is a huge cash cow."

Legal challenges to these programs have largely proved unsuccessful. In 1997, the Supreme Court ruled 5–4 against a man in Kansas who argued that civil commitment constituted a form of double jeopardy. The process was civil, not criminal, the ruling explained, and therefore not a form of punishment. In 2002, the court again upheld the practice, expanding the grounds on which states could commit someone, and leaving little hope for the roughly six thousand people currently held under civil commitment.

Many experts reject the Supreme Court's reasoning. "The underlying idea of [civil commitment] is essentially . . . punitive," Janus told me. And in 2023, an unpublished internal survey of programs in seventeen states conducted by the Sex Offender Civil Commitment Programs Network, an association of facility employees, found that patients spend far more time in "recreational [and] vocational programming" than they do receiving treatment. The survey also found that the vast majority of those who have entered civil commitment have never been released. Under Missouri's SVP law, unconditional release isn't even an option. In Kansas, only 16 of the 380 people ever committed have been discharged; 14 have received conditional release; and 65 have died in custody. Virtually everyone else remains locked up.

⊶

By the time Mick arrived at Larned, critics had long alleged that the SPTP wasn't upholding its obligation to treat patients and prepare them for societal reentry. "Many residents aren't progressing through the Program's phases on a timely basis," noted a report by the Kansas Legislative Division of Post Audit in 2005. "I don't think the state has been extremely honest about what goes on," a former SPTP clinical group leader told the *Lawrence Journal-World* that same year. "I think they're disingenuous in how willing they are to let people go through the program," he added. "That was really one of the things that caused me to leave. I couldn't any longer look at the residents and say, 'Work hard, and you'll get out.'" Another counselor, who had started working at the SPTP in 2012 and resigned two years later, has described the program as "an abomination." She told a reporter that only a handful of her ninety patients were too dangerous to be released, yet most get stuck in a "vicious cycle," ultimately boycotting treatment out of frustration.

In 2014, twenty-five SPTP residents filed a lawsuit claiming inadequate treatment. Three years later, after a resident alleged that the state had failed to conduct an annual review of his case, as required by law, for four of the first six years he was detained, the chief judge on Kansas's second-highest court wrote that the court was "deeply troubled by the general lack of attention by the district court to the periodic review component of due process."

Sean Wagner, the SPTP's administrative program director from 2014 to 2017, told me that there was a push around this time to make treatment more structured and individualized. He wanted residents to feel more incentivized to participate in group therapy, for example, and for classes to better target specific needs, such as overcoming addiction. But many staffers resisted or outright refused to implement these initiatives. He attributes this in part to widespread prejudice among the staff: "I had 237 civilly committed sexual predators, and they were basically a piece of cake compared to the 250 employees I oversaw," he told me. Half of them, he said, believed the residents "ought to be hung up by their nuts on the closest fence post." There were nurses who "thought all these guys needed to be shot." Norma Aguilera, a nurse at the SPTP in 2022 and 2023, told me that she was instructed in her orientation to view her patients as dangerous. "They pretty much put it in you to hate them," she recalled. "So when you get there and see that they're just average guys—it's the safest unit! They're being treated like they're rats or the untouchables."

It wasn't only the employees who felt the residents deserved their confinement. Once, when Wagner decided that several residents were ready for conditional release, word quickly spread through town, he said. "There were a lot of people in the community pissed off that we were even thinking about letting these guys get a job in the community."

Wagner had many disagreements with how the SPTP was run, and he believed his role there represented an opportunity to make the program more effective and humane. But, he told me, he encountered opposition to making changes at every turn, both from staffers and from his supervisors in the Department of Aging and Disability Services. Finally, in 2017, after several years of butting heads with state officials over his objections to the harshness of SPTP policies, he was reprimanded and reassigned to a different department.

In her conversations with SPTP residents, Mick often encouraged them to tell her about their experiences at the facility; in turn, some residents warned Mick that her compassion might arouse the suspicion of administrators. Still, Mick tried to speak out on their behalf when she could. Once, Mick reported, she saw a resident being moved into a room with a puddle of urine on the floor and asked that someone be sent to clean it up; another time, when she saw a staff member yelling at a resident, she suggested that her colleague take a step back and breathe.

Soon after these incidents, Mick said, she was summoned for a meeting with Brad Base, the president of Sunflower Behavioral Health, a company that contracts with Kansas to provide mental-health staffing to the SPTP. Base told Mick that he had high hopes for her future at the SPTP but, given all the scrutiny the program had been under, he preferred his staff avoid criticizing it. (Base declined to comment for this story.)

By August, Mick had come to understand just how ineffective the therapy offered at the facility was. The SPTP has three tiers of treatment through which residents theoretically progress: the first is meant to help them avoid criminal behavior; the second teaches them to lead independent lives; the third is a transitional phase focused on seeking employment and establishing a support network. Mick found the metrics for progress highly arbitrary: a patient who happened upon a difficult therapist might remain on tier one indefinitely. Some had cycled through dozens of therapists. They were taking the same courses over and over for years.

Eventually, Mick wrote to Base outlining her concerns. She was trying to work with her patients on relapse prevention, she told him, but felt there needed to be more concrete criteria for advancement through the tiers. She went on:

> Some of these guys have been there for so long, and have had so much taken away from them. They get punished for a lot, but on the flip side how can we actually try and motivate them to move forward?

Base did not reply to Mick directly. His management style, she told me, more often involved sending somewhat coded emails to his entire staff, instructing them on how to approach their work at Larned. Mick felt these messages were sometimes directed at her. "Some of you are engaging in very helpful activities with your co-workers," he wrote in one such email.

> However, before you go too far down that path, remember who our client is. We serve the State. The State is our client, not the person sitting across from us in sessions. If we are going to be effective in bringing about change to the person sitting across from us in sessions, we must first gain the trust and ability to work effectively with our client, the State.

As Mick spent more time at the SPTP, she began to take particular notice of a resident named Dustin Merryfield, whom other residents often consulted for advice. Merryfield, residents told her, had a sophisticated grasp of the intricacies of civil-commitment legislation and SPTP policies—he had self-published several books on the topics—and he had regularly helped others file complaints and understand the legal process. When Mick finally met Merryfield, she found him to be quiet, courteous, and intelligent. During his years of civil commitment, Mick learned, he had earned a bachelor's degree in theology from Liberty Bible College and Seminary, as well as certificates in computer repair, accounting, criminal justice, and paralegal studies. He regularly filed lawsuits challenging his confinement. Mick was struck by what seemed to be his wasted potential, and how his ordeal seemed to encapsulate much of what was wrong with Kansas's civil-commitment system.

Merryfield was born in 1981 in central Kansas. His father was a felon and an abusive alcoholic who was only intermittently present. At the age of ten, Merryfield began to be shuttled between various state mental hospitals and shelters. When he was fifteen, he sexually assaulted a fifteen-year-old girl. (Merryfield maintains, incorrectly, that the girl was eighteen.) He was convicted of rape and sentenced to a juvenile correctional facility for two years. Then, while on conditional release, Merryfield groped a ten-year-old girl on a playground. (Merryfield told me that he didn't know the girl's age, and that he believes he was far too immature to understand the consequences of his actions.) In 1998, he was tried as an adult and then sentenced to two years in a Kansas prison.

Toward the end of Merryfield's sentence, Mick learned, he received an evaluation from a psychologist who recommended that Merryfield needed "structured, intensive parole," in which he would live in a halfway house, find work, and be prohibited from contact with children. "The overall picture is of a young man, so overwhelmed with an inconsistent, chaotic past that he has little sense of self," the evaluator wrote.

> Judging from his attempts to normalize his past and his eagerness for an education, it would appear that he is desperately searching for meaning in his life, but hasn't found that meaning either at home or in his many placements.

Around that same time, Merryfield told me, he also received a separate evaluation, conducted by a psychotherapist named

Rex Rosenberg. Rosenberg, a former chaplain in the Christian Motorcyclists Association, was interested in demonology, and, in the '90s, had created a ninety-six-question survey that he claimed could accurately ascertain whether a person was under "demonic influence"; signs of such influence included severe depression, compulsive masturbation, homosexuality, and being "unable to read the Bible." (Rosenberg told Harper's that his demonological pursuits had no bearing on his work conducting SVP evaluations for the State of Kansas.) Rosenberg concluded that Merryfield fit the definition of an SVP. Merryfield was then committed at Larned in 2000.

By his own telling, Merryfield's time at Larned has been imperfect. In 2007, when two staff members were searching his room, he hit them with a trash-can lid, because he felt the search was unfair. In 2018, however, after maintaining a largely clean record for about a decade, he was approved to advance to tier three, and was then sent to Maple House, a reintegration facility on the grounds of Parsons State Hospital, in southeastern Kansas.

After about a year, however, a Maple House staff member accused Merryfield of making sexual remarks to her. She reported that Merryfield had complimented her looks and made sexually insinuating comments about her private life. Merryfield argued that the staff member had initiated the interaction.

To Mick, the incident—an inappropriate but nonviolent encounter with an adult following a year in close proximity—seemed like an ideal opportunity for a therapeutic intervention. "That would be a good teaching opportunity for him," she told me. Instead, in August 2019, Merryfield was returned to Larned, back to tier one. Although he committed his only crimes as a juvenile more than twenty-five years ago, Merryfield, now in his mid-forties, is still at Larned, with no release in sight.

⊶━⊶

Once a week, Mick joined her colleagues at Larned to dis-cuss new policies, any progress residents might have made through treatment, and any grievances they had recently filed. "Denied Outside recreation," read one resident's com-plaint. "Denied the ability to do a Yoga Routine," went another. Others were less specific: "Absolute denial of personal autonomy and all due process." Complaint after complaint went unresolved.

Mick found most of these to be valid grievances, while the restrictions regarding residents' privileges and behavior seemed unnecessarily punitive and arbitrary. She was particularly disturbed by how the SPTP interfered with personal and romantic relationships. Visits from those outside the facility were subject to approval. Mick recalls one staff meeting that was spent discussing whether a man on tier three—"community reintegration"—should be allowed to be visited by his girlfriend. Such situations weren't uncommon: residents' family and friends some-times introduced them over the phone to people on the outside. Relationships might develop during supervised, preapproved visits, and some residents even got married. Mick found administrators' policing of these relationships excessive, and considered them counterproductive to the independence and dignity that might have helped residents prepare for a life outside.

The longer Mick worked at the SPTP, the more disil-lusioned and angry she became. One resident showed her a letter his lawyer had sent him, explaining why his impeccable behavior in treatment was irrelevant to his prospects for release. "The States [*sic*] response is that you have been in a controlled environment and they are not willing to risk it in a non controlled environment." Mick saw this logic as circular: If therapeutic progress and good behavior within the program weren't indicators of readiness for release, what was? In September 2023, she emailed SPTP's administrators, explaining that while she respected their depth of experience, she felt she needed to call attention to problems she saw at the facility:

> I see a lot of staff here yelling at residents, being inappropriate, and not conducting themselves professionally, which I do bring attention to despite the backlash I may get. . . . As I believe that both staff and residents deserve to be treated as humans I try to model . . . empathy, warmth, as well as strong boundaries with the residents.

Meanwhile, Base continued to urge his employees to bring complaints directly to Sunflower. "They are not the State's problems, and anything that makes us look weak to the State hurts us in the long run," he wrote. "As many of you have already seen, the State is not a forgiving environment nor one that is logical. We have to do all we can to protect our name and our people."

In October, Mick received her full therapist's license. When she informed Base in a text message, his response surprised her. "I'm proud of you! That's awesome," he wrote.

> Now, we need you to be invisible, sort of, for about 4 months. We need the State, in all their

wild weirdness, to remove their focus from you
and put it back on the residents whom we serve.

Satisfying the demands of the state while still providing
treatment was a challenge, Base added:

We have to see the long game. The big picture. I
want you focused about 45% [on] treatment and
perfecting your clinical skills, 40% on learning
the political picture and how to navigate with
grace and ease, and 15% on the business side.

But Mick had little interest in the political picture, and
even less in the business side. She wanted to focus entirely
on treatment. She found herself becoming increasingly anx-
ious, worrying constantly about her patients and her job. She
never knew when she was about to be reprimanded. She had
trouble sleeping, with recurring nightmares of being chased
or locked up at Larned herself.

That November, the SPTP had a COVID outbreak. Residents were confined to their units save for brief windows of
time to shower or use the phone. Concerned for everyone's
well-being in isolation, Mick planned to deliver their mail
to their rooms. But Christine Mohr, the SPTP's clinical
program director, sent Mick an email instructing her not to
enter the units. The N95 face mask Mick was planning to
wear had not been approved by the SPTP administration,
Mohr noted—the kind of bureaucratic hang-up that Mick
told me frequently hindered work at the facility.

The next day, however, Mick learned that one of the
patients was in distress, and—after receiving permission
from a nurse, she says—she went to his unit to check on him.

While doing so, she told me, she heard her name called over the intercom, summoning her to the administrative offices. When she arrived, three security guards were waiting. They told her they had orders to escort her from the building. She had been fired, she later learned, for disobeying Mohr's instructions. They took her badge and walked her off the grounds. Mick had lasted five months.

That night, Mick phoned some of her patients to tell them she wouldn't be seeing them anymore. They would have to start treatment anew with different therapists.

"You need to stop calling units immediately," Mohr told Mick over text message. "This is unethical and unprofessional." Mick responded that it was a measure of respect that her patients deserved. "It is not," Mohr wrote back. "They're no longer your responsibility. We will address them and handle it."

⊶——⊷

After Mick was fired, she found a job as an outpatient therapist in a community mental-health program, specializing in personality disorders. Her goal is to work with teenagers who have been sexually abused and who have begun exhibiting problematic sexual behaviors of their own—those who she worries are at risk of one day ending up in a place like the SPTP. "What I'm learning is that a lot of these teenagers, all they need is just to be understood and to have a safe place to talk . . . about their trauma," Mick told me. "They're kids, and I don't think they should be called a predator or held accountable for their whole lives. All they need is treatment."

Mick also joined an informal group of advocates working to bring attention to the ongoing failures of the SPTP. Some have family members in the program, and hope to persuade state legislators to close the facility. They have been grateful for the light Mick has shed on what goes on inside. "She's brilliant, she's helpful," Eldon Dillingham, a local advocate whose son has been civilly committed for more than a decade, told me.

In April, Mick and others from the group traveled to Topeka to distribute pamphlets to state legislators. Mick handed out written testimony about the "abuse, medical and psychological malpractice, and inhumane conditions" she had witnessed at the SPTP. The pretension to treatment there was a "façade," she wrote, and the SPTP effectively a "shadow prison masking as a treatment facility. . . . These individuals are treated worse than inmates, and with absolutely no oversight regarding their rights." In her conversations with these lawmakers, Mick was surprised by how little they appeared to know about the program. Some seemed unsure which government department was responsible for it. Out of sight, out of mind: this is the attitude most people seemed to have about those in civil commitment, no matter the human cost. But Mick cannot forget what she saw at Larned. She believes that people like her former patients deserve an honest chance at rehabilitation, and she will keep fighting for their rights and dignity, no matter how unpopular this cause may be. "They told us that they'd love to see us again at the beginning of this upcoming legislative session," she told me. "We will be there."

---

*This article was produced in partnership with Type Investigations, with support from the Puffin Foundation. The reporting is also supported by a grant from Columbia University's Ira A. Lipman Center for Journalism and Civil and Human Rights in conjunction with Arnold Ventures, as well as a Lipman Fellowship.

The Memoirist and the Lie Detector

by Justin St. Germain

A few weeks before the release of my first book, a memoir about my mother's murder, I had to take a polygraph exam. The two things were not in fact related, but that was easy to forget once I found myself strapped in a chair in a windowless room on the fourth floor of a federal building in El Paso, with some polygrapher I'd just met sitting behind me, asking questions.

I'd met my examiner, whom I'll call Kevin, that morning. The federal scheduler had insisted on a 9:00 A.M. appointment even though I lived four hours away, which meant I'd spent the previous night alone in a Motel 6 by the highway in El Paso, eating Del Taco and reflecting on the decisions that had led me to spending the night alone in a Motel 6 by the highway in El Paso, eating Del Taco. Technically, I was there because I'd applied for a job with Customs and Border Protection. But the truth seemed much more complicated than that.

I didn't get much sleep, and showed up at the federal building early, dressed in what I imagined the government meant by comfortable clothing: black dress pants, plain white oxford, no tie. I looked like a banquet waiter. One other guy was in the waiting room when I walked in. As we sat there past the scheduled time of our appointments, we struck up a desultory conversation. Like me, he'd been in the hiring process for years, had driven down from Albuquerque the night before, and seemed nervous. He asked if I'd done any research on the polygraph. I said no, and asked him the same question. He said no. We were getting our first lies out of the way.

The government's guidelines had repeatedly stressed that we should not do any research before our polygraph. Their insistence struck me as odd: if the machine detects lies, why would it matter? I'd spent much of the previous week googling polygraphs. I was in the middle of denying it to my new friend when the door opened and Kevin appeared.

He was around sixty, short, portly, bald, with a silly goatee and wire-rimmed glasses, wearing a baggy gray suit and a shirt in one of those colors I never can keep straight, puce or mauve or periwinkle, a little too festive for the occasion. Kevin was squinty and smug, with an air of hollow authority that reminded me of my middle-school principal. He didn't even step into the waiting room, just swung the door open and shouted my full name. I stood and shook the hand he extended. He squeezed too hard and said I could call him by his first name, as if he were doing me some great favor.

Kevin led me down a drab hallway to a door on the left that led to my first disappointment. I'd been expecting the sort of tableau you see in cop movies, some dank cellar with a dangling bulb and a two-way mirror on the wall for me to stare defiantly into. Instead we entered a bare, sterile room with office chairs on either side of a desk. Wires ran from the computer on the desk across the room to a hardbacked chair festooned with cuffs and straps and sensors.

We sat in the normal chairs. Kevin leaned back in his, twirled a pencil, and said, "Let's get started." I knew this bit, the casual tone and performative warmth. I was a college professor, sort of, and I did this same bit on the first day of classes, trying to make my students trust me. In that first fluorescent moment, staring into Kevin's beady eyes, I had a premonition: I was going to fail my polygraph exam.

⌐═══○

Joan Didion once wrote that it's easy to see the beginnings of things, and harder to see the ends. That has not been my experience. Ends are obvious: divorce, death, getting fired. Beginnings, on the other hand, seem subjective. If ends are facts, beginnings are truth: relative, random, subject to belief.

The story of my exam, for example, could begin two years before I met Kevin, when President Obama signed an act requiring polygraph screening for applicants to certain federal agencies. Or two years before that, when I started writing a memoir and began to understand what it means to tell the truth. Or it could begin with the polygraph itself, the kind of story America likes best: a simple one that isn't all that true. The polygraph's most commonly credited inventor is John Larson, an employee of the Berkeley Police Department, who developed a new device for interrogations in 1921. Larson was twenty-nine at the time, and, like me, a strange candidate for law enforcement: he might have been America's first cop with a PhD.

His degree was in physiology, the science of the body's systems. The then-prevailing scientific belief saw crime as biological, either hereditary or the result of a physical defect. Larson explored both possibilities. His undergraduate work tried to find familial patterns in fingerprints that predicted criminality. In grad school, Larson shifted his focus to thyroid deficiencies. The results were disappointing, so he turned to machines. Larson read an article about using blood pressure to detect deception, and decided to improve on its author's technique by designing a machine that could do so more objectively. The polygraph was born.

The truer story is, as usual, more complicated. Larson's machine was not so much an invention as it was an amalgam of existing devices. He didn't believe it detected lies and didn't call it a polygraph: Larson referred to his machine as an "emotion recorder." His protégé and rival, Leonarde Keeler, would later come up with the term polygraph to help commercialize the device.

Polygraph organizations like to say the word means "many writings," which is halfway true. It's a neologist portmanteau of the Greek terms meaning exactly that, and the machine does indeed create many writings. But to claim the word means only and exactly one thing is to make the same mistake with language polygraphers habitually make with facts: believing that they're static and absolute. Language, like truth, is neither. Words evolve and change over time and mean different things in different contexts. Polygraph has six different definitions, according to the *Oxford English Dictionary*—three of which predate the machine—and they range from a letter grouping in cryptography to a person imitating another to a writer of various works. (Which I guess makes this an essay about a polygraph taking a polygraph.)

More to the point, polygraph does not mean "lie detector." Larson himself repudiated that term for the rest of his life.

But that fact didn't get in the way of a good story. Once the polygraph was adopted by police across America and heralded in the popular media, it took on a mythical new name: the lie detector. And as soon as the lie detector became famous, a bunch of men fought with each other for decades—mostly in their memoirs—over who was its true inventor. In his book *The Truth Machine: A Social History of the Lie Detector*, Geoffrey C. Bunn devotes an entire chapter to the question of who invented the device and offers enough credible candidates to field a baseball team: everyone from Carl Jung, who helped pioneer the field of psychology, to Étienne-Jules Marey, who did the same for cinematography. As Bunn puts it, with magisterial restraint, it was a "curious and notable fact that the lie detector's principal actors mistrusted each other intensely." Maybe they should have taken a polygraph to resolve the question.

My polygraph test was the final step in a process that had begun three years earlier, when I started applying for government jobs. At the time, I was living in San Francisco, teaching at Stanford, and was nearly finished with the book. While my job sounded impressive, it paid forty thousand dollars a year and was located in one of the most expensive areas of the country. I was in the second year of a two-year contract and had been trying unsuccessfully to get a real teaching job for years, something tenure-track, or at least a lecturer gig in a more affordable city, one with benefits and some semblance of job security.

When I was "on the market," as they say, I applied to teaching jobs in Fairbanks, Alaska; Birmingham, Alabama;

Spokane, Washington; Camden, New Jersey; Cullowhee, North Carolina; and on and on. I spent a lot of time back then browsing Wikipedia pages for cities I'd never been to, trying to convince myself I could live there. It was a moot point. Despite dozens of interviews, I couldn't get a professor job. My memory has condensed the experience into one vivid example, when the writing faculty of a football powerhouse down South made me fly to Chicago, in January, on my own dime, so I could sit in their hotel suite sweating through my freshly pressed suit while they asked a series of oddly combative questions for an hour and a half, after which they never bothered to contact me again to tell me that I didn't get the job I wouldn't have taken if my life depended on it.

Somewhere along the way, I decided to give up on academia and find a less demoralizing line of work, something with better pay, more stability, maybe even a union. I applied to be a technical writer, an FBI agent, a cop. I didn't have any luck with those, either. My brother suggested the Border Patrol. He was an agent, and so were a half dozen of my childhood friends and my former baseball coach. They were always hiring. The starting pay was nearly double what I made at Stanford, with much better benefits, and I might be able to move back to Arizona.

Most of my old friends from home thought joining the Border Patrol was a good idea. I could be closer to family, make a living, maybe even buy a house. My social circle in San Francisco was another story. By then, I'd been in academia for more than a decade, surrounded by white liberals from wealthy backgrounds. When they heard I was trying to join the Border Patrol, my new friends all said the same thing: *why?*

I didn't understand the question, and soon determined it was a matter of perspective. For people who grew up wealthy, or even middle-class—whatever that means—the proper career path seems to be to find a job that's rewarding, fulfilling, whatever. I'd done every job I'd ever had for one reason, the same reason I was trying to join the Border Patrol: money. Did I want to drive around the border in an SUV detaining people? Of course not. But I didn't want to help tech billionaires write their memoirs, either. At least the Border Patrol paid a living wage.

But the Border Patrol is *racist*, my friends said. And that might be true. But cries of racism rang hollow coming from people who worked in academia, one of the whitest industries in America. The Border Patrol is a hell of a lot more diverse than the average writing faculty.

Their underlying point was right, though: if I joined the Border Patrol, I'd be complicit. But I was already complicit. The longer I spent in higher ed, the more it seemed like an engine driving American inequality. At least the Border Patrol gave working-class people a path to economic mobility without being saddled by a lifetime of student loan debt. My brother had begun his career at the same time I'd started grad school. Nine years later, he made twice as much as I did, owned a house and a new Acura, had health insurance and a retirement account and the whole American dream. Meanwhile, in the three years since I applied to the Border Patrol, I'd taken another teaching job in Albuquerque, making forty-five grand, with shitty benefits and no long-term security. Besides, I still hadn't decided to actually join the Border Patrol. I hadn't been offered the job.

By the time I went to El Paso, I'd passed a four-hour written exam, a physical, a fitness test, an oral interview, and a background check so intensive that they'd talked to my co-workers, every neighbor in my apartment building, and my high school teachers. Once I passed the background check, I waited more than a year for the call from the polygraph office.

That call would be the first sign that the government and I had different ideas about truth. First, I got an email from a scheduler saying he'd been trying to reach me. I hadn't received any messages, so I knew that wasn't true, but had no way to prove it. I called the office and spoke to another man, who said he was a quality control agent, and that he'd call me back soon with a date and time for my appointment. He never did. Then I received a letter saying I'd been removed from consideration for refusing to take the polygraph. I called Mr. Quality Control. He accused me of lying, but grudgingly scheduled my appointment. So there I was, in a building full of liars, about to have mine detected.

⸎

Kevin started off by reminding me of the rules. One of them was that I could not discuss my test with anyone afterward. I'm sure he would have told me that I couldn't write about it either, although I made sure not to ask. Clearly the government believed, despite all historical evidence to the contrary, in its power to control information. I believed my right to free speech was inalienable. In that sense, I guess this essay is a lie detector, too: we're going to find out who was right.

Kevin ran me through some questions that might be on the test. Some were pedestrian, my name and address and so on. Others were bizarre: questions about bestiality, child porn, terrorism.

When he got to a question about my past drug use, Kevin's tone changed. His smile fell and he held eye contact. The interrogation had begun. I told him the same well-rehearsed thing I'd told my background investigator: *I experimented with drugs a few times in high school and college.* It was a lie. Kevin seemed to detect it.

"What do you mean by few?" he asked.

"Not many."

"Could it mean five?"

"I guess it *could.*"

"Don't be a smartass."

I looked around the room. It couldn't be just me and Kevin. Surely there was a witness somewhere, a hidden camera, a recorder, anything to prove we actually said what his report would say we had. Later I would learn that federal polygraph protocol requires examiners to make audio recordings of exams, and that many examiners have been accused of ignoring that requirement, as well as an array of other sordid and unprofessional practices. I don't remember Kevin saying anything about a recording, or seeing a device. But there's no way to say for sure.

Kevin sighed elaborately and asked the maximum number of times I could have used illegal drugs. "Was it six? Eight?"

"Sure," I said. "It was a long time ago."

"Could it be ten?" he asked, with a smug little grin, and finally I caught on.

"No. Definitely not ten." If Kevin wanted a fixed and certain truth, I'd give him one.

He wrote "6–8 times" on his notepad.

"I said it could have been that many, not that it *was.*"

Kevin said to let him do his job, and a shroud of dread descended. The test hadn't even begun, and I'd already found myself at epistemological loggerheads with the federal government. Kevin thought he'd convinced me to tell the truth, which was that I'd done drugs between six and eight times in my life. I thought there was no truth to tell. I didn't remember how many times it was. A few minutes earlier, Kevin had said there was no maximum threshold for drug use that would disqualify me—a bald-faced lie I had not yet detected—but I wasn't about to say that the real number was closer to a hundred. So the lie became the truth: I'd done drugs six to eight times.

Almost immediately, I began to believe it. As I sat there watching Kevin scribble notes, a handful of specific drug experiences returned to me. The first time I got high and drunk at the same time, in eighth grade, and spent the night in my friend David's bathroom with my head on the toilet seat while he tried to convince his mom that I had food poisoning. When Charlie taught me the trick where you blow the smoke through a paper towel tube with a fabric softener sheet rubber-banded over the end. The first line of meth I ever snorted, off a Bone Thugs CD case in Jeremy's bedroom. The cooks at my first restaurant job going around at closing time on busy nights, handing out key bumps. The eight ball I went in on with two ex-con dishwashers at my second restaurant job, who told me they'd pay me back double in a week, but then Mike got stabbed and I realized I wasn't cut out for that life. I never saw that money or the drugs, so maybe that one didn't count.

But that was all during one relatively short period of my life, when I was a shithead teenager. I'd come so far since then. I was a college professor; technically a visiting assistant professor, but still. My memoir was about to come out. The sitting president at the time had admitted to using marijuana and cocaine in *his* memoir. Why should I be banned from a job for being a small-time delinquent twenty years ago?

Remove those few wayward years and it was true enough that I'd only done drugs a few times in high school and college. As we say in the memoir business, it was *my* truth.

My new profession, memoirist, had a complicated relationship with truth, to put it mildly. Fake-memoir scandals have erupted more or less continuously as long as America has existed, from James Frey and his contemporaries, to the so-called autobiographies of Howard Hughes and Davy Crockett, to fantastical captivity narratives of the colonial era and dubious accounts of European explorers in the New World. Sometimes it seems like every notable American figure wrote a fictionalized memoir—even Wyatt Earp, the patron saint of my hometown. (*Frontier Marshal*. It's a hoot.) I fudged plenty of facts myself, combining real people into composite characters, changing the order of events. Most memoirists do the same. The point of the genre isn't accuracy or precision. The point is to tell a good story.

The same applies to the polygraph. There's no real evidence for the machine's accuracy. Its purpose is to monitor the body's physical response to stimuli, but the body's response to lying is indistinguishable from its response to any other stimulus. Even the telltale spike in the polygraph chart, itself largely a myth created by TV and movies, can indicate anything from a heart problem to sexual attraction. (Indeed, the machine's inventors used it to detect both of those things. Larson married one of his first test subjects, and Keeler discovered a heart defect while testing the machine on himself.)

But from the early years of the machine to the present day, its proponents have told the same story of an infallible machine that detects lies. Polygraph organizations routinely estimate its accuracy at nearly 100 percent. Most of those estimates are invented out of thin air, and the few based on data suffer from an obvious sampling error. As early as 1939, Walter Summers—yet another purported inventor of a lie detector—pointed out the fundamental flaw on which all polygraph statistics are based: they "fail to relate the number of instances in which deception was actually practiced in a manner which eluded the examiner and the instrument." You can't detect the lies you can't detect.

Independent studies suggest a polygraph exam is roughly as accurate as a coin flip, and that polygraph operators find as many as half of innocent subjects guilty. The scientific case against the polygraph is so compelling that the National Academy of Sciences, the American Psychological Association, the Congressional Office of Technology Assessment, and the United States Supreme Court have dismissed it as unreliable. A federal law forbids using the polygraph to screen applicants to private companies. For most jobs in America, an exam like mine would've been against the law.

In fact, the only people who seem to believe the polygraph is accurate are its operators. Every study I've found that supports the machine's ability to detect deception was funded or performed by polygraphers. They've formed half a dozen different organizations dedicated to spreading the lie of the lie detector. Their websites are ironically similar to the polygraph itself: archaic, slipshod, rife with bias and bullshit. The International League of Polygraph Examiners calls the device's invention "officially one of the greatest of all time," and claims the accuracy of contemporary polygraphs is close to 100 percent. The American Polygraph Association, which claims to be the largest organization of polygraphers, has a section of its website devoted to Polygraph Validity Research.

It begins by stating the organization "*believes* that scientific evidence supports the validity of polygraph examinations." The site includes a link to what seems to be the entire basis of that belief, the "Meta-Analytic Survey of Criterion Accuracy of Validated Polygraph Techniques." The document was prepared by a team of polygraphers, and it reads about how you'd expect. I made it far enough to learn a few astounding facts, including that until 2012, the American Polygraph Association did not require members to use methods supported by published research. In other words, for the first ninety-one years of its existence, polygraphers literally had no scientific standards. Luckily for me, they came up with some just in time for my exam.

The lie detector was like any true story in America: the facts didn't matter as long as a lot of people believed it. And we wanted to believe it: the notion of a lie detector existed long before the polygraph did. Tellingly, it first appeared in fiction. Bunn traces its first known usage to Charles Walk's 1909 detective novel *The Yellow Circle*, in which a character fantasizes about having a machine he calls a lie detector: "With its aid one can plumb the bottomless pits of a chap's subconscious mind, and fathom all the mysteries of his subliminal ego." In 1914, seven years before anyone claimed to have invented a polygraph, G. K. Chesterton mocked the notion of a lie detector in his mystery story *The Mistake of the Machine*, comparing it to the Dark Ages belief that blood would flow from a victim's body if their murderer touched it. Bunn lists many other instances of lie detectors appearing in fiction long before anyone claimed to have invented one.

Meanwhile, the popular American media seemed obsessed with the idea of machines that could see inside our heads, hearts, and souls. Fourteen years before Larson's polygraph debuted, *The New York Times* ran an article rhapsodizing about Jung's electric psychometer. That "mysterious little machine" purported to detect emotions, not lies; still, the article foretold a future when it would be used to detect guilt, making criminal courts superfluous. Four years later, the same paper ran a two-page profile of the "big-hearted" men, Edward Johnstone and Henry Goddard, who'd been doing the "self-sacrificing work" of testing the psychometer on developmentally disabled children at an institution in New Jersey. Under Johnstone's supervision, Goddard hooked kids up to a machine like Jung's. Their intent was to study and eradicate "feeble-mindedness"; Johnstone was a noted member of the American eugenics movement. But the article breathlessly predicted a future in which the lie detector would replace the "impedimenta" of American justice, like judges and juries.

When the story started circulating that a cop with a PhD had invented a lie-detecting machine, a myth became a widely reported fact almost overnight. Within a year, the *San Francisco Examiner* claimed, "everyone has heard of the 'lie detector.'" By then, polygraph results had already been banned from American courts, by a judge who was less enthused about the prospect of a machine replacing juries. It would be the first of many official dismissals of the polygraph. But it didn't dampen the media's fascination with the so-called lie detector—and, by extension, the American public's.

That fascination was furthered by the polygraph's sister inventions, psychology and cinematography, which were created by some of the same men at around the same time. In addition to his psychometer, Jung also helped create the field of modern psychology. Marey developed a different forerunner of the polygraph, as well as chronophotography, an important step in the development of cinema. Marston pioneered the idea of detecting lies based on physical responses, and later became a Hollywood censor and wrote a guide for aspiring screenwriters. His academic mentor, Hugo Münsterberg, helped lay the theoretical groundwork for the polygraph, and also published one of the earliest works of film theory.

The rise of psychology helped drive a cultural fascination with discovering the inner workings of the mind—especially the criminal mind—a desire the lie detector satisfied. Meanwhile, cinematography, the notion that we could document and preserve reality itself, had embarked on its ongoing project of destroying our cultural distinctions between fiction and fact.

Throughout its history, the polygraph has moved freely between the two realms. As it spread to police departments across the country, who used it to investigate real crimes, the machine also began to appear in advertisements and movies. The machine may have made its screen debut in the 1926 silent-film serial *Officer 444*, alongside Vollmer, who played an idealized version of himself, a criminologist using science against evil. By the 1930s, Marston was using the polygraph to screen-test Hollywood films, including *Frankenstein*—ironic, considering that Larson once compared his invention to the Monster—and to sell razor blades, gasoline, and cigarettes. In 1941, Marston invented Wonder Woman, a female superhero whose primary power was a Lasso of Truth, similar to a lie detector. Marston called the

comic "psychological propaganda," and it was hugely effective: within a year, Wonder Woman had her own comic book
with a circulation of half a million. In 1946, Keeler starred in
a noir movie alongside his version of the machine. The first
TV show called *Lie Detector* debuted in the fifties; there have
since been a handful of others, both scripted and reality, not
to mention a continuous stream of polygraph appearances in
film and television. While writing this essay, I watched lie
detectors play prominent roles in two different TV shows. In
one, the polygraph is accurate; in the other, it isn't.

Kevin slid a blank sheet of paper across the desk and told me
to draw the number five inside a black circle. I did, and slid
it back. Kevin drew other numbers in other circles and said
now he was going to hook me up to the machine.

He told me to take off my shoes and empty my pockets,
then directed me to the chair. I sat on one sensor and put
my feet on two others. Kevin wrapped two cords around
my chest, slid a sphygmomanometer over my left arm, and
stuck metal clamps on my right index and ring fingers. As
he pumped up the cuff, Kevin asked if I was comfortable.
He didn't seem to be joking.

He sat behind his desk and said he was going to point to
all the numbers on the paper and ask if I'd written them. I
should say no every time, even for the one I'd written. He
did. I did. He unhooked me, led me to the desk, and pointed
to the lie on the computer screen. It looked like a lot of
squiggly lines to me.

"Now we can take a break," Kevin said. I looked at the
clock, which wasn't visible from the polygraph chair; we'd

only been in the room for half an hour. Kevin smiled inscrutably. "Bathroom and water only. Be back in ten minutes."

I wandered into the hallway, drank from a fountain, leaned against another beige wall, and tried to calm down. I was not then in a great place, psychologically speaking. I stayed up until sunrise a few nights a week, spent days on end inside my apartment, often went blank with anxiety in front of my classes, and was preoccupied by a vivid and persistent vision of myself swan-diving off my balcony. I would later be diagnosed with various conditions and embark upon a reasonably successful therapeutic journey, but right then, in that hallway, I was freaking the fuck out. My shirt clung wetly to my chest, where I could see my heart beating as if it was trying to escape, like the alien in *Alien*. If I had a heart attack in the chair, what would that look like on the polygraph readout?

I'd tried to learn techniques for managing anxiety. Most of them didn't work—picture a beach, my ass—but a shrink I'd briefly seen had suggested imagining the worst possible outcome, and that seemed helpful. The idea was that you embrace the notion of failure and realize it wouldn't be so bad, thereby relieving the pressure not to fail.

I tried it. What if I failed the poly? I'd go back to Albuquerque, keep teaching, apply for more jobs. This was my backup plan, which made me luckier than pretty much everyone else applying. Then again, that was not the worst-case situation. One problem with that exercise is that I could always come up with something worse. What if I got in a car accident on my tired four-hour drive and spent the rest of my pain-filled life alone in my rented house in Albuquerque? What if I passed the poly, got the job, and actually took it—got sent to some borderland armpit like Ajo or Wellton where I'd have to herd other human beings into the back of trucks? Woke up two or ten or thirty years down the road and didn't recognize myself?

By the time Kevin came to get me, a few minutes sooner than the ten I'd been promised, I'd almost accepted my imminent failure. If my anxiety didn't make me fail the test, something else would. I remembered something from my sorta-research about Catholics failing the polygraph at higher rates. Technically I was Catholic, baptized and confirmed, now lapsed, but that only made things worse. Maybe I'd ask Kevin how to become a polygrapher. How much training did it require? Did he enjoy it? How much money did he make? Later, I'd search around online and find out that the average polygraph examiner makes even less than I did at the time. Then again, the training only takes ten weeks, and there are actually jobs in that field. I'd been training for years to be a nonfiction professor and still had no idea what truth actually meant; maybe I should've just taken a polygraph course and become an official federal arbiter of facts, an asshole demigod like Kevin.

I shouldn't be so hard on Kevin. Judging by his clothes and demeanor, he probably came from a similar background to mine. Maybe polygraphing was his version of teaching, a thing he did to pay the bills because it was better than his other options. Maybe he had a whole life to maintain, a family, a little house in some cul-de-sac on the West Side, two Toyotas and a swing set.

While Kevin strapped me back into the chair, I wondered what he told himself at night, trying to sleep, after watching applicants lose their best hope for a career to his machine. Kevin seemed like a smart guy, way too smart to believe in the simpleminded fantasy of a machine that detects lies. But that wasn't his decision. It was his employer's. And why is our government the only major employer in the world that uses polygraphs to screen prospective hires?

The answer to that question is based on a lie. Even the United States government isn't dumb enough to believe the polygraph works. The machine's real purpose is symbolic, as an icon of the power of the state. Law enforcement agencies don't use the machine to detect lies. They use it to coerce confessions.

In its early days, the polygraph was considered a more humane version of the infamous "third degree," the interrogation procedure it largely replaced, which involved beating the shit out of a suspect until they confessed. The third degree was itself a variation of another quintessentially American tactic, outright torture. The parallels between torture and the polygraph are obvious: the latter's arcane parts and procedures, its use of restraints and stimuli, the gratuitous periods of waiting for what the subject knows is coming. The polygraph creates the very stress it's designed to detect, then presents it as evidence of deception, which often leads its subject to confess. If the subject confesses, that confession effectively *becomes* the truth, whether it's true or false or somewhere in between.

And the polygraph has a long history of coercing false confessions. It may begin with its maiden voyage in 1921, when Larson tested his new device on the residents of an all-female Berkeley dorm that had experienced a rash of petty thefts. Thanks in part to the polygraph, a suspect admitted to most of the thefts and withdrew from the university. But the crimes continued, and Larson himself doubted the veracity of her confession.

Not long after, Larson tested a man named Henry Wilkens who was accused of having his wife killed. The polygraph helped to exonerate Wilkens despite evidence of his guilt. After that, police began to doubt the polygraph's utility, and some departments refused to use it. (The media had no such qualms: it continued to trumpet the infallibility of the "electric detective.")

A year after the Wilkens case, a young Black man named James Frye retracted his confession to killing a Washington, DC, doctor, claiming it was coerced. Using his variation of the lie detector, Marston examined Frye and declared him innocent. But the judge prevented Marston from testifying as an expert at trial, and an appeals court upheld the ruling, instituting what became known as the Frye rule, which has largely prevented polygraph results from being admissible in American courts ever since.

But the machine remains useful for extracting confessions. And the conflation of confessions and truth is yet another lie, one that's kept the polygraph alive for the last century as a peculiarly American delusion. Confessions are usually presumed to be true and treated as such in legal settings. But recent research suggests that false confessions are common, especially in the context of police interrogations.

Despite a growing body of evidence, including hundreds of exonerations based on DNA evidence, most people don't believe in false confessions. A recent article in the *Journal of the American Academy of Psychiatry and the Law* explains why:

> Most lay people believe in what has been referred
> to as the myth of psychological interrogation:

that an innocent person will not falsely confess to police unless he is physically tortured or mentally ill . . . the myth of psychological interrogation persists because most people do not know what occurs during police interrogations, and because they wrongly assume that individuals do not act against their self-interest or engage in self-destructive behavior, such as falsely confessing to a crime that they did not commit.

The likelihood of a false confession increases when interrogators use certain tactics, especially elements of the so-called Reid Technique, a procedure created in the 1950s by John E. Reid. I didn't know it at the time, but Kevin used elements of the Reid Technique in my test. He conducted it in a small, barely furnished, cold room; seated me in a hard, armless, straight-backed chair; and repeatedly encroached on my personal space.

Reid first used his technique (along with a polygraph) in 1955, to extract a confession from a man named Darrel Parker who was suspected of killing his wife. Parker was convicted and sentenced to life in prison. He served fifteen years before being released on appeal because Parker's confession was ruled to have been coerced. Eighteen years after Parker's release, a man on death row for other crimes confessed to the murder; he did so by showing his lawyers a passage of his memoirs that described the murder in detail, a passage the legal system apparently assumed to be true.

Neither those nor the Reid Technique's subsequent high-profile failures, including the $2M settlement of a 2012 civil case by a wrongly convicted man named Juan Rivera, have prevented it from being adopted by police departments across

America. The company founded in Reid's name, John E. Reid and Associates, claims its technique is "the most widely used approach to question subjects in the world," and recently registered a trademark on the term.

The Reid Technique™ involves a number of tactics, from creating an anxiety-inducing environment to a list of specific steps. According to Saul Kassin, perhaps the foremost American expert on false confessions, the purpose of those tactics is to "get suspects to incriminate themselves by increasing the anxiety associated with denial, plunging the subject into a state of despair and then minimizing the perceived consequences of confession."

Like the polygraph, the Reid Technique isn't designed to find the truth. Its purpose is to coerce confessions. Research suggests the Reid Technique may actually make interrogators *worse* at detecting truth. In an independent study, interrogators trained in the Reid Technique were less accurate, although "they were more confident and cited more reasons for their judgments."

The polygraph itself is not required for the Reid Technique, but it helps. Together, they have a long and checkered history of producing false confessions. In 2013, the *Chicago Tribune* found a pattern of false confessions obtained via polygraph exams and the Reid Technique, by examiners who routinely ignored accepted standards, including failing or refusing to record interrogations.

Kevin said the first battery of questions would cover my character, and asked if I had any questions. I did, but too many, and where to start? So I said no, and Kevin started the exam.

He asked me a battery of eight questions four times in different orders. By the time I typed notes on my phone after the test, I'd already forgotten one of them. The other seven were:

1. Have you misrepresented your past drug use?
2. Have you lied about participating in serious crimes?
3. Have you falsified info on forms?
4. Have you ever cheated to get ahead in your personal life?
5. Have you ever made disparaging comments about your supervisor?
6. Is the light on?
7. Have you taken a drink of water today?

Except for the last two, all of them seemed open to interpretation. For instance, I absolutely had misrepresented my past drug use, but only the number of times, not the drugs or the fact of doing them. And could my estimate be a lie when there's no way to know the exact answer? What crimes are considered serious? What counts as cheating? Who gets to say? Has any employed person in America not made a single disparaging comment about a supervisor?

The first time through the questions, I tried to follow Kevin's direction to answer quickly, yes or no, and to abide by his somewhat contradictory instructions to breathe normally while staying absolutely still. The second time through, my voice began to crack, and I swallowed.

"Stop!"

I turned my head to see who he was yelling at.

"Stay completely still!"

I turned back to the wall and tried to comply. Kevin kept yelling, asking combative and rhetorical questions: was I *trying* to beat the test, did I *want* to fail? I tried to calm myself by imagining something peaceful, although that was probably considered a countermeasure, and anyway, it didn't work: I visualized ripping off the electrodes and punching Kevin. I tried the box-breathing technique I'd once learned from a veteran stepdad. That worked better. Possibly too well. Soon I caught myself nodding off.

That probably sounds like a lie. How could someone under that much stress be sleepy? Have you ever been inter-rogated? I don't mean metaphorically, having a difficult conversation, confessing something to a spouse, parent, priest, boss. I mean actually interrogated, by a profes-sional. No lawyer, no witnesses, nobody on your side. And he has a machine that says he's right, not to mention the backing of the Department of Homeland Security, a vast and unaccountable agency built on the lie that policing and surveilling Americans will protect us from terrorism. Suddenly, this part of the Border Patrol application pro-cess made a grim kind of sense: I was getting a little taste of how an immigrant might feel. Except I deserved it. I'd signed up for this.

If you haven't been in that situation, maybe you think, like I did before it was proven otherwise, that you'd be one of the exceptions. You'd beat the polygraph, like people do on TV. But that's the thing: you can't beat the polygraph, because the polygraph isn't a lie detector, isn't a test, isn't even a machine. It's a fact, part of a story power tells itself to justify its power. Maybe you can beat the machine—they don't detect lies, so it's not that hard—but you can't beat an entire country that believes in it.

As Kevin went through the questions again, I sank into a fugue, part paranoia and part exhaustion, and lost track of time. Not what time it was—the whole idea of time. There was no past or future, only an endless present of sitting in that windowless room, strapped to a chair, wired to a machine, staring at a beige wall while a stranger I couldn't see asked the same questions, over and over. I forgot why I was there, who I was, the truth and what it meant. At some point, I heard a sort of flutter, and my vision vibrated and jumped, as if someone had changed the reel. My mind floated up to the corner of the room and observed the proceedings from a cool remove. My memory of the rest of the test is from a vantage point outside of my body.

Jung defined this phenomenon as dissociation, the loss of a fixed and coherent identity. Reports of similar experiences were largely ignored in early psychology, but more recent studies suggest dissociation is fairly common, and can be triggered by drugs, trauma, stress, or nothing at all. Jung said dissociative states could prevent a subject from recalling important facts, among other things. "We talk about being able to control ourselves," he wrote. "But self-control is a rare and remarkable virtue."

The polygraph showed me I was neither rare nor remarkable. By the final time through the battery, I no longer knew what was true. For example: the first three times Kevin asked if I'd ever disparaged a supervisor, I'd rationalized, telling myself "disparaged" was a strong word. It means to regard as having little worth, and older definitions meant to dishonor or degrade; did Kevin know it came from the Old French *disparagier*, to marry unequally? Certainly, I'd made fun of some bosses, and respected few, but I hadn't disparaged my supervisors, per se. The fourth time he asked me the question, a crystalline memory popped into my detached head, a moment a few years before when I told my then-girlfriend that my then-boss was a fucking idiot.

"No," I said. Kevin moved on.

Later I would learn that I wasn't the first lie detector subject to report experiencing dissociation. I'm not even the first one to write about it. As an undergraduate at Harvard, Gertrude Stein worked in a laboratory run by Hugo Münsterberg, who came up with the earliest scientific rationale for lie detection. Stein's first published work, an 1894 essay originally written for her sophomore composition class titled "In the Psychological Laboratory," was an account of her experiences in the lab, including an instance of being connected to one of Münsterberg's primitive predecessors of the polygraph. The essay's third person narration and distinctive syntax are both harbingers of Stein's future work, and her knowledge of the machine seems to have informed her later experiments in "automatic writing." (It's also worth noting that her autobiography has fictional elements.)

But her account interests me for other reasons. She describes the experience of being subjected to an exam in front of a group of students like so:

> Strange fancies begin to crowd upon her, she feels that the silent pen is writing on and on forever. Her record is there she cannot escape it and the group about her begin to assume the shape of mocking fiends gloating over her imprisoned misery. Suddenly she starts, they have suddenly loosened a metronome directly behind her, to observe the effect, so now the morning's work is over.

What it describes sounds like dissociation, or exactly what I felt when I was subjected to the polygraph.

The scientific literature suggests dissociation during polygraph exams is fairly common. In 1996, the polygrapher Donald J. Krapohl wrote an article for *Polygraph*, the official organ of the American Polygraph Association, that addresses the phenomenon. The article is typical of polygraphers' attempts at justifying their profession in the sense that it's paranoid, authoritarian, proto-fascist, and presents the opinions and experiences of a single polygraph operator as if they're commandments carved into tablets. Krapohl begins with a blithe, moralistic tirade about "the phenomenon of mendacity" that "pervades every class and culture." Lying, he claims, is endemic to certain types of people, having "served to defend or expand the interests of uncounted generations of monarchs, merchants, spouses, debtors, knaves, and saints."

Kraphol attempts to codify four classes of countermeasures. The first, Physical Countermeasures, includes any instance in which a polygraph subject "use[s] movements in hopes of masking their reactions or misdirecting the examiner." Of course, a polygraph subject might move for any number of reasons during an exam, including as a natural reaction to the very discomfort and stress it's designed to cause; no examiner or machine can determine *why*. And one wonders why a test so supposedly accurate can be fooled by something as simple as flexing a muscle.

The second category, "Mental Countermeasures," includes imagery, hypnosis, biofeedback training, placebos, and even personality. Notably, dissociation is considered a mental countermeasure. Here, again, is the rub: if the subject dissociates during a polygraph, who's to say whether it's intentional? Even Krapohl acknowledges that "the outward appearance of a dissociating subject is quite similar to that of a cooperating test subject." In other words, nobody can tell if another person is dissociating, much less why. Even the person dissociating may not know; I certainly didn't at the time. Studies suggest dissociation is often an unconscious response to intense stress of the sort the polygraph is designed to create in its subject. The polygraph works by stressing you out, but if the stress it causes in turn causes the subject to dissociate, they can be failed for trying to cheat.

⚓

Kevin gave me another break. I spent it in the waiting area, staring out over the rooftops of El Paso. The window faced east, so I couldn't see the border, but the border is like the truth: you know when you're close to it. After a few minutes, Kevin came and led me back into the interrogation room, where he sat me down and said I'd failed. The machine detected deception in my answers to either the drug question or the falsifying information question. I was amazed: he couldn't even tell which question I'd lied about? And why hadn't he detected my lie about disparaging my boss?

Kevin went on to say that I must have researched tactics to defeat the poly. My swallowing seemed to bother him to the point that he considered it evidence of deception. I said my mouth had been dry, but Kevin ignored me, telling stories about his brother who'd done drugs and other applicants who said they'd gotten high a thousand times. I didn't know it at the time, but his psychological tactics were all elements of the Reid Technique: repeated, unwavering assertions of guilt; attempts to excuse or minimize the suspected crime;

constant interruptions; professed sympathy; and, of course, outright lies.

Kevin said he was almost positive that my drug use wasn't over the threshold. Earlier, he'd told me there was no threshold, and it dawned on me that Kevin wasn't much of an interrogator without his machine. He kept fishing, accusing me of various lies, interrupting whenever I tried to deny, suggesting things I may have forgotten: didn't I ever do any pills when I was a bartender? Did I really only do meth once or twice? He began pointing to the computer screen and picking up other deceptions. He detected possible lies in my academic record—I told him I'd gotten a 3.0 GPA at a state school, and why the hell would anybody lie about that?—and questioned whether I really had a master's degree, even though I'd provided transcripts as part of my background investigation.

He accused, I denied, and it became the worst kind of male interaction, a matter of pride. He was lying, I was lying, everything we said was both true and false, depending how you looked at it. I wasn't even hooked up to the machine anymore, so I didn't understand why we were still talking. He'd already said that I failed. Couldn't we call it a day?

As Kevin's one-man theater dragged on, I thought about the long drive ahead of me, and began to understand why people make false confessions. It's not because you don't know the truth. It's because the truth doesn't matter. When the person across the table has all the power, what's the point of arguing? It was pretty clear by then, a few hours into a test I'd already failed, that Kevin didn't give a damn what was true. He wouldn't be satisfied until I confessed. But fuck Kevin and his machine. I wasn't confessing.

Kevin paused, and I thought we might finally be done until he asked about my mother's murder: was there anything I hadn't told him about *that*? It broke the spell. I dissociated in reverse, came fully into my body. My chest relaxed, my heart quieted, and I saw the situation clearly for the first time. Kevin was just some dickhead with a grift, doing a job based on lies for a government that practically invented them. Did I know anything about my mother's murder? I'd spent five years writing about it. I was the world's foremost authority on the subject. But I wasn't telling Kevin. If he wanted to know, he could buy the fucking book.

I asked if I was free to leave. He shrugged. As I stood and went for the door, he asked if I would come back for another test with him if necessary. Sure, I said. I'd love to. It was the last thing I would ever say to Kevin, and I wanted to make sure it was a lie.

When I got home, I checked the internet forum and read a post by the guy who'd been sitting with me in the waiting room. He'd failed, too. His story was almost exactly the same as mine, except his test took twice as long. He must have tried harder than I did to tell the truth.

Three weeks later, my book came out, and I once again found myself answering questions. Whenever someone asked about truth, I'd say that I consulted the historical record when possible, but that the book was mostly based on memory. Sometimes, despite myself, that old cliché slipped out: *it's my truth*. I'd think about the polygraph, Kevin's endless questions, his assumption that a fixed, detectable truth existed in my memory.

Writing a book based on memory showed me it's less a font of truth than a river of lies. We may tell ourselves stories in order to live, as Didion famously said, but nobody ever quotes the rest of that passage: "We live entirely, especially if we are writers, by the imposition of a narrative line upon disparate images, by the 'ideas' with which we have learned to freeze the shifting phantasmagoria which is our actual experience." That sounds a lot like lying.

Even if we mean to tell the truth, the existing science suggests that memory is almost as unreliable as the polygraph. In 1885, the German psychologist Hermann Ebbinghaus did tests on himself and came up with his famed "forgetting curve," a chart that showed we forget more than half of information within a few days. More recent studies have found that autobiographical memory—the deliberate recollection of facts, ideas, and experiences from one's life—is not only inaccurate, but suggestible and frequently false. And factors such as depression and trauma, both psychological and physical, have been found to degrade autobiographical memory.

Then there's the issue of stress, which also seems to have a range of effects on memory. Stress hormones like cortisol and adrenaline have been shown to aid in memory consolidation, which is, more or less, the process of storing recently learned information as memories for long-term recall. But those memories can change each time they're remembered, through a process called reconsolidation: once accessed, the memory has to be rewritten, and it can be rewritten differently, revised just like a scene in a memoir. While stress may aid in memory consolidation, it has a profoundly negative effect on reconsolidation. Trauma has its own story to tell.

By the time I took the polygraph, my memory had already been rewritten. After five years of accessing and re-accessing memories of my mother and her death, I'd recently begun to understand how dangerous it is to write a book based primarily on memory. I don't mean the truth: accuracy is overrated, not to mention impossible. The real danger is the sacrifice you have to make. By writing your memories, and rewriting them again and again, draft after draft, you replace them, erase them. By the time I finished my book, after revising every word half a dozen times, I didn't remember my mother anymore. She was pages, scenes, sentences.

The polygraph works a lot like a memoir. It doesn't find the truth, it creates it. First the exam makes you doubt or forget your memories. Then, by forcing you to re-access them again and again under stress, it literally rewrites them. Since my polygraph exam, I've believed that I did drugs between six and eight times before then, even though my rational mind knows that isn't true. My experience of being polygraphed showed me that not only does the polygraph not detect lies, it manufactures them.

More than two million polygraph exams are given every year in America; it's a two-billion-dollar industry. No other country in the world uses the poly to nearly the extent that we do, and most don't use it at all. Why are we the only ones who build machines to detect the truth, and believe that they can, despite all evidence to the contrary? Why do we need to believe in a truth so simple it can be detected by a machine?

The lie detector is a myth. Everyone who doesn't make money off polygraphs agrees on that. But myths exist for a reason, to explain collective phenomena, to explain us to ourselves. Myths create a sense of community through shared belief. Judging by our obsession with lie detectors—and the fact that we continue to call them that, more than a century into this charade—the myth of a simple, detectable truth is one of the few beliefs most Americans do still share.

The lie detector came straight out of science fiction, and drifted into the realm of fact at the beginning of a century in which a succession of groundbreaking technologies would shatter and reshape our cultural conceptions of what was possible: Edison's bulbs, Bell's telephone, Ford's mass-produced cars, the Wright Brothers' airplane. By the time the polygraph came along, a credulous American public was used to tales of revolutionary, terrifying innovations that were going to change their lives forever. Some of those technologies were transforming reality itself. Electricity was spreading across the country, quite literally changing the way people saw the world. So were telephone and radio access, which did the same for how we heard it. The polygraph's siblings, cinema and psychology, were transforming the way people saw themselves. Meanwhile, Modernism—the artistic movement responding to those changes—was roiling the arts in every medium, revising our expressions of lived and imagined reality; the United States government banned James Joyce's *Ulysses* the same year the polygraph debuted.

How it must have felt to be a human then. A man my age in 1921 might have remembered reading dime Westerns by candlelight as a boy, riding a horse to school, a time before voices—much less humans—could travel through the air. He'd seen the Progressive era rewrite the rules of society, including the victory of women's suffrage the year before. He might have fought in the first World War. By the time the polygraph was invented, he may have owned a car or had access to a telephone, if he was wealthy. But he still got his news from newspapers or neighbors. He didn't own a screen.

Can we blame him for believing in a simple kind of truth that a new device could find?

A century later, I'm awash in new technologies, and deeply confused about what to believe. I was a young adult when smartphones arrived, in college when Facebook debuted, and dimly remember an early childhood before the internet changed everything. In the last few years, as of this writing, the COVID-19 pandemic has altered American life in ways nobody comprehends. Nobody trusts the media anymore, and appalling numbers of Americans refuse to believe in fundamental, verifiable facts. Meanwhile, conspiracies ricochet around the internet, gathering believers.

It's hard not to see this moment as a parallel of the polygraph's invention, another time when technology has done a number on whatever shared sense of truth America once had. That erosion has worsened our cultural and political divisions, which often hinge on what kind of truth we believe in: relative and constructed, or absolute and fixed. A century ago, the polygraph was born from the latter belief. But the notion of objective truth seems quaint and naive in our era of fake news and algorithms, when the only truth that still exists is ours, a custom reality created for us and delivered to our devices. We're all memoirists now, shouting our stories into the void. We're all polygraphers, staring at the screens of our truth machines, proving ourselves right.

A few months after the exam, I got the official news: not only had I been found unsuitable for employment, I also had no right to appeal the decision and was barred from reapplying for a minimum of three years. The consequences of my polygraph exam were finally clear, the only real truth revealed in the whole process: I was never going to be a federal agent.

I wasn't alone. I soon found out that Customs and Border Protection job applicants had a polygraph failure rate of 68.1 percent, more than double that of other law enforcement agencies. The CBP commissioner at the time said those statistics showed the polygraph was working and blamed the quality of the applicants. It struck me as a strange rhetorical strategy to suggest that his agency attracted applicants so much worse than those of any other law enforcement body in America, but what did I know: I was one of those applicants. One article described polygraph subjects being accused with no evidence of cheating on their wives and having cartel connections, in exams lasting eight hours or longer. Other law enforcement agencies called CBP's conduct excessive, and Jeff Flake, then a Republican Senator from Arizona, suggested that operators were being forced to fail applicants to justify their own jobs.

A few months after my exam, I got an email officially notifying me of my failure.

I replied to the email and asked for a copy of the polygraph report. The CBP representative told me I'd have to file a Freedom of Information Act request. I did. They ignored my request for four months, in violation of FOIA. When I threatened legal action, they denied my request for other reasons, both of which were lies.

I filed another FOIA request and was still waiting for a response when the Office of Personnel Management announced that it had suffered a data breach. The personnel files of millions of federal employees and applicants had been stolen by Chinese hackers. An investigation ensued, and the

Inspector General accused OPM officials of lying about the hack. Multiple high-ranking officials, including the director of OPM, resigned in the aftermath.

Eventually I received a letter from the replacement director alerting me that I'd been affected by the hack. (In the letter, she admitted that her own background check had also been compromised, as if that was supposed to make me feel *better.*) The most sensitive imaginable document about my life—one that included all of my personal and financial information, as well as a complete history of my jobs, residences, and relationships—had been stolen. The government's solution was to offer free credit monitoring to those affected.

As of this writing, it's been more than a decade since my polygraph exam, and the government still hasn't sent me a copy of the report. But at least now I know the truth is out there. It's on a hard drive somewhere in China.

The Problem with Erik: Privilege, Blackmail, and Murder for Hire in Austin

by Katy Vine and Ana Worrel

A spoiled heir to an auto-dealership empire responded to a threatening text by ordering two murders. Four years and a jury trial later, what motivated his ruinous decision remains a mystery.

E rik Maund had always lived the high life, as you might expect of a man whose surname had been blasted on TV ads for decades. By the time he was in his forties, he was an executive at Maund Automotive Group, a car sales business whose first dealership was opened by his grandfather Charles Maund. "If you say the Maund name in Austin in a 7-Eleven, two people say, 'I bought a car from him,'" said Wallace Lundgren, a retired Chevrolet dealer. Austinites could probably recognize the major names in the car business better than they could identify any local politician. And members of the city's old power circles would recognize Erik—a six-foot-three white guy with short brown hair, a boxy head, and heavy-lidded eyes tucked under a straight brow—as a likely heir to the business.

He and his wife, Sheri, a former dealership office worker, had raised two kids to the cusp of adulthood and lived in a seven-thousand-square-foot white brick mansion next to the Austin Country Club, where he teed off regularly with a close-knit group of friends. He owned a boat and a lake house. On Sundays he often enjoyed brunch at the club with his family.

But on March 1, 2020, as the world was rattled by reports of a highly contagious virus turning up in nation after nation, Erik received a text that demanded his attention. It came from a stranger who knew about a night Erik had spent with an escort in Nashville a few weeks earlier and wanted money to keep quiet.

Certain aspects of Erik's life were less than picture-perfect. He was a gambler, sometimes losing thousands of dollars on a golf game. He treated the country club as his local bar, favoring Ketel One and tonic with lime. At times he struck others as clueless about his privilege. And he wasn't above paying an escort for her services.

In February, while he was preparing to visit his son at college in Nashville, he'd messaged an escort who went by the name "Layla Love" and whom he had met at least once before, on an earlier trip. "Hey darling!!" he wrote. "I was thinking Wednesday night around 9:30 at the JW Marriott. 90 minutes would be great so we're not rushed. If all sounds good, let me know and I'll text you Wednesday when I get to Nashville. Erik"

Two days later, Erik met with Layla Love as planned; he made reservations with a different escort the following night. Afterward, he returned to Austin, where he went back to his routine at the dealership and the country club, in what would be the last few weeks of normalcy before the COVID-19 lockdown.

And then that text appeared on his phone. The message is now lost to the digital ether, but as court testimony would later establish, the sender threatened to expose him. Get me $25,000, the blackmailer demanded, or I'll tell your wife everything.

"Let me get you in touch with a divorce lawyer. That's what I would have told him," said someone who knew Erik. That was one possible course of action: Erik could have told his wife everything. Or he could have called the cops. He could have just paid up. After all, he was worth millions of dollars, and the sender might have gone away.

He chose a fourth option, one that would cost him a lot more money and, ultimately, his freedom. Four years and a jury trial later, it's still hard to pinpoint just what motivated his ruinous decision. At first glance, Erik comes off as a spoiled heir missing a moral compass, who in trying to outwit a blackmailer wound up guilty of murder. As you look closer, a striking feature of the story is that Erik and many others involved, culprits and victims alike, were trying to chase away their demons with fantasies and desperate schemes—until all these delusions collided, leaving two people dead.

One of those victims was Holly Williams, the escort who called herself Layla Love. Though the work was lucrative, it left her vulnerable. She'd installed security cameras outside her front door and inside her apartment, and on the afternoon of March 10, the interior footage shows that she was acting peculiarly, sneaking around. Petite, wearing a black tank top with her midnight-black hair ponytailed, Holly crept out from the bedroom holding a door brace. She passed the tall floor vase in the dining room and the black and white photo of a longhorn steer above a navy sofa, with fluffy pillows placed just so, in the living room. Using her left foot, she scooched aside a woven welcome mat and quietly secured one side of the brace to the floor and the other below the doorknob.

Outside her door, about forty minutes later, a man knocked, crossed his muscular arms, and knocked again. "Hey, Holly. Holly, if you're in there," he said. "Just a couple questions then I'm done. No worries."

She didn't respond and tiptoed back to the kitchen, waiting for him to leave.

Holly was a magnetic beauty in her early thirties, with Kardashian-style thick lashes and full lips, who was always in the mood for dancing, whether it was the goofy Carlton snap-step from *The Fresh Prince of Bel-Air* or some steady bouncing to electronic dance music (EDM). If she couldn't find a friend to join her for a night on the town, she'd head to the clubs solo and make new acquaintances, staying out till dawn, drawing guys like moths to her glow. "It was like a Marilyn Monroe movie, where the men come up and light her cigarette," said her friend Marie Carroll. "There's six men around her. And that's how it was whenever we went out. Everyone just swarmed her, especially the men."

Marie connected with Holly back in 2018, through a mutual friend who figured they could bond over their training as aestheticians—though as Holly admitted to Marie, she wasn't paying her rent by selling laser treatments or Botox injections. She drew much of her income from working as an escort, a service she publicized on secure websites such as Preferred411 and Slixa. As for why Holly had chosen that work, "I think a lot of it was that need to be told, 'You're beautiful,'" said Marie. The money was good too: some guys, whom she called her "whales," would pay her $20,000 or $30,000 for a weekend.

Even so, the work felt risky. "The benefit is you get presents, and you can get whatever you want," she had told Marie. "You can travel, you can get a car, furniture, or whatever. But it's not worth it if you just feel like you're in danger constantly." Holly was cautious. She charged enough to keep the riffraff away: $1,500 a session for one person; $2,500 for a couple, according to trial testimony. She could always reach out to other escorts on her sites and ask if this or that client was "safe." Still, she never knew exactly what was going to happen when she was alone with a guy.

A few months after she met Marie, Holly fell for a tall, lanky redhead named Bill Lanway, and she withdrew from her friendships as her world melted into his. According to friends and recovered texts that would later become evidence, the two started traveling to EDM shows and taking party drugs together. He'd call her Holly Ann or "baby girl," and she'd call him Will or, affectionately, "punk." Bill assured her that she was "absolutely mesmerizing" and texted her that he was proud of her "for being a strong independent woman and for facing all u have in life and still coming out on top"—something she needed to hear. She responded, "I'm glad u can see the good in me because I sure as hell can't. Nor can my family. I keep making all the wrong decisions and repeating the same mistakes. I can't help but feel like a failure in life or like as if I'm being punished for not changing my lifestyle & the people I associate with."

As they drew strength from each other's support, they also revealed their scars. She had an estranged relationship with her mother, and he had a heartbreaking past he rarely told anyone about: his father had stabbed and killed his mother when he was a toddler, and he'd been raised by an aunt. In 2011 he'd lost his five-year-old daughter, Maddie, to cancer. The two traumas, his friends believed, lay behind the endless partying.

Bill likely didn't know about Holly's escort business until they'd been dating awhile, when he snooped around on her phone. By then, he couldn't easily walk away. His feelings for her had grown too strong. Plus, he'd become financially dependent on her; he'd even moved into her apartment. While he made a little money delivering Amazon packages and dealing for private, high-stakes poker games, he didn't have a reliable source of income. So what could he say about her line of work? "He kind of confided in me about it," said Bill's best friend, "and then I was like, 'Man, Bill. What the hell? How do you deal with that?'"

He dealt with it poorly. The couple began fighting, and by April 2019, Holly had involved the police, filing an order of protection against Bill. The complaint alleged that he stole the SIM card out of her phone, punched the windshield of her car, and hit her in the mouth. She later dropped the request.

Bill kept going through Holly's phone, and one day, he found her client list and zeroed in on a local radiologist who'd been seeing Holly every few months for years. Bill texted the doctor anonymously, instructing him to stop seeing Holly or Bill would tell his wife and his employees.

In the months that followed, the couple's behavior followed a pattern of violent escalation and reconciliation.

After one fight, Bill broke into Holly's apartment, snatched her dog, and dropped it off next to a busy highway, where a car ran over it. Holly trashed Bill to her friends and reset the keypad locks. Then, as usual, she and Bill made up.

By early 2020, Holly was trying to get her life on track: paying bills, hiring an accountant to help with her taxes, screening new clients. On February 3 she texted Bill, "I hope you don't go back to your jealous ways and start bitching at me anytime I have to do work stuff. Just remember, I would not be in this position and would not have to put myself out there to gain new clientele if you hadn't run off my consistent, longtime clients."

Her message must not have sunk in, because Bill texted the wife of the radiologist. (The radiologist dealt with the personal fallout, eventually coming clean to his wife.)

Around this time, a friend of Holly's named Matt Garrett, whom she'd known since her teenage years, had a sudden urge to call her. Matt lived an hour away, and he hadn't talked with Holly in six or seven months. He was a competitive bodybuilder with "antihero" tattooed on his knuckles. He considered himself an empath, and he'd just had an ominous dream. "Look, I don't know how to tell you this, but I think your boyfriend is going to kill you," he told Holly on the phone. He could understand her surprise, but he felt compelled to let her know. "Yeah, do with it what you want." That was the last time he talked with her.

A contingent of aging car dealers and other businessmen regularly gathers at a Central Austin hangout they call the Shithole, basically a painted concrete man cave behind a

Shell station, overseen by Salem Joseph, a longtime gambler and self-titled "Head Motherf—er in Charge." Over the years it has drawn former UT football stars and other local luminaries, lending it a certain allure. That might explain why Erik Maund used to stop by once in a while, though he rarely sat down. "Afraid he might get diseased," said Salem's brother Joe Joseph.

The Shithole crowd represents an older generation of hustlers and scrappers, some of whom had known Charles Maund, the founder of the family business. On one of the days we visited, a massive TV playing ESPN was mounted over a dripping sink. Wooden floors offset the gas station vibe, while a handful of men sat around a table cutting chunks off a block of Costco cheese.

While Erik was raised in a wealthy part of West Austin, playing on the golf team at Westlake High School, his grandfather came from tougher stock, they said. Charles Maund grew up poor in Hemphill, Texas, two hours' drive north of Beaumont, and according to his 2002 obituary in the *Austin American-Statesman,* his parents had both died by the time he turned fifteen. He was sixteen years old, pumping gas for a living, when a local banker lent him $500 to buy a used car. Charles fixed it up and sold the car for a profit.

A few years later he started selling cars in earnest, and in 1957, when he turned 30, he moved to Austin and opened his first dealership, Charles Maund Oldsmobile-Cadillac. "They called him Lucky. How he got the dealership, we never figured that out, because Cadillac was so particular," said Wallace Lundgren, the Chevrolet dealer and Shithole regular. "He was a fun guy. Not the kind of fun you brag about, but we drank lots of whiskey, and we really had a good time, you know?" Wallace thought for a second. "Well, we didn't kill anybody."

Charles Maund built an empire of dealerships over the decades, selling Cadillacs, Toyotas, Volkswagens, and other vehicles. He eventually passed that empire along to Erik's father, Doug, though it sounds as if Charles never completely dropped certain conditioned instincts. In one hard-to-imagine incident that came up in multiple interviews about the Maunds, Charles and Doug got into a knife fight at the Austin Country Club. "That's common knowledge," Wallace said, though neither he nor anyone else could say what the fight was about. Doug never quite developed his father's street smarts, friends said.

As luck would have it, though, the path was laid for Erik. The middle child of three born to Doug and Janis Maund, Erik attended St. Edward's University, in Austin, and the National Automobile Dealers Association Academy, in Virginia, before going to work in the family business. According to a former employee named Justin Wright, Erik could be ruthless to anyone who crossed him; otherwise, as a manager at the family's Volkswagen dealership, he coasted on his name. "So his part was, no s—, just sitting in his office dipping [snuff] and looking at the internet," Wright said. "He was just kind of like an asshole figure in the background, always." At the country club, his reputation wasn't so much lazy or vindictive as it was occasionally tone-deaf. Once, when a fellow member of the country club asked him about the Camry hybrid that his dealership sold, Erik responded quite earnestly that his dad's butler liked the one he had bought.

He had a prenuptial agreement, so had he told Sheri about his dalliance in Nashville, he wouldn't have risked losing his fortune in a divorce. Yet exposure would've been devastating to his reputation and to his family—including his mom and his sisters, all of whom were well regarded. Looking for advice, Erik turned to a trusted colleague, Charles Maund Toyota's general manager, Jim DiMeo. Erik had confided in Jim before when he'd had issues with gambling or women. Someone had sent a message, Erik said, wanting money.

Jim had an idea: maybe the dealership's new security person, Gilad Peled, could help. Though he'd only just started a relationship with the Maunds, he claimed to have served in the Mossad, the Israeli intelligence agency. Built like a boulder, with a neck as wide as his shaved head, he looked like a badass.

Gil and Erik linked up at the dealership, Erik explained the situation, and at first Gil suggested going to the police. But when Erik explained he didn't want the embarrassment, Gil reassured him that everything would be fine. "I got this," he said.

Gil Peled considered himself a fixer. In 1999 he moved from his homeland of Israel to the US, and in 2007 he became a US citizen. He served as a tank commander in the Israeli army and claimed at various times to have worked as a member of a special-forces unit and as an operative for the Mossad foreign intelligence service. He also boasted about negotiating hostage and extortion threats for a Russian billionaire and for the Mexican government. In 2011 he landed a flashy Hollywood job: bodyguard for Charlie Sheen.

Sheen's former personal assistant, Steve Han, said that when he first met Gil, it was hard for him to take the man seriously. Gil always wore sunglasses, and he acted like his job was to stand around flexing his gigantic muscles. "Gil played the role of bodyguard protecting his client very seriously, but it's like, who's he protecting him from, a soccer mom that just wants a photo?" Steve said. Once, when Sheen was visiting Colombia, Gil saw to it that Sheen and his entire crew were transported in bulletproof vehicles. "I wouldn't say he was a fearmonger," Steve said, "but it was in his best interest if the world was a scary place for someone like Charlie."

In 2014, Sheen fired Gil, who wasn't a favorite of Sheen's fiancée, and the Israeli American and his family moved to Austin, where he had relatives. While his wife established a salon in an upscale shopping center, Gil struggled to secure the kind of wealthy clients and steady business he'd rounded up in Los Angeles. Though he had a talent for projecting success, he'd overdrawn his business bank account, and he was facing foreclosure on his home. In late February 2020 he had eleven dollars in the bank.

By this time, he'd found temporary work providing security at Charles Maund Toyota. He was hired mainly to deter run-of-the-mill vandalism—nothing that required his claimed level of expertise. But now Gil had a new mission: to figure out who was extorting Erik and put an end to the threats.

Erik gave Gil the blackmailer's phone number and the name mentioned in the message, Layla Love. Gil asked an acquaintance who worked at a private security firm to help him out, and by the next day, he had identified "Layla Love" as Holly Williams, of Nashville, who had an on-again-off-again boyfriend named William Lanway. Someone should approach William and Holly and negotiate with one or both of them, Gil told Erik. The encounter wouldn't be violent, and it wouldn't be illegal. It would mostly require on-the-ground surveillance, Gil said. He could arrange a few days of that for $50,000.

To surveil Holly and Bill in Nashville, Gil wanted all-stars—"the best money can buy," as he later called them, guys he didn't have to "second-guess or micromanage," though some on the team of military vets he assembled would decide that achieving the objective justified extreme tactics. He didn't have to look far to find someone who could run the operation from Austin. Just a few miles from Gil's house lived the perfect candidate, a guy whose wife was friends with his wife: Bryon Brockway. He'd deployed all over the world conducting special operations on behalf of the US Marines and the CIA. His voicemail greeting used to say he couldn't answer because he was "currently taking over the world."

Brockway boasted an extensive network of military contacts. His first hire was Adam Carey, a tall and lanky 29-year-old former Marine with hollowed-out cheeks and a dirty blond buzz cut. In Adam, he saw a kid who was eager for action. All too eager, as it turned out. Adam had done prison time for impersonating a police officer.

Brockway's next hire was a man who'd served as an Army Ranger, whose real name we've agreed not to use. We'll call him Red. He was recommended to Brockway by a mutual friend in the contract security world. In Red's telling, he'd been "blown up" by improvised bombs a few times and somehow walked away. If the plan was just to monitor a young woman's apartment, Adam and Red seemed a bit overqualified.

On March 7, 2020, Adam hopped in his black Ram truck, Red boarded a flight, and they met in Nashville to begin investigating. They didn't have the blackmailer's name, just a number. Adam set up a phone app called Pinger to anonymously text that number, then he reached out to Holly through one of her online escort sites, pretending to be a potential client. Both tactics went nowhere.

Figuring they could learn more by observing Holly and attempting to contact her when she was alone, Adam and Red staked out her apartment. After the first two days, they determined—as anyone would have—that Bill was a frequent visitor, if not a live-in boyfriend. In a report to Gil, Red wrote that he didn't believe Holly could be part of the blackmail scheme since it would be "professional suicide" for Holly "to intentionally breach the client's trust." Bill was a different story. "Mr. Lanway has previously demonstrated his controlling nature over Ms. Williams," he wrote, possibly in reference to posts she'd made on social media about her troubles with Bill. Red wasn't positive, but he suggested Bill had initiated the extortion and was acting alone.

Then Adam made a drastic proposal. He could eliminate the client's problem, he said, for $50,000 or $60,000. Unsure whether that was a joke, Red brushed him off at first, but then Adam kept casually suggesting things like zip-tying Bill to the steering wheel to get him to talk. He even went to Walmart and bought cable ties and burlap. And rather than continue to stake out the apartment from their rental car, Adam bushwhacked his way into a wooded area beside the complex and observed Holly's building from there. Red started thinking Adam was cavalier and unprofessional, "a loose cannon."

Soon he wouldn't be the only member of the team to hold this opinion. Because of the lack of progress, Bryon added yet another member with extensive military training: Tony Repinski, a 13-year veteran of the Navy SEAL Team Six. The one thing Tony was concerned with when he signed on to the Nashville trip? Stupidity. He must have been disappointed, then, to have encountered stupidity right off the bat. Hours after landing in Nashville, Tony said in testimony, he was sitting in his car surveilling Holly's apartment when—unannounced—Adam Carey opened Tony's back door, hopped in, and tossed a pistol in Tony's lap.

"What the f—?" Tony said and threw the gun back at him. To his thinking, this was just a surveillance operation. Adam continued the tough-guy banter. His temperament was immature, bordering on alarming, Tony thought. He didn't want to be held accountable for anything Adam did. Keep that guy away from me, Tony told Red.

It's all too easy, in retrospect, to see how the killings might've been avoided. Erik might have sought help from someone other than the Toyota dealership's freelance security man. Gil could have managed the job directly rather than delegating it to the ex-CIA husband of one of his wife's friends. Bryon, in selecting his team, could've given less priority to experience in Afghanistan and more to experience doing shoe-leather investigative work in the Nashville area.

Instead, the job of finding and talking to a blackmailer devolved into a gruesome show of machismo. By chance, in a Kroger parking lot on the afternoon of March 10, Red spotted Holly's white Acura, which Bill had taken without asking. Red called Adam and Tony, and Adam, once he'd arrived, let the air out of the car's tires. After Bill left the store, the three of them approached him. But Bill didn't appear intimidated. He just slammed the car door, looked Red in the eye, flipped him the bird, and drove away on the leaking tires. Presumably, the team concluded that Bill wasn't interested in talking.

It seems Bill didn't immediately tell Holly about his encounter when he returned the car. But when he did share what happened, she didn't believe his story, texting the next day, "You seriously think I'm going to believe some random person had the desire to come up to a random car for no good reason and let out the air?? Why!" Bill had a history of flattening her tires. It was part of a pattern. They'd fight, then he'd break something of hers, just so she'd come back to him, asking him to fix it.

"I almost got into a bad car accident!" she wrote. "My tire is putting off some major steam from me driving on it while it was flat! You could've killed me!"

Four days after the surveillance began, Gil's team members were no closer to having a face-to-face conversation with Bill or Holly. Red was heading out for another job, and Tony was getting ready to leave the following morning. Deciding he'd done enough outsourcing, Bryon left Austin and flew to Nashville himself.

What he didn't know was that Bill, too, had decided to step it up.

On the evening of March 11, Erik was at home when his landline rang. An unfamiliar voice was on the line, and Erik knew it was the blackmailer.

Erik freaked out—that's what Gil would later tell a jury. We don't know what was said on the call, but Bill also texted that he needed $25,000 by 8:00 that night, or he'd tell Sheri everything. The threat elicited no response.

"You lied to me Erik," Bill texted. "It's 8 now. I will follow through with everything. Thank you."

Just before midnight, as Tony was packing up his things in a Hampton Inn in southwest Nashville, he asked Bryon to come to his room. He had a sinking feeling about this job, and he wanted to warn Bryon about Adam's attitude. But Bryon showed up with Adam by his side.

Tony pivoted. Maybe we should ask the police to do a wellness check on Holly, Tony suggested, in case Bill was somehow controlling her actions.

Bryon and Adam told Tony they'd been hatching an alternative. They didn't get into specifics. They'd be moving forward without him, on to plan B.

Back in Austin, Gil Peled drove in the darkness toward Erik's house, passing stores and schools facing uncertain futures. A week earlier, the city had canceled the South by Southwest festival. Grocery stores were besieged by customers stocking up on toilet paper and hand sanitizer.

Outside the house, Erik opened the passenger door and slipped inside.

The guys on the ground had an offer, Gil said: they would take Bill out. He didn't mention the fee he'd discussed with Bryon—two shooters, at $60,000 per shooter, for a total of $120,000.

Whatever negotiation skills he'd picked up over the decades seemed to have abandoned Erik in this moment. "How much does something like that cost?" he asked. "Five hundred thousand?"

Yes, Gil said, $500,000 would cover it.

At that point, the team believed Bill was acting alone. Holly's texts with Bill, later obtained by investigators, would seem to back that up. Two months earlier, she'd filed a police complaint against Bill, and after he returned her car with flattened tires, she texted him that she was planning to confirm her statement with the district attorney. She added that she'd thrown his belongings outside and suggested he come pick them up before she doused them in bleach. "Have FUN in PRISON!" she wrote. "See you in court on the 16th motherf—er!"

The words hardly indicate two people acting in cahoots. On the contrary, Bill may even have been heading to jail, which would've complicated his blackmail attempt if it didn't end it entirely.

Yet at some point between midnight on March 11 and the morning of March 12, someone on the team—we still don't know why—decided that Holly was in on the blackmail attempt. So Adam and Bryon offered a new deal: $200,000, which the two shooters would split, to kill Holly Williams and Bill Lanway. Gil then set a new price with Erik: $750,000.

On the morning of March 13, a construction worker arrived at his jobsite a few miles away from Holly's apartment. Down in a ditch alongside a gravel road, he spotted a white Acura. He walked closer. Inside, he saw two bodies: a petite woman with black hair hunched over the rear floorboard and a large man fully inverted in the passenger seat.

Detectives from the Metro Nashville Police Department conducted the first investigation of the murders. They pulled bullet fragments from the Acura and gathered prints from interior and exterior blood spatter. They began scouring the couple's social media accounts and text messages. They also retrieved surveillance footage from Holly's apartment.

In video from outside the apartment recorded just before they were killed, Holly and Bill can be seen exiting the apartment together, even though just hours earlier they were sending acrimonious texts back and forth. Something has reunited them. Cautiously, they creep out the front door—first Holly, in a black knit hat, followed by Bill, in a blue ball cap—and walk down the short, dimly lit pathway to the parking lot.

Earlier, Adam had moved the camera to face Holly's door, so that it wouldn't record what happened in the parking lot. Nevertheless, the camera continued to pick up sounds from there. That recording, in the words of Brooke Farzad, one of the prosecutors on the case, "was very, very difficult to listen to."

You can hear them get into a vehicle. You can hear that vehicle start up. Then Bill yells "What the f—?" Shots follow. Loud banging noises accompany high-pitched screaming. Holly begs, "Please God, help me. Help me!" Bill's voice goes silent. You can still hear Holly screaming for several minutes before the car drives away and her screams trail off.

Investigators obtained Bill's Pinger messages and from those identified Erik Maund as a person of interest. Once they learned that he was a wealthy car dealer in Texas, they decided it was time to contact the FBI.

Special agent David Som had been with the bureau since 2008. He has short black hair, a thin frame, a smooth complexion, and a methodical manner, and for almost a year after he was handed the case in 2020, he pieced together every bit of relevant information he could. While Som didn't agree to an interview, prosecutor Rob McGuire, who worked with him on the case, told us, "We really wanted to try to find, wherever possible, hard evidence that told us one way or the other whether a person was involved or not. And that takes time."

Once Adam Carey was identified as a suspect and Erik Maund was identified as a person of interest, Som tried to figure out who they were talking to in February and March of 2020. He gathered phone records and made a connection to Gil Peled. Then he tried to figure out who Gil had been talking to. Eventually, he learned that Erik Maund had transferred $150,000 to Gilad Peled the day of the murders, which was "very significant," said McGuire.

In January 2021, a search warrant for Gil's iCloud account allowed Som access to a critical piece of evidence: a "situation report" from Red, reporting on the surveillance of Holly and Bill. The murders, Som realized, stemmed from an effort to surveil these two victims.

"By the summer of 2021, we had really done everything that we knew to do covertly," said McGuire. "There were no more bank records to search. There were no more phone records to obtain. There was no more iCloud data to gather. And we had a decision to make." What they'd uncovered pointed toward Erik but fell short of an airtight case against him. They still felt like they could get more, better evidence.

What Som needed was a confidential source, someone he could leverage. And he was in luck. Red had just applied for a job at a federal agency that required a security clearance. Som met him at the interview, inside a government building in Virginia. At first Red pretended he didn't know anything about a double homicide, but as the conversation continued, he realized he was in a tight spot. Trapped, Red agreed to go undercover, though he was terrified of being found out.

"Hey, been a minute," he texted Adam. "Had a potential job come up, similar in nature to last March. Client is willing to throw a lot of money at it. This is in the very early stages just wanted to know if it's something you're interested in."

"Always interested," Adam responded.

With Agent Som hovering nearby, recording, the two men switched to the phone. Red, following Som's instructions, told Adam he needed his advice. Adam weighed in on pricing and tricks of the trade—bring long gloves, he said, and if there's a site where you plan to dump the bodies, be sure to scout it ahead of time. Afterward, make the weapon vanish like pixie dust.

A few days later, Red and Adam met in person at a brewpub in Raleigh, North Carolina, but in the interim Adam had talked to Bryon and had grown nervous. He patted Red down. Before long, though, he began venting about Erik and other clients like him. "Man, why don't these guys hire SOF [special operations forces] dudes to go get them the right prostitute? Right?" Adam said. "Like just bring me along on your travels. I'm gonna bring you a chick that's gonna do everything you want and this will never happen."

"Yeah, it's not hard," Red said. "It's just idiots with money being f—king idiots with money."

Red also met with Bryon, first at a noisy Austin brewery, then retreating to Bryon's car to have a more private conversation. There, Bryon started recalling the particulars of the crime.

He and Adam had shot both Holly and Bill in the apartment parking lot, he explained, but while Bill stopped responding, Holly was still conscious.

They drove her Acura down the highway to a quiet site they'd scouted earlier in the day, he said, and Adam took over from there.

"He finished it in the back seat," Bryon said. "And he totally got my respect for that. A lot of guys with females they'll f—ing have a bleeding heart."

When Som and McGuire heard the recordings, they knew they had their case. In November 2021 they sought indictments for Bryon Brockway, Adam Carey, Erik Maund, and Gilad Peled.

Keeping a low profile was easy enough in the pandemic months that followed the murders. Even for Erik. "What else are you going to do?" said Shithole owner Salem Joseph. "You're not going to tell everybody what happened." Erik paid off the $905,000 (the fee for the murders plus taxes) and even hired Gil's company, Speartip, to provide overnight security at the Toyota dealership. When Erik went hunting, he'd save Gil deer meat. Gil would buy ammunition for Erik and others in his circle. And when Sheri Maund found a suspicious number for a "Brandon Love" in Erik's phone (it's unclear if "Brandon Love" was Erik's code for "Layla Love"), it was Gil whom Erik asked to provide a fake polygraph test.

On December 7, 2021, Erik agreed to help his fixer in turn. He was preparing for an upcoming hunting trip with friends when Gil sent him a text. "Hey bro when you get a chance can you please review Speartip on Google."

Erik gave the company five stars. "Speartip is very professional and on top of it," he wrote. "They get the job done in an expedited time. Couldn't imagine using anyone else!!"

Three days later, the FBI brought the hammer down. In San Diego, agents arrested Bryon Brockway as he was headed to his son's Marine Corps boot camp graduation. On the opposite coast, the FBI arrested Adam Carey and searched his small North Carolina home, where agents found almost $60,000 in bundled cash hidden around the place. Down in Austin, ten FBI agents surrounded Gil Peled at the airport and took him in for questioning.

Gil must have known he had to outmaneuver the others. With the feds watching, he picked up his phone, opened his Signal app, and dialed Erik's number.

"Man, we have a problem," Gil said on the recorded line. Erik was with a hunting buddy, driving up Interstate 35, but he pulled over to the side of the road, got out of the car, and walked down an embankment. He didn't spot the FBI agent who'd been following him at a distance.

Gil told him that one of the Nashville shooters wanted an extra $25,000 to keep quiet. Erik was wary and retrieved a drink from his car. Once he was back on the line Gil assured him that Bryon would try to calm the guy down. But if the shooter didn't comply, he asked, did Erik want Bryon to take care of it?

"Give me a number," Erik said.

"One hundred," Gil said.

"Honestly, I think I'd rather take care of it permanently than do the twenty-five," Erik said.

Still living in a world where he paid to have troublesome people killed and moved on with his life, Erik said he'd wire $150,000 to Speartip, "like we did last time." He then continued his drive until officers arrested him near San Marcos.

When news of Erik's murder-for-hire charges hit Austin, many in the country club set wondered if authorities had trumped up the charges. "The way they'd defend him is to say: He didn't say 'kill them,' he'd say 'take care of it,' and it was misinterpreted," said one Austin Country Club member. The guys at the Shithole were dumbfounded. "I could not believe it," said Joe Joseph. Salem had a similar reaction. "I don't believe it. No way," he said.

A few Maund haters surfaced online, including Justin Wright, who'd worked with him at a VW-Audi dealership. "He definitely wasn't the brightest bulb," Wright wrote on a Reddit thread. A disgruntled restaurant service worker

who'd waited on Erik and his father for a few years com-
mented, "They're all a bunch of pricks and I hope he rots."

In the aftermath of the arrests, the Maunds sold their car
business to a Fortune 300 company called Group 1 Automotive for an undisclosed amount. It's possible the family
was compelled to sell. "They lost the Toyota dealership over
this deal," said Wallace, who spoke from experience, having
owned a Chevrolet dealership. "There's a [clause] in all of our
agreements with Chevrolet . . . and they stick to it. If you get
in some kind of jam, like this, you're done."

The sale would give the Maunds an influx of cash. Erik
hired a team of high-powered attorneys who must have
buoyed his confidence. Erik's father, Doug, had hope—
"more hope than was reasonable," said the Austin Country
Club member, adding that Doug would wrestle the phrase
"when Erik gets home" into conversations.

Erik's loyal friends stayed in touch with him, calling him
and sending him books to pass the time in jail, as he waited
for his day in court alongside Adam and Bryon.

The prosecution painted Erik as cold-blooded, stressing
that in his recording with Gil, he talked as if he were
"speaking to the help." Erik's attorneys countered that Erik
just told Gil to "take care of the problem," and when the
FBI approached Gil, Gil made up a story to save himself.
"Gil Peled could take a small problem and turn it into a
big problem and put a price tag on it," said one of Erik's
attorneys. To explain Erik's demeanor in the undercover
recording, they explained that Erik had been drinking all
day—and the day before.

In November 2023, inside a federal courthouse in Nash-ville, Adam, Bryon, and Erik were tried for murder for hire. (Angling for leniency, Gil had already pleaded guilty.) There were times during the eleven-day trial when Erik appeared relaxed, smiling and even laughing in conversations with his attorneys. But on the last day, a jury foreman announced that Erik was guilty of the murder-for-hire charge. As Erik listened, he sat still, as if he were trying to remember to breathe.

Bryon and Adam were found guilty of the same charge, and two additional ones: conspiracy to commit kidnapping, and kidnapping with death resulting. Each count carries a mandatory life sentence. A sentencing hearing will be held later this year, though appeals are in process.

As the verdict spread on text threads and social media posts, Wallace Lundgren noticed a shift in the mood about the trial. "The day before, you could get guys to argue with you that he was going to walk, and he didn't do it," he told us. The day after? "We haven't heard a peep from anyone."

Erik was now heir to a stockpile of money—some forty million dollars—he'd never see again. At the Shithole, his downfall epitomized a younger generation's foolishness. "If Charlie Maund was alive today, none of this would've hap-pened," Joe Joseph said. Charlie would have gotten him a divorce lawyer, paid up, and moved on. "Charlie, he came up the hard way. He knew about all that stuff."

But you don't need to have come up the hard way to understand that Erik had better options. As he tried to protect his family (and himself) from scandal, he thrust himself into a worse and much more public one. Erik and Sheri separated just a few weeks after the murders, with plans to divorce. His parents and siblings attended his trial, but Sheri and the kids were nowhere in the room. As for embarrassment, well, the country club set probably knew about the verdict within hours, while the car empire he was meant to inherit vanished.

If you drive around Central Texas today, you'll eventually see a truck with a Charles Maund Toyota license plate holder, marked by the company's logo—the shape of Texas colored like the state flag. Some day, years from now, a driver might see one of those and wonder: Whatever happened to Charles Maund Toyota? A silence will follow. And that will be Erik Maund's legacy.

The Heiress at Harvard Who Helped Revolutionize Murder Investigations— and the Case She Couldn't Forget

by Patricia Wen

Frances Glessner Lee didn't want to be known as a "rich woman who didn't have enough to do." In her 60s, she became a pioneer of forensic science.

O n an afternoon in July 1940, several day laborers were walking through the woods in Dartmouth, Massachusetts, searching for blueberries on their lunch break. About 12 feet off the trail, under the branches of a pine, one of them stumbled across what looked like a brown burlap sack. As he edged closer, he realized with horror it wasn't a sack at all. It was a dead body.

Police officers arrived at the grim scene. The victim appeared to be a young woman, but her corpse was significantly decomposed. Not far away was a secluded dirt road known as a Lovers' Lane for parking couples wanting privacy. A rifle shooting range was also nearby—a half-dozen .22-caliber cartridges were found near the woman's body. A heavy rope encircled her neck and was tied to her wrists. She wore a brown plaid dress and one of her silk stockings bound her ankles.

It was the most brutal murder the local police had seen in years. Detectives of the era received little training in crime scene investigation, and they were in over their heads. It was time to call in, perhaps begrudgingly, the forensic scientists from Harvard Medical School—the "college boys," as the officers sometimes put it.

The teletype message arrived at 2:30 that same afternoon, July 31, summoning staff from Harvard's new department of legal medicine. Dr. Alan Moritz and his colleagues drove from Boston to Dartmouth right away, and were relieved to find police hadn't disturbed the body. A Harvard pathologist had once arrived at a home to find officers scrubbing blood evidence from the wall—they didn't want to bump against it and stain their uniforms.

Examining the scene closely, Moritz knew there was much to do, including a careful autopsy, leaf and insect analysis, and experiments with the rope. But he could already conclude this much, judging by the broken stems of nearby underbrush—she'd likely been murdered elsewhere, and dragged by the feet to this spot.

Although it would eventually become clear that life hadn't been kind to this young woman, she would receive one of the most advanced death investigations of the time. And it would be largely thanks to the most unlikely of figures: a strong-willed, unconventional heiress in her 60s named

Frances Glessner Lee, who was on a mission to revolutionize murder investigations. In the years to come, Lee's life, and the woman's death, would connect the two in unexpected ways.

Lee stepped into the male-dominated world of detective work later in life, like a real-world Miss Marple from Agatha Christie's novels. Lee, who favored brimless hats and dark dresses, was described in 1949 by a reporter as "motherly looking" and "amply girthed." But a police detective she trained offered a more telling description. She was "unquestionably," he said, "one of the world's most astute criminologists."

Lee was the driving force behind Harvard's new department of legal medicine, the first program of its kind in the United States. She'd pursue her mission of professionalizing murder investigations with single-minded focus, despite significant odds stacked against her at Harvard and in local police departments across the country. She contributed much of her personal fortune, political acumen, and even her artistic talents to making sure all victims—man or woman, rich or poor—got investigations that were full and fair.

With resolve as deep as her pockets, she'd will the department into existence, be appointed an official consultant, and be named a founder of crime scene investigation. And among her many other accomplishments, it would turn out, was engineering a way to make sure the woman in the woods would not be forgotten.

Frances Glessner Lee's quest to reform homicide investigations started at a low moment in her life. A divorced mother of three adult children, she had grown weary of her image as a rich woman with too much time on her hands.

Born in 1878, Lee grew up on one of the most affluent streets in Chicago, in a 17,000-square-foot mansion that is now a museum. Her father's fortune came from building International Harvester, the maker of agricultural and construction machinery. She and her older brother were both bright and received a rigorous education at home by tutors, including learning multiple languages. He went off to Harvard, but she wouldn't go to college. Her parents believed "a lady didn't go to school," she once told a reporter years later.

Lee was also taught how to run a household, be a generous hostess, and pursue crafts such as needlework. She showed an aptitude for noticing the smallest details and significant artistic talent, according to *18 Tiny Deaths*, a biography of her by Bruce Goldfarb. For her mother's birthday, she once made a scale model of the 90-member Chicago Symphony Orchestra, where each musician was recognizable and had a miniature instrument and tiny musical score.

In her late teens, Lee was sent on a 14-month grand tour of Europe, then introduced to Chicago high society as a debutante in November 1897. Just shy of her 20th birthday, she married a Southern lawyer named Blewett Harrison Lee, a distant relative of Robert E. Lee. They had three children, but Lee felt chronically unhappy and hemmed in by the marriage. In her mid-30s, she took the then-unusual step of obtaining a divorce. She'd never marry again.

Over the years, Lee adopted New England as her home, dividing her time between her family's 1,400-acre summer estate, The Rocks, in Bethlehem, New Hampshire, and the Ritz-Carlton hotel in Boston. In this city in the early 1930s, a series of conversations with Dr. George Magrath, a close Harvard classmate of her brother's, inspired a new intellectual passion—the investigation of murder.

Magrath was a longtime Suffolk County medical examiner who, over his career, testified in some 2,000 court cases and investigated 21,000 deaths. A dapper dresser, he cut an unusual figure in town. He wore pince-nez for glasses, smoked a pipe, and lived for years at Boston's private St. Botolph Club, then on Newbury Street. He ate only one meal a day—at midnight.

Lee liked him immediately.

She listened, enthralled, as Magrath shared stories of complex autopsies, many of which revealed surprising causes of death missed by bumbling police. In some cases, murders were masked as suicides; at other times, police mistook suicides for murders. His passion for the inner workings of the human body—and what clues they reveal about death and a person's place in society—mesmerized Lee.

She began to join Magrath at autopsies and crime scenes, poring through murder case files and tracking state-by-stage legislation related to death investigations. She and Magrath shared a vision of the system of trained medical examiners—which had existed in Suffolk County in Massachusetts since 1877—going nationwide.

Lee wanted it to replace the patchwork system of coroners, typically funeral directors, political appointees, or elected officials with no medical training making critical decisions about causes of death. That system dominated the country in the 1940s. Today, more than half of Americans live in areas governed by coroners.

In 1931, at the age of 53, Lee gave $4,500 a year (about $90,000 in today's dollars) to fund a Harvard Medical School professorship for Magrath, the first such forensic science position in the country. She'd soon donate a library in Magrath's honor with 1,000 volumes she'd collected, including the memoirs President Garfield's assassin penned while he awaited the gallows.

But her role went deeper than money. With her own desk at Harvard, she worked as Magrath's teaching assistant, and later was named a consultant. To Lee it felt like finally, in middle age, she was contributing something important—that she had a mission. "For many years I have hoped that I might do something in my lifetime that should be of significant value to the community," she once told a reporter. She "was sincerely glad to find that my opportunity to serve lay here at Harvard Medical School."

The intense ties between Magrath, the lifelong bachelor, and Lee, the long-divorced heiress, sometimes raised eyebrows. "At times Lee bordered on the coquettish, referring to herself in unpublished writing for Magrath as 'Ye Saucy Scrybe,'" Goldfarb writes in Lee's biography, "and yet in correspondence between the two, they never used terms of endearment. Lee always called him Dr. Magrath, and to him, she was Mrs. Frances G. Lee."

As Magrath's health began failing—he died in 1938 at 68—Lee's obsession with forensic science did not diminish. She donated the equivalent of about $5 million to start the department of legal medicine, a place to teach cutting-edge methods in blood spatter analysis, gunpowder chemistry, and more. She suggested to Harvard she might be willing to write an even larger gift into her will, perhaps as much as $22 million in today's dollars.

Lee's new department, she vowed, was not to be corrupted by politics or other outside influences. "We testify for no party," its official credo read, "neither for the prosecution nor for the defense but for the Truth alone."

When Lee stayed at the Ritz, she'd eat meals at her usual table overlooking the Public Garden. On August 1, 1940, if she'd been reading *The Boston Daily Globe*, she'd have found it weighty with portents of looming war. Lowering the draft age was in discussion, and the US House had just passed the biggest appropriations bill in history, $5 billion to build warships and warplanes. The 23-year-old son of the ambassador to Great Britain had just published his Harvard senior thesis, "Why England Slept." His name was John F. Kennedy.

But above all the stories, above everything on the front page of that evening's edition, stretched a headline in bold capital letters: GIRL, 22, TRUSSED AND SLAIN.

The victim discovered in the Dartmouth woods two days earlier had been tentatively identified as Irene Perry, a 22-year-old single mother who couldn't have come from a background more different than Lee's. If not for the shocking brutality of Perry's murder—and the provocative circumstances around what the press nationwide immediately dubbed the "Lover's Lane Slaying"—it's doubtful her death, like her life, would have risen to the notice of the newspapers at all.

Perry was 15 years old when her mother died, and dropped out of school to care for her father, four brothers, and eight sisters, news reports said. When she was around 20, she had a baby on her own. The Catholic immigrant family—"Perry" was an Anglicized version of their Portuguese name—lived in a modest home in New Bedford, where Perry's father worked at the country club as a greenskeeper. Hers was a hard life. Later, some said she dreamed of disappearing to Europe where she could start anew.

She'd last been seen on the evening of June 29, when she left her 2-year-old son, Donald, at home and headed to a store about a half mile away to run an errand, with a dollar from her father in hand. A slim woman with dark hair and large, deep-set eyes, she wore a brown plaid jacket and dress and a blouse with puffed sleeves. It was the last time her family saw her alive.

Perry's father didn't report her missing until the next day. She'd had boyfriends, and apparently this wasn't the first time she hadn't returned home at night. A month later, he got a heart-stopping call: Police asked him to come to a funeral parlor to look at a body. His daughter's remains were badly decomposed, but he recognized her clothes.

It would be up to Dr. Moritz and the Harvard forensic scientists to make a positive identification, using evidence they'd gathered from the crime scene and her body. They'd also be tasked with solving a series of mysteries that stacked like nesting dolls.

When did Perry die and where?

How was the murder committed and who was the culprit?

And why would anyone want to kill Irene Perry in the first place?

⊶

Lee didn't know anything about living a life as hard as Perry's, but she knew what it was like to be a woman in the early 20th century. How the wishes of a girl's parents, and then a woman's husband, could circumscribe a life. What it was like to dream of a new start in a new place. How it felt to be looked down upon.

"Chief amongst the difficulties I have had to meet," Lee once wrote in a private letter, "have been the facts that I never went to school, that I had no [professional degree] letters after my name, and that I was placed in the category of 'rich woman who didn't have enough to do.'"

Still, Lee had a preternatural ability to prevail when people made the mistake of underestimating her, including in the halls of Harvard Medical School, which didn't admit female students until 1945.

In 1935, she decided the department of legal medicine needed more office space, training her eye on a set of offices occupied by the pharmacology department. When her written request to the dean for that space was rebuffed, she took her case to Harvard's president—he also resisted.

She waited three months and then wrote to the president again. "I do not feel that I can let our decision pass without a protest," she wrote, "and request that you give this problem a little further study."

She got the office space.

Lee tangled with medical school leaders in other ways, including over priorities for the department. She believed Harvard should play a larger role in training police officers, so they could improve their ability to spot clues at crime scenes and gather and protect evidence for medical examiners. But Harvard leaders were more focused on research and teaching—plus, they found assisting the local police expensive—and largely dismissed the police work she supported.

Lee had a theory about one of the reasons why. "Men are dubious of an elderly woman with a cause," she observed. "My problem is to convince them that I am not trying to butt in or run anything. Also, I have to sell them on the fact that I know what I am talking about."

As Lee pushed for change, in Massachusetts and across the nation, she tapped influential people. She once arranged a meeting with FBI director J. Edgar Hoover to discuss forensic medicine. And she developed a close relationship with Malden-born Erle Stanley Gardner, author of *The Case of the Fenced-In Woman* and other Perry Mason mysteries. He'd become a booster of her cause, and he later dedicated a novel to her.

Lee's goal was to eliminate human bias from death investigations. "[F]ar too often the investigator 'has a hunch,' and looks for and finds only the evidence to support it, disregarding any other evidence that may be present," she wrote in an article for a criminology journal. "This attitude would be calamitous in investigating an actual case."

⸺⸻⸺

For nearly two weeks after Irene Perry's body was discovered, Dr. Moritz and his colleagues at the department of legal medicine worked feverishly. This was one of the new department's first major cases, and Lee knew high-profile investigations could demonstrate the importance of forensic medicine across the country.

To understand the circumstances of Perry's death, the scientists would need to summon all the disciplines at their disposal, including medicine, chemistry, entomology, and botany.

Moritz confirmed the body was Perry. In addition to her clothing, everything else matched: her height (about 5-foot-2), her estimated weight (100 to 110 pounds), and her short brown hair. Dental characteristics made it certain.

A key question was this: Did Perry die the night of June 29, 1940, when she disappeared, or days or weeks later? The answer could help police rule out suspects—or identify a killer.

At the crime scene in Dartmouth, the scientists found that the plants trapped beneath Perry's body, including lowbush blueberries, had reached full leaf—and then abruptly stopped growing. Considering when that stage was reached for that species, her body must have been left there sometime after June 15. Meanwhile, the insect larvae found on Perry were in a stage of development that put her time of death at four or more weeks before she was found. Combining this analysis with the date of Perry's disappearance pointed to a time of death very close to when she was last seen.

Moritz knew the heavy rope found wrapped around the victim's neck and wrists required careful observation.

To determine if Perry was strangled to death, he measured the first loop of rope around her neck. It was 10.5 inches. That was likely tight enough to kill her, but her neck was so decomposed Moritz couldn't be sure. He assembled 50 female volunteers between the ages of 18 and 25, so he could measure their necks. None had a neck circumference less than 12.5 inches.

When Moritz and his staff tightened a rope on the necks of these volunteers, they found merely a half-inch caused "great discomfort," and 3/4 inch "could not be tolerated." The evidence showed Perry was a "victim of homicidal strangulation," Moritz wrote in his report.

A close examination of Perry's skeletal remains yielded one last surprising finding: Fetal bones. At the time of death, Perry was pregnant with her second child.

"Irene Perry was unmarried," Moritz wrote in his report, issued on August 10. "The finding of the bones of an unborn three-month-old fetus in the abdominal cavity of the dead woman provides a possible motive for her death."

In the understated tone of a scientist, he noted a new avenue deserving of inquiry: "The desirability of attempting to learn the identity of the man responsible for her pregnancy is obvious."

On the night of August 26, police arrested Frank Pedro, a 25-year-old New Bedford laborer, and charged him with murder. They had interviewed dozens of people, and finally zeroed in on Pedro because of the unique characteristics of the rope in the murder.

Investigators had traced it to a manufacturer in New York, where a strand of rope had been accidentally made with 24 threads, rather than the usual 21. After that manufacturing mistake, the rope was trucked to a Long Island wholesaler, and then to a job site at an estate in Rhode Island where Pedro's relative worked. The same rope—the same 24 threads—was found in Pedro's basement, police said.

The forensic scientists and police had uncovered the evidence. The rest was up to the legal system of the day.

Reporters were in the Bristol County Superior courthouse in May 1941, when Pedro's trial began. Newspapers had been covering every unseemly twist of the case, drawing an increasingly unsympathetic picture of a promiscuous young woman, one who'd had her first child out of wedlock and was pregnant with another. Records show lawyers were concerned potential jurors might be swayed by the salacious details they'd read.

Judge Walter Collins presided over the trial, swearing in 12 jurors who would ultimately decide if the defendant was guilty. As was customary at the time, it would be limited to men—women in Massachusetts were barred from sitting on criminal juries until the 1950s.

Prosecutors outlined their case: Perry's murder was likely committed shortly after her disappearance on June 29, 1940, and at some place between her home and the rifle range. She was killed somewhere else, then dragged into the woods. Dr. Moritz was called to the stand, testifying that "the probable cause of death was strangulation."

The rope found in Pedro's cellar and around Perry's neck "were identical in every respect," a police captain said from the witness stand.

Prosecutors also pointed to the motive. Pedro was a married man, with a baby boy at home. He'd admitted during police questioning that he had been romantically involved with Perry for several years—that he had "illicit relations with the girl over an extended period," in the words of a news story. They'd even gone parking near Lovers' Lane, he admitted, in the area where Perry's body was discovered.

The forensic evidence and the police interviews appeared strong. When court-appointed defense lawyer Philip Barnet began his interrogations, however, he worked to introduce doubt into key aspects of the government's case.

Barnet put Pedro on the stand to profess his innocence. He told jurors that he'd ended his relationship with Perry some months before her murder, in March 1940, because he was married, had a child, and, as he put it, "didn't want trouble with his wife." Pedro insisted Perry never told him she was pregnant.

Barnet called his own rope specialist to the stand, who said the piece in Pedro's house was different from the type found around Perry's neck. In fact, Barnet disputed that

Perry had been strangled to death at all. What if the scene was staged to look that way?

Barnet presented another theory that had the potential to turn the jury against Perry. The victim, he suggested, may have died from an "attempted illegal surgery"—a reference to a botched abortion—that was later covered up to look like a murder, perhaps by whoever performed the procedure.

After hearing testimony over two weeks, the jury deliberated for less than two hours. Foreman Frederick Kerry, a Taunton shop owner, delivered the verdict: "Not guilty."

⁂

Records don't show if Lee and the Harvard experts were surprised by the verdict, or if law enforcement thought a guilty man went free. Perry's name disappeared from the headlines. Her son, Donald, would be raised by her extended family.

But in the months that followed, Lee plunged with obsessive energy into a massive, multiyear project largely focused on deaths like Perry's. It would combine Lee's childhood training in the "women's work" of sewing and crafting with her later-life passion for crime scene investigation.

She created 18 immensely detailed, dollhouse-like dioramas of crime scenes. But these were not toys. They were tools to train detectives. To come up with her scenarios, Lee studied real life case files and police photographs.

"My whole object," she once explained, "has been to improve the administration of justice, to standardize the methods, to sharpen the existing tools as well as to supply new tools, and to make it easier for the law enforcement officers to 'do a good job' and to give the public 'a square deal.'"

Lee called them The Nutshell Studies of Unexplained Death, after a police saying: "Convict the guilty, clear the innocent, and find the truth in a nutshell." The point was to learn to look closely at the evidence.

In a miniature bathroom scene, a woman is dead in a bathtub, her stiff legs splayed out and water running over her face. *Did she have an accident? Or did the rigor mortis in her legs suggest she was killed elsewhere and moved into the tub?* In a kitchen, a dead woman lies near an open oven door. *Was this a case of suicide due to the gas or a clever imitation?* At the scene of a fire evidence pointed toward the blaze starting beneath the wife's bed. *Was the husband capable of murder?*

Lee spared no time or expense in making her nutshells, spending months and as much as $135,000 in today's money on each. She personally made many of the items within the crime scenes, working with her carpenter in New Hampshire. Tiny pencils contained real lead, a police whistle can emit a shriek, and one room had a miniature Sherlock Holmes novel.

The minutely detailed models didn't portray the elegant spaces of Lee's own life—the mansions, the Ritz, the Chicago Symphony—but environments where working-class people lived and died, predominantly women. Lee is unlikely to have used the word feminist to describe herself, her biographers say, yet her dioramas often seem to point to the oppressed place of women in society.

"Her actions were much louder than her words," says Susan Marks, a documentary filmmaker whose second film about Lee's life will be screened in October at The Rocks estate. "Her actions were very much that women's voices had to be heard." In making the dioramas, Marks continues, "She chose quite a few situations in which women are murdered, including in places where they are supposed to be safe."

Lee's carpenter helped with construction, but Lee insisted on creating the victims herself. She took immense care with them, knitting tiny stockings with straight pins, placing a knife in a woman's chest, painting a face in the precise shade of red indicative of carbon-monoxide poisoning.

It's not a coincidence that Lee's murder scenes are often set in kitchens, bedrooms, and living rooms, explains Corinne May Botz, a photographer and author of the book *The Nutshell Studies of Unexplained Death*. "The nutshells can be viewed as precursors to the women's movement," she writes, "because they depict the isolation of women in the home and expose the violence that originates and is enacted there."

The nutshell studies would become the centerpiece teaching tool of one of Lee's most lasting legacies: one-week seminars designed to teach state and local police officers from across the country about medical forensics. The seminars would include presentations from experts on the latest advances in criminology, then conclude with training on her nutshell studies.

Lee presided over her invitation-only annual seminars like a regal chairwoman. They included a multicourse banquet at the Ritz with elaborate flowers arranged by Lee herself. The hotel spent thousands of dollars on gold-leaf dinnerware to be reserved only for the seminars, at her insistence. (She was "probably the fussiest patron the hotel ever had," the general manager later said, "and we loved her.")

One year, Lee allowed her friend Gardner, the novelist, to attend one of her seminars. Lee's instructors accomplished feats of deduction "little short of astounding," he wrote, and said students could learn more from her crime scenes in an hour than in "months of abstract study."

Gardner would never dare put one of Lee's graduates in one of his novels, he noted—that detective would solve the mystery a hundred or so pages before Perry Mason.

⚬⚊⚬

In the summer of 1946, Lee's nutshell studies captured the attention of an editor at *Life* magazine, which published photos and an article about them. That story, in turn, caught the eye of filmmakers at Metro-Goldwyn-Mayer.

The MGM executives reached out to Lee and Moritz, suggesting a film about the Harvard department. They offered a working title, *Murder at Harvard*, and submitted a draft script that featured "Mrs. Lee" as a central figure in improving the way homicide investigations were handled.

"Confirming our telephone conversations," MGM's Samuel Marx wrote to her in February 1948, "we feel that an interesting motion picture of a semi-documentary nature can be made dealing with your work in the field of crime."

Lee was pleased her department was gaining notice, but never liked lavish amounts of media attention on her. She wanted the department's work on behalf of the public to take center stage. When meeting with MGM, she said she had just the right story to focus on. It was a murder case she hadn't been able to forget, even nearly a decade after it ended without justice for the victim.

Don't focus on me, Lee said. *Focus on the Irene Perry case.*

The Hollywood executive listened.

"After our very pleasant dinner," Marx wrote Lee later in 1948, "I went to New Bedford, Massachusetts, and investigated the Irene Perry case in which the Department of Legal Medicine played such an important part of the solution."

The script was written and the movie went into production.

By 1949, the Harvard department of legal medicine was weakening. Dr. Moritz left Harvard to head a pathology center in Cleveland, and remained influential in the field. After President John F. Kennedy's assassination, he gave expert testimony on the autopsy.

Moritz's replacement struggled to run the program with a firm hand. "In my opinion," Lee wrote, "the Department is rapidly dying on its feet."

In the years to come, she worked hard to get the medical examiner system adopted in more states, but found local resistance throughout the country. She also struggled with serious medical issues, including breast cancer. Her fears about mortality caused her to be more open about some of the challenges—especially as a woman—that she faced in her work.

"For me, it has been a long, discouraging struggle against petty jealousies, crass stupidities, and an obstinate unwillingness to learn that has required all the enthusiasm, patience, courage, and tact that I could muster," she wrote to her trusted advisers. "Also, being a woman has made it difficult at times to make the men believe in the project I was furthering."

She appeared to reserve her harshest criticism for Harvard, saying it had a deserved reputation of being "old fogeyish and ungrateful and stupid." She decided in the end against giving the school any money in her will, and urged her advisers to monitor her previous gifts closely. "Harvard is clever and sly and will need to be watched constantly or she will take advantage of you and apply any funds you may grant her to her own purposes," she wrote.

In 1962, at age 83, Lee died of complications from cancer. She was buried at Maple Street Cemetery in Bethlehem, New Hampshire. At The Rocks, a few miles away, the state installed a historical marker calling her the "mother of forensic science."

Some of her fears about Harvard soon began coming true. The university shuttered the department of legal medicine in 1966, and her nutshell studies were handed over—"on loan for an indefinite period," says a university spokesman—to the Maryland medical examiner's office, which had close ties with Lee. The Magrath library was folded into the main one at the medical school. The professorship she'd endowed sat vacant for many years, and for the last two decades the position has focused on bioethics.

When the Smithsonian American Art Museum in Washington, DC, opened an exhibit of Lee's nutshell studies in 2017, some Harvard physicians broached the idea of bringing the dioramas to a Boston museum. But the proposal got mired in questions of logistics, and still-unresolved legal issues over who actually controls them.

The Maryland medical examiner's office, however, has continued Lee's tradition of holding the homicide training seminars. This year's installment, in October, will include expert-led sessions on strangulation, poisoning, and other causes of death. As is customary, the program will feature investigations of Lee's nutshells.

Lee's files at Harvard are full of letters from medical examiners and police officers from across the country, saying they are deeply indebted to her for making them more observant detectives, even as the field of forensics has come to include DNA analysis and other advances she never could have dreamed of.

"This was the essence of Frances Glessner Lee," says Thomas Andrew, a former chief medical examiner in New Hampshire. "Look at what the scene tells us."

<hr />

Irene Perry was buried at New Bedford's St. John the Baptist Cemetery, in an unmarked grave that is numbered 976.

Helen Craig, now 79, is Irene's only surviving sibling, the child of Irene's father and his second wife. She tries sometimes to visit her half sister's grave. She says her father spoke little of Irene's death, but understands why. "He was heartbroken by it," she says.

Relatives say Perry—and her murder—were almost never openly discussed at family gatherings, and some surmise it was because her case had the whiff of scandal. "Nobody talked about it," says Charles Lackie, a retired Dartmouth police sergeant whose grandmother was Perry's sister. "It's like it never happened."

But for those who look closely, Irene Perry's death and life are memorialized in a different way. MGM had followed Lee's advice, and focused not on her, but on the case of a working-class woman from an immigrant family in New Bedford.

"Irene Perry's case is exactly the kind of death that would have been overlooked," says Goldfarb, Lee's biographer, "if not for Lee's determination that all victims, regardless of their background, receive rigorous investigations."

Renamed *Mystery Street*, the film premiered nationwide in 1950, receiving many positive reviews. Starring a young

Ricardo Montalban as a detective from the local Portuguese community, it was the first forensic-science procedural put to film. It was also the first commercial movie filmed in Boston, with scenes of Beacon Hill and Harvard Square. (The original title, *Murder at Harvard*, was changed after the university complained it would sully its brand.)

Although *Mystery Street* is fictionalized—the victim isn't a dark-haired woman named Irene, but a blonde named Vivian—it includes many similarities to the Perry case. The skeletal remains of a young Massachusetts woman are discovered in a remote area, and the killer remains on the loose. Harvard pathologists led by Dr. McAdoo, modeled on Dr. Moritz, use forensics to establish the facts of her murder. When examining her skeleton, they find the tiny bones of a fetus.

The biggest difference may be that, in the movies, the Perry character gets the Hollywood ending that no amount of forensic science could deliver her in real life. Though police initially apprehend the wrong man, they successfully chase down the real killer. He's a married man, a father, and had been the victim's lover. After she confronted him about ignoring her, saying she was "in a jam," he shot her.

The movie also portrays the hard life of single working women at the time, struggling to pay rent and seeing relationships with men as one way to gain stability in their lives. It is Vivian's boarding house roommate, Jackie, who first reports to police that she has mysteriously disappeared. Jackie worries something terrible has happened to her.

When investigators interview her, she reflects on how hard life could be for women like her and Vivian.

"Girls like us," she says. "Mostly there's nobody to look out for us."

The BTK Killer's Daughter. Gabby Petito's Parents. JonBenét's Dad.

by Luke Winkie

America turned their darkest moments into a never-ending spectacle. I went to see just how far that's gone.

The Gaylord Opryland Resort is an artificial oasis in the barrens of northern Nashville, Tennessee. Colossal palm trees reach toward the glass ceiling in the hotel's verdant conservatory, sealing the grounds in a perpetual equatorial humidity. A few Disneyland-esque waterfalls crash into the rippling stream that circles the miniature shopping concourse below; it includes what the resort refers to as the "only Jack Daniels restaurant in the world." This has traditionally been a setting for country music, particularly the historic Grand Ole Opry. But on this summer day, it provided a jarring contrast to an entirely different kind of event. As hundreds gathered nearby, Tara Petito stepped up to a microphone and imagined out loud what she might have said to Brian Laundrie, the man who murdered her daughter.

"He robbed our daughter, our beautiful Gabby, of her life, her future. He robbed her of the chance to ever know what it's like to walk down the aisle with the love of her life, to bear children, to grow old," she said, grief flickering—then smoldering—in her throat. "He is a horrible excuse for a human being. If Brian was alive today, any words out of his mouth would be lies."

The disappearance of Gabby Petito was one of the most pervasive crime stories of 2021. The 22-year-old was traveling across the United States over the summer in a camper van with her fiancé, Laundrie, with the intention of documenting their journey in blooming, hashtaggable snapshots on #vanlife Instagram. But Petito vanished during the trip, stirring up a whirlwind of speculative press, condemnation of police malpractice in domestic violence cases, and anger at the elisions of social media. Petito's body was discovered in a Wyoming park three weeks later, and in October, Laundrie—who had since disappeared himself—was found dead by a self-inflicted gunshot wound, alongside a notebook in which he admitted to the crime.

The frenzy that consumed Gabby's murder turned the mixed Petito family—her stepmother Tara, her stepfather Jim, and her biological parents, Nichole and Joe—into celebrities. They have thousands of social media followers and have been featured in countless glossy magazine interviews and cable specials.

Now here they were in Nashville, at CrimeCon, one of many stops of a live true-crime circuit that subsumes families like these for years after the unthinkable happens to someone they love, providing them a forum to recount their sorrow and suffering to eager audiences. Even three years after Gabby's murder, everything the Petitos will say at CrimeCon is treated like breaking news. By the end of the convention, recaps of the family's appearances will be published by Fox News and CNN.

CrimeCon, now in its eighth year, fashions itself as the singular nexus for the large and loosely defined true-crime community, aiming to summon a fandom that exists primarily online—through twisting subreddits, gumshoeing podcasts, and lengthy comment threads on the *20/20* Facebook page—into physical space. The convention drew 6,000 guests this year, an uptick from the 5,000 who attended 2023's event in Orlando. Tickets started at $229 and are tiered between standard, gold, and "platinum" packages, with the latter offering fast-track lanes, private lounges, and exclusive memorabilia from the event's "talent," many of whom are the family members of murderers and murder victims alike. The CrimeCon imprint has been successful enough that Red Seat Ventures, the company behind the convention—as well as a larger portfolio that includes flagship podcasts from Bari Weiss and Megyn Kelly—is set to expand. It has already made landfall in the United Kingdom, and this winter, it will take to the high seas for the annual CrimeCruise.

The patrons get their money's worth. Over the course of a single weekend, Nashville's CrimeCon clientele—young and old, but overwhelmingly white and female—will orbit through a variety of keynotes and panels. Nancy Grace and Chris Hansen are on the docket, as are the authors of whodunits, like Aphrodite Jones. Elsewhere, you'll find emergent stars, like the pseudonymous hosts of the ludicrously popular *Small Town Dicks* media brand, and Anthony Ames, a former

NXIVM member who now co-hosts the true-crime podcast *A Little Bit Culty*.

But looming above the rest of the field, haunting every corner of this event, are the victims and the people connected to them. John Ramsey, father of JonBenét Ramsey, is a headliner, as are Denise Huskins and Aaron Quinn, the couple who were implicated, then exonerated, in a wild kidnapping scheme that was recounted in the hit Netflix true-crime docuseries *American Nightmare*. Further down the bill you'll find Summer Shiflet, the sister of Lori Vallow Daybell, who received a life sentence for the murder of her children and another woman. On the second day of the convention—a few hours before Shiflet was scheduled to speak—Daybell's husband would be sentenced to death for the crimes. Undaunted, Shiflet took the stage. "When I heard those words, it was everything I needed to hear," she said to a packed house in the main theater, in an exclusive response to the news.

The convention does not compensate its guests for their appearances. Most of them are expected to pay for their travel and lodging. Still, these victims flock to CrimeCon to make their bereavement public and consumable. They will spend the weekend addressing their life-altering tragedies in a variety of different panels, Q&A sessions, meet and greets, and cocktail hours. They will be flagged down by badge-holders concealing morbid curiosities. They will be wreathed with condolences, pose for pictures, and autograph the inside covers of their memoirs. All the while, they will be reacquainted with the terrible way they've become famous.

Tara Petito is, unsurprisingly, a superstar in this world. Laundrie "murdered our daughter, drove back to his family's home, and then went on vacation while Gabby lay cold, out in the wilderness, with the grizzly bears," she said during her session. "Thinking about the pain our baby girl had to endure is truly agonizing. Visualizing her final moments over and over again is a pain I wish on no one. The trauma it causes is unexplainable. Sometimes I feel like I've downed a bottle of pills, but I'm completely sober. All because of that piece of garbage."

This was CrimeCon in its basic essence: powerful, tender, and undeniably lurid. It left me with a question I couldn't stop asking in Nashville: What on earth brings people like Petito here? She has repeated this story many times since her daughter was murdered. She has sat down with Dr. Phil and Sean Hannity. She has told *People* magazine that she feels as if her daughter is sending her messages from the heavens. Yet, still, she's once again reliving the worst event of her life—not just as a victim and a survivor, but as a CrimeCon dignitary. I embarked on a surreal weekend to find out why.

A few hours before Tara Petito's panel, right after CrimeCon opened its doors, guests were funneled into one of Opryland's immense auditoriums, which would serve as the convention's marquee dais for the rest of the weekend. The lights dimmed over a phalanx of identical chairs, all pointed in the direction of two gargantuan projection monitors hovering over a spartan stage. *CSI*-flavored yellow text beamed across the screens, underlaid with the urgent clacking of a laptop keyboard. "Through all the tales of triumph and tragedy, we are here to remind you that these aren't just stories," read the text. "These are real families. Real lives."

What followed was a medley of cable news clips, edited together in warp speed, providing a recap of the past year in crime. The *Rust* shooting was mentioned, for which Alec Baldwin had not yet been cleared, along with the potential unmasking of Tupac Shakur's killer and the long-awaited release of Gypsy Rose Blanchard. The audience cheered the heroes and heckled the villains, right on cue, with an obvious fluency in all order of unsolved mysteries. The Delphi murders case, for which a trial is finally imminent, got a huge ovation. The montage rounded out with a series of heartening conclusions: criminals busted, missing people recovered, truths revealed. The show had come to life. Eminem's "Lose Yourself" poured out of the speakers.

Joe Petito, Tara's husband, would later tell me he had been scared to come to CrimeCon the first time. After watching the introduction video, I understood why. Joe had feared that people were attending this convention to gawk at him, focusing on, in his words, the "gory details" of his daughter's killing. The whole Petito family grasped the bitter irony of their presence, he said. Jim Schmidt, Gabby's stepfather, recalled the years his wife had spent as a true-crime junkie, basking in the enthralling puzzle of a provocative murder, savoring the careful distance from the pain. "You see the stories and are like, *That's not real—how did that happen?*" he told me. "And before you know it, you're living it."

Joe has come around, though. This is now the second CrimeCon the Petitos have attended. Joe treats the weekends like a vacation. "People are looking for inspiration; they're looking for help with their own lives," he said. "I was pleasantly surprised by how giving the people here are."

The panel that featured Tara was called "Finding a Voice: Victim Impact Statement Readings." Typically, victim-impact statements are read in court before sentencing occurs. The idea is to allow survivors a chance to color a perpetrator's crimes with their own accounts, pairing clinical procedure with visceral experience. Five women had volunteered to speak at this panel, two of whom were reciting the same statements they had delivered at the trials where their own perpetrators met justice. The other three were never afforded the opportunity in court. So they intended to use this venue, and its ticketed audience, to conjure an alternate timeline where they could look into the eyes of the person who had caused them so much misery.

One of the volunteers was Mo Silva, the daughter of Deanna Butterfield, who was raped and murdered by William Huff, the Bay Area prowler, in 1987. Her body was found in the picnic area of a Berkeley park. Her killer wasn't sentenced until 2018, some 30 years later. Silva was choking back tears even before she began reading at the lectern. She had been just four years old when her grandmother called her to the living room and informed her that her mom was sick. Silva suggested a trip to the pharmacy to get medicine that might heal her. Then her grandmother told her the truth.

"My heart sank, and I began to cry," she said. There was a long pause, and Silva began to visibly wither under the lights, matching the stifled sobs that slipped out of the audience. "Just as I am now. Because I knew I would never see her again."

By the time Silva and I spoke after her speech, she had regained her composure. She was wearing a silver butterfly pendant, joining some that float down a half-sleeve tattoo on her right arm. (Her mom had had a small butterfly tattoo on her chest.) The panel was Silva's one and only CrimeCon duty. She had depicted her suffering, with excruciating clarity, for a crowd of onlookers who could never understand, and now the job was complete. I had the same question for her as I had for the others: Why would anybody do this to themselves?

"CrimeCon is focused on the front part of crime, but we're forgetting about the end, and that's the aftermath and the victims," she told me. "Attendees look at all these cases and want to hear about all the details, and then their interest stops. But that isn't the end. That's just the beginning of a new phase that sucks. So if you're going to do all of this, let the people see the messy part. Let them have access to people like me. Let them feel the rawness."

Away from the ballroom, in the convention's central gallery, exhibitors awaited guests. Aging mystery authors reclined behind gory paperbacks; representatives of collegiate criminal justice programs stood ready to recruit aspiring investigators; podcasters prepared promotional souvenirs—pins, brochures, and stickers—all splayed out like Halloween candy on their tables. Court TV, the former cable channel that has since been relegated to digital broadcasting, had one of the largest booths in the building, equipped with a slab of cardboard printed with the question "What's Your True Crime Obsession?" (By the end of the weekend, it was covered with sticky notes bearing all sorts of answers: "Serial Killers + Culty Things," read one. "All of It!" said another.)

Standing alone amid the pulp was a booth belonging to the National Center for Victims of Crime, a nonprofit that helps rehabilitate families languishing in the aftermath of a tragedy. Renée Williams, an advocate and the organization's executive director, distributed to those passing by a sheet detailing "eight simple rules" for being an "ethical" true-crime fan. The bullet points were boiled down to lean, punchy mantras: *Do No Harm. Respect Boundaries.* It was Williams who had orchestrated the afternoon's victim-impact statement readings, a project that she hoped would remind CrimeCon's attendees of the trauma that a highly scrutinized mystery can inflict. Williams was happy with how the readings had gone, but she had fretted about the optics of the panel for weeks before the convention. "I'm always worried if something is exploitative," she said. "Are we putting something out for someone's entertainment?"

The National Center for Victims of Crime has for years had a presence at CrimeCon, but initially, Williams said, her colleagues in the victim services sphere weren't happy about those appearances. It's a fair point. Could a commercial enterprise profiting in part off suffering performed by the invited victims sustain credible advocacy? The exhibition hall was a testament to the event's enormous contradictions. The Black and Missing Foundation, a nonprofit dedicated to raising awareness for uncracked cases involving victims of color, had a well-staffed studio near the main entrance. But the end of the promenade was marked by the convention's official merch shop, hawking T-shirts printed with slogans like "Talk Motive to Me," "Catch Killers Not Feelings," and perhaps the biggest hit at the convention, "I'm Only Here for an Alibi." Later, a select group of badge-holders would be gathered for a "Sketch and Sip" event hosted by renowned courtroom artist Bill Robles, who has immortalized everyone from Harvey Weinstein to Charles Manson at the defendant's table. The party would step to their easels, wineglasses in hand, and learn what it takes to portray a striking cross-examination of a predator.

How do you reconcile one with the other? As far as Williams was concerned, you don't. To her, the only perspectives that matter belong to the bereaved, and they had made the trip to Nashville of their own accord.

"I'm a victim advocate. I'm not their mother. I have to let them make decisions as adults," she said. "I need to trust their instincts."

⊙━━━◦

This was the third year in a row John Ramsey had attended CrimeCon, and he still wasn't quite sure why anyone would pay for a ticket. In an hour, he was due to take the convention's main stage, opposite author Paula Woodward and a box of tissues, for a high-profile panel titled "Searching for Truth." His six-year-old daughter JonBenét's notorious murder and all that came out of it have given him plenty of time to contemplate the enduring fascination with the case.

"Some of the attendees are these amateur detectives who treat it like a real-life board game," he said. "They stop me in the halls. They say they only came to the convention just to meet me. I'm almost embarrassed by it. I'm not that great. I've not done anything spectacular."

Ramsey is 80 years old, and JonBenét has been dead for nearly three decades. Nobody at CrimeCon has been in the spotlight longer than he has. Ramsey's media portfolio includes appearances on *Dr. Phil*, The *Dr. Oz Show*, and a memorably uncomfortable Barbara Walters interview in 2000, in the still-simmering aftermath of the crime. He has also published two books—the first defending himself from those who suspected his family's involvement in the killing, and a second reflecting on the combined grief of JonBenét's murder and the death of his wife Patsy from ovarian cancer in 2006. This has all helped ensure that the lurid interest in JonBenét has never faded.

"I have a file on my email account for the crazy people. I put all of that stuff in there," said Jan Rousseaux, Ramsey's third wife, whom he married five years after Patsy died. Rousseaux hadn't been anywhere near Colorado during Christmas 1996, but missives from the dedicated, and the unhinged, bombard her inbox all the time.

"The other night, his phone kept vibrating. *Bzzt. Bzzt. Bzzt.* Finally, I got up because I thought someone we know might be in trouble," Rousseaux said. "But no, it was a woman in Canada, sending a series of photos and texts—11 of them—saying, 'I am your daughter. I am JonBenét.'"

Ramsey believes that this is a good problem to have. Police investigations tend to be malleable to scrutiny, and if you trust his account—that a roving invader broke into his house, tortured and murdered his daughter, and stashed her body in the basement—then you must also trust that Ramsey is being honest when he says that he is doing everything in his power to focus the fraught nature of his celebrity on the objective of finding JonBenét's killer. Ramsey makes sure to read all the unhinged emails that Rousseaux detailed, even the ones that are erratic and dissertation-length. "You're always looking for that little nugget that isn't public information," he said.

"I want to clear the cloud," Ramsey said when asked why he keeps saying yes to things like CrimeCon. "My family needs the cloud removed. It's not going to change my life at this point, but for them, it will."

In Nashville, I learned that Ramsey is correct about the advantages of his stardom. Maggie Zingman, a 69-year-old from Oklahoma whose pink horn-rimmed glasses protrude from curtains of silver hair, would do anything to swap places with him. She has a slain daughter too. Her name was Brittany Phillips. Zingman often wears an oversize pin displaying Phillips's high school portrait. On this day, it's dangling heavily from her collar.

In 2004, Phillips was raped and murdered in her Tulsa apartment. She was 18, and she was buried on her 19th birthday. Investigators never came up with a suspect, nor did any national reporters sniff around to ramp up the pressure. So, when Phillips's case went cold, Zingman took matters into her own hands. She plastered her SUV with pictures of her young daughter and printed the number of a tip line along its doors. Zingman has been driving across the country, on and off, since 2007, searching for a lead. That odyssey had now brought her to CrimeCon. Standing next to Zingman was a life-sized cardboard cutout of her daughter. "Do You Know Me?" reads the text near her head. "I'm the Girl Next Door."

Zingman is not a featured speaker at this year's event. She will not be appearing on any panels or conducting any book signings or meet and greets. Therein lies the problem. Despite her best efforts, the slaughter of Brittany Phillips has never achieved nearly the same resonance as other American tragedies. This fact has left Zingman alone with the most horrible of mortal sensations: a twinge of envy as she watches the zeitgeist wash over the bereaved mothers who happen to have a more famous dead daughter.

"Do I get jealous? Yes. Is it hard? Yes. But I can't be ashamed about it. It's human nature. I see the Petito family talking to all of these people: Chris Hansen, Paul Holes, John Walsh. National news attention is the only thing that's going to change my case and if my story could get in their hands," Zingman told me. "There are thousands of us out there. I'm from middle America. My daughter had gone away to college. She had a chemistry scholarship. She was beautiful. But that's too normal."

Candice Cooley, the mother of Dylan Rounds—a Utah teen whose murderer pleaded guilty to the crime earlier this year—told me at the conference she had been in Zingman's position until she got "lucky," in the grimmest sense of the word. Cooley's calls to her local news stations had gone unreturned for weeks after her son's disappearance—until one day she began to weave his biographical details into her plight. Rounds had left home at 17 to start a farm on his grandfather's property. The color of his life was enough to overcome the algorithm. Suddenly, Rounds's story was everywhere.

"We gave him a brand. Gabby was the blogger, and Dylan was the farmer. Unfortunately, that's what it takes," Cooley said. "Our Facebook group exploded to 20,000 people after that, and that's when the media grabbed it." She was wearing a gray sweatshirt embellished with the logo of her foundation, Dylan's Legacy: two stalks of wheat crisscrossing under a sunflower. "It's almost like you have to market your missing child," she said.

In 2023, when some of the details surrounding Rounds's murder were still murky and hot on the tabloid circuit, CrimeCon sprang for Cooley's flight and hotel so she could attend the convention. Cooley was assigned to a meet-and-greet session that she found unpleasant and dehumanizing. "I had people coming up to me that I don't know, telling me that they loved me, and they want to hug me, and that they love my son so much," Cooley said. "I felt like a circus monkey," she added. "It's like you're put on display. Like, *Oh, you paid $300 extra just to meet me.*"

Lately, Cooley's friendships with the other big names on the true-crime junket had strengthened, to the point where the promise of a reunion with them was one of the main reasons she traveled to Nashville. Cooley has grown particularly close with the Petitos. Now that their cases have been mostly settled, their shared focus has turned to families of missing children who have never been showered with the same attention—absorbing, then reflecting, the spotlight.

It was here that I began to understand one part of the enduring gravitational pull victims experience with CrimeCon. Even as the Tara Petito panel focused on the still-raw aftermath of her daughter's murder, Jim Schmidt and Joe Petito, Gabby's stepfather and father, respectively, appeared on another panel, which spotlighted Indigenous women who had been disproportionately victimized by violent crime. Sitting next to them onstage was Vangie Randall-Shorty, a Navajo woman whose son Zachariah Juwaun Shorty was abducted and killed in New Mexico by an unknown person in 2020. Joy Sutton, the panel's host and the woman behind the podcast *Untold Stories: Black and Missing*, asked Joe what he made of "missing white woman syndrome," a term used to describe how preoccupied the news apparatus can become with the disappearance of someone who fits Gabby's precise demographic background. Joe replied with several factors that he thinks led to the media circus—a gap in the tabloid cycle and, yes, perhaps the color of her skin.

It was extraordinary to watch him analyze the horrific death of his daughter from such a vantage point, considering how heavily the loss still weighs on the Petito family. Jim told me that since Gabby went missing, pretty much everything makes him cry. There's a cheesy Publix commercial in particular that reveals the extent of his heartbreak. "It's about a stepdad and a daughter," he said. "It goes through the years, and the daughter is saying, 'Thanks, Dad.' High school graduation: 'Thanks, Dad.'" Jim's voice trailed off, and his eyes began to well up.

"That's what happens!" Joe said. "I walked into a room where my wife was watching *90 Day Fiancé*. I sat down to watch just for a few minutes. The first thing I saw on the TV happened to be a dad walking his daughter down the aisle. And I started bawling."

If the two of them are to share this domain—with the specter of their catastrophe waiting to pounce—then perhaps it makes sense that the Petitos are doing whatever they can to give this new life meaning, or at least to be dutiful custodians for other bereaved parents who have recently joined, in Jim's words, "the club."

"It's validating," he said. "Everybody knows our story. But we're here alongside other victims, to elevate them. And that's how we always frame those sessions."

"It's our purpose," Joe said.

<hr/>

At the victim-impact session—the same one where Tara Petito and Mo Silva spoke—there was also Kerri Rawson, the famous daughter of the BTK killer, Dennis Rader. She was there to break some unsettling news in the case.

After reviewing Rader's coded diaries as part of an ongoing police investigation to uncover more of his crimes, she discovered evidence that she, too, had been sexually abused by her father. The revelation lined up with a buried memory. Rawson was two years old when the incident happened, she believed. She has a faint recollection of a large man hulking over her childhood bedroom, which contextualized the lifelong problems she's had with her neck.

Rawson said she confronted Rader with the charges in prison, where he is serving 10 consecutive life sentences. He told her it was a "fantasy."

This latest twist in the BTK saga quickly made headlines across the true-crime media ecosystem. Reports of the horror immediately popped up on NewsNation and the *New York Post*.

A couple days later, in a bit of whiplash, I came to see Rawson sign some books in the convention's meet-and-greet room. She sat in front of a paperboard backdrop stamped with the CrimeCon logo; yellow caution tape stretched over a black-and-white thumbprint.

The heaviness of the material didn't affect the mood in the lobby. Rawson was breezy and hospitable. One of the first fans in line to meet her was Candy Griffin, a realtor from Texas. She had started following Rawson's writing career on Facebook and Twitter after they first met in the VIP lounge of last year's CrimeCon, where the two had hit it off immediately. They have had remarkably similar lives, Griffin thought. Both have lived in the exact same region of rural northeastern Kansas. She connected with how Rawson wrote about loss. Griffin is surprised that they didn't meet ages ago.

"My father wasn't a serial killer," Griffin said. "But there are a lot of things that interlink us."

The dissonance continued. On Sunday morning, the final day of the convention, the booths in the exhibition hall were already being packed into boxes. Most of the victims had caught flights out of Nashville, and by the afternoon, CrimeCon had vanished without a trace. But in its dying embers, you could find a brand-new placard set up in the Opryland foyer: CrimeCon 2025 in Denver had just been announced. Tickets are on sale now.